Benchbook

for U.S. District Court Judges

SIXTH EDITION

Federal Judicial Center

The Federal Judicial Center produced this *Benchbook for U.S. District Court Judges* in furtherance of its mission to develop and conduct education programs for the judicial branch. This *Benchbook* is not a statement of official Federal Judicial Center policy. Rather, it was prepared by, and it represents the considered views of, the Center's Benchbook Committee, a group of experienced district judges appointed by the Chief Justice of the United States in his capacity as chair of the Center's Board. The committee was assisted by Federal Judicial Center staff.

Published by Michigan Legal Publishing Ltd.
Grand Rapids, Michigan
www.michlp.com
ISBN: 978-1-64002-062-7

Preface

From the first edition in 1969 to this sixth edition more than forty years later, the Federal Judicial Center's *Benchbook for U.S. District Court Judges* has provided a concise, practical guide to situations federal judges are likely to encounter on the bench. Although the *Benchbook* is written primarily for district and magistrate judges, bankruptcy judges also may find useful information in many of the sections. The *Benchbook* covers procedures that are required by statute, rule, or case law, and it offers detailed guidance from experienced trial judges on these requirements and other matters that arise in the courtroom. New judges in particular should benefit from the *Benchbook*, but even experienced judges may find useful reminders about how to deal with routine matters, suggestions for handling more complex issues, or helpful starting points when they face particular situations for the first time.

This edition contains several significant additions, two of which come at the request of committees of the Judicial Conference of the United States. The Advisory Committee on Criminal Rules, then chaired by Judge Richard C. Tallman (9th Cir.), requested that we add a section on prosecutors' duty to disclose favorable information to defendants under *Brady v. Maryland*, 373 U.S. 83 (1963). Working with Judge Reena Raggi (2d Cir.), Judge Tallman's successor as chair, the *Benchbook* Committee developed a primer on *Brady* that addresses such issues as the basic duty to disclose exculpatory information, the elements of a *Brady* violation, and the timing of disclosures. New section 5.06 includes an extensive discussion of later Supreme Court and appellate case law interpreting and applying *Brady*; links to the Department of Justice's disclosure policies and the Center's report to the Advisory Committee in 2011 on *Brady* and Federal Rule of Criminal Procedure 16; and a list of sample cases in which disclosure of *Brady* material was required.

The *Benchbook* also has a new section on civil pretrial case management, section 6.01, which was the result of a joint request by the Committee on Rules of Practice and Procedure, then chaired by Judge Lee H. Rosenthal (S.D. Tex.), and the Advisory Committee on Civil Rules, then chaired by the late Judge Mark R. Kravitz (D. Conn.). The committees prepared a detailed outline of civil case management from the period before the Rule 16 conference through the final pretrial conference, focusing on the judge's role as an active case manager. They were assisted by Professor Steven S. Gensler (University of Oklahoma College of Law); Judge David Campbell (D. Ariz.), then chair of the Discovery Subcommittee of the Civil Rules Committee; and the Reporters to the Civil Rules Committee, Professors Edward Cooper (University of Michigan Law School) and Richard Marcus (University of California, Hastings College of the Law).

Another major change to the *Benchbook* is a completely revised section on sentencing. The Center has received many requests for a sentencing "script" that judges can follow, and section 4.01 now contains an extensive colloquy for the sentencing hearing.

Other significant additions are a new subsection on restraining disruptive defendants (often referred to as "shackling"), a *Padilla* warning to noncitizens on the possible immigration consequences of a guilty plea, a similar warning to sex offenders about collateral consequences they may face, and expanded jury instructions on the use of social media.

It is important to emphasize that while much of the material in the *Benchbook* comes from case law, federal rules, and statutes, the particulars of the procedures suggested here represent only the recommendations of the *Benchbook* Committee. The information provided is deemed to be accurate and valuable, but it is not intended to serve as legal authority and should not be cited as such. And because circuit law may vary, particularly with respect to procedures, judges should always familiarize themselves with the requirements of their circuit's law.

One other change should be noted. Largely because of budgetary constraints, the Center will distribute printed copies of the *Benchbook* only to new judges. A limited number of paper copies will be available to judges upon request, but otherwise the *Benchbook* will be available electronically on the Center's website.

The materials presented in the *Benchbook* were prepared by experienced judges. The book is reviewed, updated, and added to by each succeeding Committee in collaboration with Center staff. The Center would like to thank the members of the *Benchbook* Committee, who are appointed by the Chief Justice. The Committee is chaired by Judge Irma E. Gonzalez (S.D. Cal.) and includes Judge Paul L. Friedman (D.D.C.), Judge Robert Holmes Bell (W.D. Mich.) (also chair of the Committee on Criminal Law), Chief Judge James F. Holderman (N.D. Ill.) (the FJC Board Liaison to the *Benchbook* Committee), Judge John W. Lungstrum (D. Kan.), and Chief Judge Patti B. Saris, Chair of the United States Sentencing Commission. Special thanks go to Judge Friedman, who took the lead in drafting the new section on *Brady* disclosure, Judge Saris for doing the same with the revised section on sentencing, and Judge Gonzalez for organizing and overseeing all of the changes. We also thank Judge Barbara J. Rothstein, previous Director of the FJC, who worked with the Committee during the initial drafting of these revisions, and Senior Research Associate Laural Hooper of the Center's Research Division, who shared her extensive knowledge of *Brady* disclosure issues.

We hope you find this edition of the *Benchbook* to be useful, and we invite comments and suggestions for making it better.

Jeremy D. Fogel
Director, Federal Judicial Center

Contents

1.01 Initial appearance

Fed. R. Crim. P. 5

[*Note:* Under the Crime Victims' Rights Act, 18 U.S.C. § 3771(a)(2) and (3), any victim of the offense has the right to notice of "any public court proceeding . . . involving the crime . . . of the accused," and to attend that proceeding. It may be advisable to ask the prosecutor if there are any victims and, if so, whether the government has fulfilled its duty to notify them.]

The first appearance of the defendant after arrest is usually before a magistrate judge. If the defendant consents, the initial appearance may be conducted by video teleconferencing (Fed. R. Crim. P. 5(f)).

NOTE
If the alleged offense was committed in another district, see *infra* section 1.05: Commitment to another district (removal proceedings)

A. If the arrest was made without a warrant, require that a complaint be prepared and filed pursuant to Fed. R. Crim. P. 3 and 4.

[*Note:* If you have any doubts about the defendant's ability to speak and understand English, consider appointing a certified interpreter in accordance with 28 U.S.C. § 1827. If the defendant is a foreign national, regardless of immigration status, consider advising the defendant of the right to consular notification.[1]]

---

1. Although judges are not currently required to notify defendants of the right to consular notification, doing so may avoid unnecessary litigation, cost, and delay. Note that a proposed amendment to Fed. R. Crim. P. 5(d)(1) would require the court "to inform non-citizen defendants at their initial appearance that (1) they may request that a consular officer from their country of nationality be notified of their arrest, and (2) in some cases international treaties and agreements require consular notification without a defendant's request. The proposed rule does not, however, address the question whether treaty provisions requiring consular notification may be invoked by individual defendants in a judicial proceeding and what, if any, remedy may exist for a violation of Article 36 of the Vienna Convention." *See* the May 17, 2012 "Report of the Advisory Committee on Criminal Rules" *in* the Preliminary Draft of Proposed Amendments to the Federal Rules of Appellate, Bankruptcy, and Criminal Procedure, and the Federal Rules of Evidence at 205 (Committee on Rules of Practice and Procedure of the Judicial Conference of the United States, Aug. 15, 2012) (http://www.uscourts.gov/uscourts/rules/rules-published-comment.pdf). The proposed "Committee Note" to the amendment states that having a judge provide this advice is not designed to relieve law enforcement officers of their responsibility to do so, but rather "to provide additional assurance that U.S. treaty obligations are fulfilled, and to create a judicial record of that action." *Id.* at 208.

For more detailed guidance relating to the arrest and detention of foreign nationals, see Consular Notification and Access: Instructions for Federal, State, and Local Law Enforcement and Other Officials Regarding Foreign Nationals in the United States and the Rights of Consular Officials to Assist Them, *available at* http://travel.state.gov/pdf/cna/CNA_Manual_3d_Edition.pdf. See particularly the sections "Steps to Follow When a Foreign National Is Arrested or Detained" and "Suggested Statements to Detained Foreign Nationals." *See also* 28 C.F.R. § 50.5(a) ("Some of the treaties obligate the United States to notify the consular officer only upon the demand or request of the arrested foreign national. On the

B. For a felony charge, inform the defendant
    1. of the nature of the complaint against him or her and of any affidavit filed therewith;
    2. of the defendant's right to employ counsel or to request the assignment of counsel if he or she is unable to employ counsel (see *infra* section 1.02: Assignment of counsel or pro se representation);
    3. of the defendant's right to have a preliminary hearing (Fed. R. Crim. P. 5(d)(1)(D) and 5.1; 18 U.S.C. § 3060);
    4. under what circumstances the defendant may secure pretrial release;
    5. that the defendant is not required to make any statement;
    6. that if the defendant has made a statement, he or she need say no more;
    7. that if the defendant starts to make a statement, he or she may stop at any time (*Miranda v. Arizona*, 384 U.S. 436 (1966)); and
    8. that any statement made by the defendant may be used against him or her.

    Fed. R. Crim. P. 5(d)(1).

C. For a misdemeanor charge, the procedure is similar. See Fed. R. Crim. P. 58(b)(2). The defendant must also be informed of the right to trial, judgment, and sentencing before a district judge unless he or she consents to trial, judgment, and sentencing before a magistrate judge.

D. Determine whether the defendant has had a reasonable opportunity to consult with counsel. Allow further consultation if needed. Fed. R. Crim. P. 5(d)(2).

E. Determine whether to detain or release the defendant (see *infra* section 1.03: Release or detention pending trial).

F. Schedule a preliminary hearing and/or detention hearing, if applicable.

G. For release or detention of a material witness, see 18 U.S.C. § 3144.

H. If the person is before the court for violating probation or supervised release, see Fed. R. Crim. P. 32.1. *Morrissey v. Brewer*, 408 U.S. 471 (1972); *Gagnon v. Scarpelli*, 411 U.S. 778 (1973); Fed. R. Crim. P. 5(a)(2)(B).

I. If the offense was committed in another district, see Fed. R. Crim. P. 5(c)(3) and *infra* section 1.04: Offense committed in another district. If the defendant was arrested for failing to appear in another district, see Fed. R. Crim. P. 40 and *infra* section 1.05: Commitment to another district (removal proceedings).

---

other hand, some of the treaties require notifying the consul of the arrest of a foreign national whether or not the arrested person requests such notification.").

Other FJC sources

David N. Adair, Jr., The Bail Reform Act of 1984, at 11–15 (3d ed. 2006)

1.02 Assignment of counsel or pro se representation

18 U.S.C. § 3006A; Fed. R. Crim. P. 44; CJA Forms 20, 23

[*Note:* Under the Crime Victims' Rights Act, 18 U.S.C. § 3771(a)(2) and (3), any victim of the offense has the right to notice of "any public court proceeding . . . involving the crime . . . of the accused," and to attend that proceeding. It may be advisable to ask the prosecutor if there are any victims and, if so, whether the government has fulfilled its duty to notify them.]

If counsel has not been assigned by the magistrate judge before the defendant's first court appearance, assignment of counsel should be the first item of business before the judge.

[*Note:* If you have any doubts about the defendant's ability to speak and understand English, consider appointing a certified interpreter in accordance with 28 U.S.C. § 1827.]

A. If the defendant has no attorney:
  1. Inform the defendant
    (a) of his or her constitutional right to be represented by an attorney at every stage of the proceedings;
    (b) that if he or she is unable to afford an attorney, the court will appoint one without cost to him or her (18 U.S.C. § 3006A, Fed. R. Crim. P. 44); and
    (c) of the offense with which he or she is charged.
  2. Ask the defendant
    (a) if he or she understands his or her right to an attorney;
    (b) if he or she wishes and is able to obtain counsel; and
    (c) if he or she wants the court to appoint counsel.
B. If the defendant requests appointed counsel:
  1. Require the completion of a Financial Affidavit by the defendant on the appropriate Criminal Justice Act form.
  2. Inform the defendant that he or she is swearing to the answers to the questions on the affidavit and that he or she may be penalized for perjury if he or she gives false information.
  3. Determine whether the defendant is unable to afford privately retained counsel. If the defendant qualifies financially for court-appointed counsel, make that finding and sign the order appointing counsel.

Section 1.02: Assignment of counsel or pro se representation

C. If the defendant does not want counsel:

The accused has a constitutional right to self-representation. Waiver of counsel must, however, be knowing and voluntary. This means that you must make clear on the record that the defendant is fully aware of the hazards and disadvantages of self-representation.

If the defendant states that he or she wishes to represent himself or herself, you should ask questions similar to the following:

1. Have you ever studied law?

2. Have you ever represented yourself in a criminal action?

3. Do you understand that you are charged with these crimes: [state the crimes with which the defendant is charged]?

4. Do you understand that if you are found guilty of the crime charged in Count I, the court must impose a special assessment of $100 and could sentence you to as many as ___ years in prison, impose a term of supervised release that follows imprisonment, fine you as much as $____, and direct you to pay restitution?

[Ask the defendant a similar question for each crime charged in the indictment or information.]

NOTE: The assessment is $25 for a Class A misdemeanor, $10 for a Class B, $5 for a Class C or infraction.

5. Do you understand that if you are found guilty of more than one of these crimes, this court can order that the sentences be served consecutively, that is, one after another?

6. Do you understand that there are advisory Sentencing Guidelines that may have an effect on your sentence if you are found guilty?

7. Do you understand that if you represent yourself, you are on your own? I cannot tell you or even advise you how you should try your case.

8. Are you familiar with the Federal Rules of Evidence?

9. Do you understand that the rules of evidence govern what evidence may or may not be introduced at trial, that in representing yourself, you must abide by those very technical rules, and that they will not be relaxed for your benefit?

10. Are you familiar with the Federal Rules of Criminal Procedure?

11. Do you understand that those rules govern the way a criminal action is tried in federal court, that you are bound by those rules, and that they will not be relaxed for your benefit?

[Then say to the defendant something to this effect:]

12. I must advise you that in my opinion, a trained lawyer would defend you far better than you could defend yourself. I think it is unwise of you to try to represent yourself. You are not familiar with the law. You are not familiar with court procedure. You are not familiar with the rules of evidence. I strongly urge you not to try to represent yourself.

13. Now, in light of the penalty that you might suffer if you are found guilty, and in light of all of the difficulties of representing yourself, do you still desire to represent yourself and to give up your right to be represented by a lawyer?

14. Is your decision entirely voluntary?

[If the answers to the two preceding questions are yes, say something to the following effect:]

15. I find that the defendant has knowingly and voluntarily waived the right to counsel. I will therefore permit the defendant to represent himself [herself].

It is probably advisable to appoint standby counsel, who can assist the defendant or can replace the defendant if the court determines during trial that the defendant can no longer be permitted to proceed pro se.

Other FJC sources

Manual on Recurring Problems in Criminal Trials 1–7 (Tucker Carrington & Kris Markarian eds., 6th ed. 2010)

1.03 Release or detention pending trial

18 U.S.C. §§ 3141–3148; Fed. R. Crim. P. 46

[*Note:* Under the Crime Victims' Rights Act, 18 U.S.C. § 3771(a)(2) and (3), any victim of the offense has the right to notice of "any public court proceeding . . . involving the crime . . . of the accused," and to attend that proceeding. It may be advisable to ask the prosecutor if there are any victims and, if so, whether the government has fulfilled its duty to notify them. Victims also have a right "to be reasonably heard at any public proceeding in the district court involving release" of the defendant. § 3771(a)(4).]

A. Preliminary
   1. Ask the defendant:
      (a) What is your full name?
      (b) How old are you?
      (c) Do you have an attorney?
         [If the defendant is unrepresented by counsel, inform the defendant of his or her right to counsel, and appoint counsel if the defendant is qualified (see *supra* section 1.02: Assignment of counsel or pro se representation).]
   2. If you are not sure the defendant understands English, ask the defendant:
      Are you able to speak and understand English?
      [If the defendant has an attorney, ask counsel if he or she has been able to communicate with the defendant in English. If you doubt the defendant's capacity to understand English, use a certified interpreter. See 28 U.S.C. § 1827.]
   3. Ask the U.S. attorney whether the government wants to move for detention under 18 U.S.C. § 3142(d) or (e). If the motion is made, hold the appropriate hearing. This may require a continuance (not to exceed five days on the defendant's motion, three days on the government's motion, except for good cause). 18 U.S.C. § 3142(f). If the motion is not made, proceed to the bail inquiry.

B. Bail inquiry[1]
   1. Review any pretrial services report provided by the probation office.
   2. Hear information relevant to considerations for fixing bail:

---

1. Paragraphs B through F of this section cover procedures for setting bail when detention is not requested, or when detention is denied and conditions of release must be set. The information obtained under paragraphs B through E is also relevant to deciding whether to detain the defendant under 18 U.S.C. § 3142(f). See paragraph H *infra.*

      (a) the nature and circumstances of the offense charged, including whether the offense is a crime of violence or involves narcotics;

      (b) the weight of the evidence against the accused;

      (c) the history and characteristics of the accused, including

         (i)   character, physical and mental condition, family ties, employment, financial resources, length of residence in the community, community ties, past conduct, history of drug or alcohol abuse, criminal history, and record concerning appearances at court proceedings;

         (ii) whether, at the time of the current offense or arrest, the defendant was on probation or parole or on release pending trial, sentencing, appeal, or completion of sentence under federal, state, or local law;

      (d) the nature and seriousness of danger to any person or the community if the accused is released.[2] 18 U.S.C. § 3142(g).

      (e) In a case involving domestic violence, stalking, or violation of a protective order, give the alleged victim an opportunity to be heard regarding the danger posed by the defendant. 18 U.S.C. § 2263.

      (f) Give any other victims present in the courtroom "an opportunity to be reasonably heard." 18 U.S.C. § 3771(a)(4).

  3. If a secured bond or surety bond is being considered, inquire about the defendant's financial resources and, if appropriate, the sources of any property to be designated for potential forfeiture or offered as collateral. See 18 U.S.C. § 3142(c)(1)(B)(xii), (c)(2), and (g)(4).

C. If there is a pretrial services agency in your district (18 U.S.C. § 3154), use the report of the interview by the pretrial services officer as an aid to fixing bail. If you do not have a pretrial services agency, consult the probation office.

D. In developing information from the defendant relevant to bail, the following questions are typical:

[*Note:* This information is usually included in the pretrial services report and is based on an interview of the defendant and independent verification of the information provided.]

  1. Are you married?

  2. Do you have any children?

  3. Are you living with your spouse or children? Do you support your spouse or children?

---

2. A crime victim has the right "to be reasonably protected from the accused." 18 U.S.C. § 3771(a)(1).

4. Do you support or live with anyone else? Who?

5. Are you employed?

6. How long have you worked for your current employer?

7. What is your average weekly or monthly take-home pay?

8. Do you own an automobile?

9. Do you have a savings account, bonds, stocks, or similar liquid assets?

10. Do you own or rent your home?

11. Do you own any other real property?

12. How long have you lived at your current address?

13. How long have you lived in this city [state] or the surrounding area?

14. Do you have a telephone? Where can you be reached by telephone?

15. Do you possess a passport?

   [*Note:* The defendant might be asked to deposit his or her passport with the marshal (or bailiff) as a condition of bail.]

16. Do you owe anyone money? Do you have to make mortgage payments, time payments, or other periodic payments?

17. Are you regularly receiving medical treatment?

18. Have you ever been treated or hospitalized for mental illness?

E. Ask the U.S. attorney for the defendant's rap sheet (fingerprinting record) to determine past convictions and the issuance of bond forfeiture warrants indicating prior failure to appear for scheduled court hearings.

[*Note:* This information is also typically included in the pretrial services report.]

F. Set bail with appropriate conditions, 18 U.S.C. § 3142(b) or (c), or hold a detention hearing under § 3142(f). If you do not hold a detention hearing:

1. In setting bail, determine whether appearance and community safety can reasonably be ensured by releasing the accused on personal recognizance or on an unsecured appearance bond with only the condition that the accused not commit a crime while on release.

2. If you determine that further conditions are necessary, set them. Do not set a financial condition that the defendant cannot meet.

3. Explain the conditions to the defendant.

4. Execute a release order and obtain the defendant's written acknowledgment of the conditions of release and the consequences of violation.

5. Tell the defendant when to appear in court again, or explain how he or she will be advised when next to appear in court.

6. Explain to the defendant, as 18 U.S.C. § 3142(h)(2) requires,

   (a) that failing to appear in court as required is a crime for which he or she can be sentenced to imprisonment (18 U.S.C. § 3146);

   (b) that if the defendant violates any condition of release, a warrant for arrest may be issued, and he or she may be jailed until trial and may also be prosecuted for contempt of court (18 U.S.C. § 3148);

   (c) that committing a crime while on release may lead to more severe punishment than he or she would receive for committing the same crime at any other time (18 U.S.C. § 3147); and

   (d) that it is a crime to try to influence a juror, to threaten or attempt to bribe a witness or other person who may have information about this case, to retaliate against anyone for providing information about the case, or to otherwise obstruct the administration of justice (18 U.S.C. §§ 1503, 1510, 1512, 1513).

7. As required under § 3142(h)(1), include in the release order a written statement that clearly sets forth all the conditions of release to which the defendant is subject. Also, "state in writing, or orally on the record, the reasons for an order regarding the release or detention of a defendant." Fed. R. App. P. 9(a)(1).

G. If temporary detention for up to ten days is sought under 18 U.S.C. § 3142(d):

1. Ask the U.S. attorney to state the factual basis for the motion.

2. Give the defendant's counsel an opportunity to respond.

3. Determine whether the defendant fits within one or more of the categories set forth in 18 U.S.C. § 3142(d)(1).

4. If the defendant fits within one or more of these categories, determine whether he or she "may flee or pose a danger to any other person or the community." 18 U.S.C. § 3142(d)(2). If so, detention is mandatory.

5. If detention for up to ten days is not ordered, proceed to the release inquiry. If detention for up to ten days is ordered:

   (a) Direct the U.S. attorney to notify the appropriate officials immediately and to notify the court and the defendant's counsel immediately if any such official expressly declines or fails to take the defendant into custody.

   (b) Fix a date and time for a bail hearing to be held in the event that the defendant is not taken into custody by any such official.

   (c) Execute a temporary detention form.

H. If pretrial detention has been sought under 18 U.S.C. § 3142(e), conduct the required hearing under § 3142(f) (see § 3142(g) and paragraphs B through E *supra* for factors to consider):

1. Make findings of fact and state the reasons for the decision. If detention is ordered, these must be written. 18 U.S.C. § 3142(i)(1). See also Fed. R. App. P. 9.

2. If detention is not ordered, set bail, if any, impose conditions of release under § 3142(b) or (c), and issue a release order pursuant to 18 U.S.C. § 3142(h). See paragraphs B through F *supra*.

3. If detention is ordered, execute a pretrial detention order that meets the requirements of 18 U.S.C. § 3142(i).

Other FJC sources

David N. Adair, Jr., The Bail Reform Act of 1984 (3d ed. 2006)

1.04 Offense committed in another district

Fed. R. Crim. P. 5(c)(3), 20

[*Note:* Under the Crime Victims' Rights Act, 18 U.S.C. § 3771(a)(2) and (3), any victim of the offense has the right to notice of "any public court proceeding . . . involving the crime . . . of the accused," and to attend that proceeding. It may be advisable to ask the prosecutor if there are any victims and, if so, whether the government has fulfilled its duty to notify them.]

The following procedure applies if the defendant and the government consent to transfer the prosecution of an offense committed in another district to the district where the defendant was arrested or is being held. Fed. R. Crim. P. 20(a).

A. Preliminary

Have the oath administered and ask the defendant:

1. What is your full name?

2. How old are you?

3. How far did you go in school? What is your employment experience?

    [If you are not sure the defendant understands English, ask the defendant:]

4. Are you able to speak and understand English?

    [If the defendant has an attorney, ask counsel if he or she has been able to communicate with the defendant in English. If you doubt the defendant's capacity to understand English, use a certified interpreter. See 28 U.S.C. § 1827.]

5. Are you currently or have you recently been under the care of a physician or a psychiatrist, or been hospitalized or treated for narcotics addiction? Have you taken any drugs, medicine, or pills or drunk any alcoholic beverage in the past twenty-four hours?

    [If the answer to either question is yes, pursue the subject with the defendant and with counsel to determine that the defendant is currently competent to waive proceedings in the district where the offense was committed.]

6. Do you have an attorney?

    [If he or she does not have an attorney, inform the defendant of the right to counsel and appoint counsel if the defendant qualifies. See *supra* section 1.02: Assignment of counsel or pro se representation.]

B. Obtain a waiver of indictment if one is required (see *infra* section 1.06: Waiver of indictment).

C. Explain that the defendant's case cannot be handled in this court unless he or she wishes to plead guilty or nolo contendere. [*Note:* For juveniles, see 18 U.S.C. § 5031 and Fed. R. Crim. P. 20(d).]

D. Question the defendant to ascertain on the record that the defendant understands he or she is agreeing to

    1. plead guilty or nolo contendere;

    2. waive proceedings in the district in which the crime was allegedly committed; and

    3. be proceeded against in this court.

E. Explain to the defendant and ask if the defendant understands that

    1. he or she has a right to be tried in the district where the crime is alleged to have been committed;

    2. he or she cannot be convicted or sentenced in this court unless he or she consents freely; and

    3. if he or she does not consent to be proceeded against in this court, he or she may be proceeded against in the district in which the crime was allegedly committed.

F. Obtain the defendant's written statement incorporating the understanding described above.

G. Obtain the written consents of the U.S. attorneys.

H. Take the defendant's plea. [*Note:* All points should be covered in taking the plea, as in an ordinary arraignment. See relevant portions of *infra* sections 1.07: Arraignment and plea and 2.01: Taking pleas of guilty or nolo contendere.]

I. If the defendant or the government does not consent to proceedings in this court, follow the procedures in Fed. R. Crim. P. 5(c)(3) for transfer to another district. See also *infra* section 1.05: Commitment to another district (removal proceedings).

1.05   Commitment to another district (removal proceedings)

Fed. R. Crim. P. 5, 32.1, and 40

[*Note:* Under the Crime Victims' Rights Act, 18 U.S.C. § 3771(a)(2) and (3), any victim of the offense has the right to notice of "any public court proceeding . . . involving the crime . . . of the accused," and to attend that proceeding. It may be advisable to ask the prosecutor if there are any victims and, if so, whether the government has fulfilled its duty to notify them.]

A. Arrest of an individual in this district for an alleged offense committed in another district (U.S. attorney will have filed a Petition for Removal) Fed. R. Crim. P. 5(c).

   1. Ascertain from the U.S. attorney or arresting officer, or from court file materials received from the charging district

      (a) where the alleged offense was committed;

      (b) when the defendant was arrested and whether the arrest was with or without a warrant; and

      (c) whether an indictment has been returned or an information or complaint filed.

   2. If the arrest in this district was without a warrant (which rarely occurs):

      (a) The defendant cannot be ordered transferred until a complaint and warrant are issued in the charging district.

      (b) The complaint must be filed promptly. See Fed. R. Crim. P. 5(b).

   3. If it is not evident, ask the defendant if he or she can speak and understand English. If the defendant has an attorney, ask if counsel has been able to communicate with the defendant in English. If you doubt the defendant's capacity to understand English, use a certified interpreter. See 28 U.S.C. § 1827.

      If the defendant is a foreign national, regardless of immigration status, consider advising the defendant of the right to consular notification.[1]

---

1. Although judges are not currently required to notify defendants of the right to consular notification, doing so may avoid unnecessary litigation, cost, and delay. Note that a proposed amendment to Fed. R. Crim. P. 5(d)(1) would require the court "to inform non-citizen defendants at their initial appearance that (1) they may request that a consular officer from their country of nationality be notified of their arrest, and (2) in some cases international treaties and agreements require consular notification without a defendant's request. The proposed rule does not, however, address the question whether treaty provisions requiring consular notification may be invoked by individual defendants in a judicial proceeding and what, if any, remedy may exist for a violation of Article 36 of the Vienna Convention." See

4. Without asking the defendant to state his or her name or other identifying information at this time, advise the defendant of his or her
   (a) general rights under Fed. R. Crim. P. 5 (nature of charge, right to counsel, right to remain silent—see *supra* section 1.01: Initial appearance);
   (b) right to waive removal and voluntarily return to the district where charges are pending;
   (c) right, if charges are based on complaint and warrant, to
       (i) have a preliminary examination in this district;
       (ii) have a preliminary examination in the district where the charges are pending; or
       (iii) waive preliminary examination.
   (d) right to an identity hearing and the right to waive that hearing;
   (e) right under Fed. R. Crim. P. 20 to plead guilty or nolo contendere in this district if both U.S. attorneys consent.

5. If the defendant appears without counsel, appoint counsel or allow time for the defendant to retain counsel; set an appropriate hearing or examination date to allow counsel time to confer and elect options.

6. If the defendant appears with counsel or after counsel has been appointed or retained, ascertain which of the above options (4(b)–4(d) of this section) he or she desires, then sign an Order of Removal (whereby the defendant returns voluntarily) or set an appropriate examination or hearing date.

---

the May 17, 2012 "Report of the Advisory Committee on Criminal Rules" *in* the Preliminary Draft of Proposed Amendments to the Federal Rules of Appellate, Bankruptcy, and Criminal Procedure, and the Federal Rules of Evidence at 205 (Committee on Rules of Practice and Procedure of the Judicial Conference of the United States, Aug. 15, 2012) (http://www.uscourts.gov/uscourts/rules/rules-published-comment.pdf). The proposed "Committee Note" to the amendment states that having a judge provide this advice is not designed to relieve law enforcement officers of their responsibility to do so, but rather "to provide additional assurance that U.S. treaty obligations are fulfilled, and to create a judicial record of that action." *Id.* at 208.

For more detailed guidance relating to the arrest and detention of foreign nationals, see Consular Notification and Access: Instructions for Federal, State, and Local Law Enforcement and Other Officials Regarding Foreign Nationals in the United States and the Rights of Consular Officials to Assist Them, *available at* http://travel.state.gov/pdf/cna/CNA_Manual_3d_Edition.pdf on the U.S. Department of State website, http://travel.state.gov/consul_notify.html. See particularly the sections "Steps to Follow When a Foreign National Is Arrested or Detained" and "Suggested Statements to Arrested or Detained Foreign Nationals." *See also* 28 C.F.R. § 50.5(a) ("Some of the treaties obligate the United States to notify the consular officer only upon the demand or request of the arrested foreign national. On the other hand, some of the treaties require notifying the consul of the arrest of a foreign national whether or not the arrested person requests such notification.").

   (a) If the defendant waives the right to an identity hearing, have the defendant state his or her full name and age for the record.

   (b) Set the date of the hearing or examination to allow time for inquiry into possible Fed. R. Crim. P. 20 transfer.

   (c) Keep in mind Speedy Trial Act requirements (see *infra* section 1.10: Speedy Trial Act).

7. Determine whether to release or detain the defendant pending further proceedings. A request for detention or the amount of bail previously fixed in the district where charges are pending must be taken into account but is not binding. A different action, however, requires reasons in writing. Note that the defendant is entitled to only one detention hearing and may wish to reserve that right until after being transferred to the charging district.

[*Note:* If there are any victims of the offense present, give them an "opportunity to be reasonably heard" regarding the defendant's possible release. 18 U.S.C. § 3771(a)(4).]

8. Conduct hearings:

   (a) Preliminary hearing (Fed. R. Crim. P. 5.1).

   (b) Identity hearing (Fed. R. Crim. P. 5(c)(3)(D)(ii))

      (i) Hear evidence as to physical descriptions, fingerprints, handwriting, hearsay statements, telephone checks with charging district, photographs, probation officer's testimony, etc.

      (ii) The government has the burden of proof to show probable cause that the person arrested is the person named in the charging instrument.

   (c) Fed. R. Crim. P. 20 transfer plea (see *supra* section 1.04: Offense committed in another district).

9. Order the defendant held and transferred (Order of Removal), or discharged; transmit papers and any bail to the clerk of the charging district.

B. Arrest of a probationer or a supervised releasee in a district other than the district of supervision (Fed. R. Crim. P. 32.1(a)(5)).[2]

1. Determine the time and place of, and authority for, the arrest; inform the defendant of the charges; and advise the defendant of general rights (nature of charge, right to counsel, right to remain silent).

---

2. Note that the Crime Victims' Rights Act, 18 U.S.C. § 3771, may apply if the violation that caused the arrest involved the commission of a federal crime. It is not clear whether the rights of victims of the *original* offense carry over to court proceedings for violations of probation or supervised release.

2. Ascertain if jurisdiction has been or will be transferred to this district pursuant to 18 U.S.C. § 3605 (made applicable to supervised re-leasees by 18 U.S.C. § 3586). If so, proceed under Fed. R. Crim. P. 32.1 as a normal revocation case in this district.

3. If the alleged violation occurred in this district and if jurisdiction is not transferred, schedule and hold a prompt preliminary hearing af-ter counsel has been secured.

    (a) If probable cause is found, hold the defendant to answer in the supervising district, and order him or her transferred there.

    (b) If no probable cause is found, dismiss the proceedings and notify the supervising court.

4. If the alleged violation occurred in a district other than this one, schedule and hold a prompt identity hearing (unless waived) after counsel has been secured.

    (a) If, upon production of certified copies of the probation order, war-rant, and application for warrant, the defendant is found to be the person named in the warrant, hold the defendant to answer in the supervising district and order him or her transferred there.

    Or

    (b) Dismiss the proceedings and notify the supervising court if you find the defendant is not the person so named.

[*Note:* An amendment to Fed. R. Crim. P. 40(a), effective December 1, 2006, specifically authorizes magistrate judges to set release conditions for per-sons arrested under a warrant issued in another district for violating condi-tions of release set in that district.]

C. Arrest for failure to appear in another district (bench warrant) (Fed. R. Crim. P. 40(a) and (b)).[3]

When the person has been arrested in this district on a warrant issued in another district for failure to appear, pursuant to a subpoena or the terms of his or her release:

1. Determine the time and place of, and authority for, the arrest; inform the defendant of the charges; and advise the defendant of general rights (nature of charges, right to counsel, right to remain silent).

2. Schedule and hold an identity hearing (unless waived) after counsel has been secured.

    (a) If, upon production of the warrant or a certified copy, you find that the person before the court is the person named in the war-rant, hold the defendant to answer in the district where the war-rant was issued and order him or her transferred there.

---

3. Note: Rule 40(d) was added to allow an appearance under Rule 40 to be conducted by video teleconference, with the defendant's consent, in conformity with Rule 5(f).

Or

(b) Dismiss the proceedings and notify the district where the warrant was issued if you find the defendant is not the person so named.

3. The court may modify any previous release or detention order issued by the other district, but must state in writing the reasons for doing so. Fed. R. Crim. P. 40(c).

4. Note that the Crime Victims' Rights Act, 18 U.S.C. § 3771, may be applicable to this hearing.

Other FJC sources

David N. Adair, Jr., The Bail Reform Act of 1984, at 13 (3d ed. 2006)

1.06 Waiver of indictment

Fed. R. Crim. P. 6 & 7

[*Note:* Under the Crime Victims' Rights Act, 18 U.S.C. § 3771(a)(2) and (3), any victim of the offense has the right to notice of "any public court proceeding . . . involving the crime . . . of the accused," and to attend that proceeding. It may be advisable to ask the prosecutor if there are any victims and, if so, whether the government has fulfilled its duty to notify them.]

A. Preliminary

Have the oath administered and ask the defendant:

1. What is your full name?

2. How old are you?

3. How far did you go in school? What is your employment experience?

   [If you are not sure the defendant can understand English, ask:]

4. Are you able to speak and understand English?

   [If the defendant has an attorney, ask counsel if he or she has been able to communicate with the defendant. If you doubt the defendant's capacity to understand English, use a certified interpreter. See 28 U.S.C. § 1827.]

5. Are you currently or have you recently been under the care of a physician or a psychiatrist or been hospitalized or treated for narcotics addiction? Have you taken any drugs, medicine, or pills or drunk any alcoholic beverage in the past twenty-four hours?

   [If the answer to either question is yes, pursue the subject with the defendant and with counsel to determine that the defendant is currently competent to waive indictment.]

6. Do you have an attorney?

   [If the defendant does not have an attorney, inform the defendant of the right to counsel and appoint counsel if the defendant qualifies (see *supra* section 1.02: Assignment of counsel or pro se representation).]

B. Ask the defendant:

   Have you been furnished with a copy of the charge(s) against you?

C. Explain in detail the charge(s) against the defendant and make clear that he or she is charged with committing a felony.

> **NOTE**
>
> An offense that may be punishable by death must be prosecuted by indictment and therefore precludes waiver of indictment. Fed. R. Crim. P. 7(a) and (b).

D. Ask the defendant:

> Do you understand the charge(s) against you?

E. Inform the defendant:

1. You have a constitutional right to be charged by an indictment of a grand jury, but you can waive that right and consent to being charged by information of the U.S. attorney.

2. Instead of an indictment, these felony charges against you have been brought by the U.S. attorney by the filing of an information.

3. Unless you waive indictment, you may not be charged with a felony unless a grand jury finds by return of an indictment that there is probable cause to believe that a crime has been committed and that you committed it.

4. If you do not waive indictment, the government may present the case to the grand jury and ask it to indict you.

5. A grand jury is composed of at least sixteen and not more than twenty-three persons, and at least twelve grand jurors must find that there is probable cause to believe you committed the crime with which you are charged before you may be indicted.

   [Fed. R. Crim. P. 6(a) and 6(f).]

6. The grand jury might or might not indict you.

7. If you waive indictment by the grand jury, the case will proceed against you on the U.S. attorney's information just as though you had been indicted.

F. Ask the defendant:

1. Have you discussed waiving your right to indictment by the grand jury with your attorney?

2. Do you understand your right to indictment by a grand jury?

3. Have any threats or promises been made to induce you to waive indictment?

4. Do you wish to waive your right to indictment by a grand jury?

[Fed. R. Crim. P. 7(b).]

G. Ask defense counsel if there is any reason the defendant should not waive indictment.

H. If the defendant waives indictment

1. Have the defendant sign the waiver of indictment form in open court, state that the court finds that the waiver is knowingly and vol-

untarily made by the defendant and is accepted by the court, and enter an order and finding to that effect.[1]

2. Proceed to arraignment on information (see *infra* section 1.07: Arraignment and plea).

I. If the defendant does not waive indictment:

1. Ask the U.S. attorney whether the government intends to present the matter to the grand jury.

    (a) If so, detain the defendant pending indictment or continue or reset bail (see *supra* section 1.03: Release or detention pending trial).

    (b) If not, discharge the defendant.

    [*Note:* Because discharge entails a "release" of the defendant, the Crime Victims' Rights Act, 18 U.S.C. § 3771(a)(4), may require allowing any victims of the offense to be "reasonably heard."]

---

1. If the waiver was signed before the hearing, the court should examine the signatures on the form and have the defendant and defendant's counsel verify that the signatures are theirs.

1.07 Arraignment and plea

Fed. R. Crim. P. 10

[*Note:* Under the Crime Victims' Rights Act, 18 U.S.C. § 3771(a)(2) and (3), any victim of the offense has the right to notice of "any public court proceeding . . . involving the crime . . . of the accused," and to attend that proceeding. It may be advisable to ask the prosecutor if there are any victims and, if so, whether the government has fulfilled its duty to notify them.]

A defendant who was charged by indictment or misdemeanor information may waive appearance at the arraignment if a written waiver is signed by the defendant and defense counsel, the defendant affirms that a copy of the indictment or information was received, the plea is not guilty, and the court accepts the waiver. Fed R. Crim. P. 10(b).

The following procedure may be used whether the defendant appears in person or has consented to video teleconference under Fed R. Crim. P. 10(c). If the arraignment is by video teleconferencing and there is no prior written consent, begin the arraignment by having the defendant explicitly consent to conduct the arraignment by video teleconference and waive the right to appear in person.

A. Preliminary

Have oath administered and ask the defendant:

1. What is your full name?

2. How old are you?

3. How far did you go in school? What is your employment experience?

[If you are not sure the defendant can understand English, ask:]

4. Are you able to speak and understand English?

[If the defendant has an attorney, ask counsel if he or she has been able to communicate with the defendant. If you doubt the defendant's capacity to understand English, use a certified interpreter. See 28 U.S.C. § 1827.]

5. Are you currently or have you recently been under the care of a physician or a psychiatrist or been hospitalized or treated for narcotics addiction? Have you taken any drugs, medicine, or pills or drunk any alcoholic beverage in the past twenty-four hours?

[If the answer to either question is yes, pursue the subject with the defendant and with counsel to determine that the defendant is currently competent to enter a plea.]

6. Do you have an attorney?

>   [If not, see *supra* section 1.02: Assignment of counsel or pro se representation).]

B. Ask the defendant:
    1. Have you received a copy of the indictment [information]?
    2. Have you had time to consult with your attorney?
    3. Do you want the indictment [information] read, or will you waive the reading of the indictment [information]?

       [Have the indictment [information] read if the defendant so desires.]
    4. How do you plead to the charges?

C. If the defendant's plea is not guilty:
    1. Set motion and/or trial dates according to your local Speedy Trial Act plan.
    2. Continue or reset bail (see *supra* section 1.03: Release or detention pending trial).

D. If the defendant indicates a desire to plead guilty or nolo contendere, see *infra* section 2.01: Taking pleas of guilty or nolo contendere.

1.08 Joint representation of codefendants

Fed. R. Crim. P. 44(c)(2)

[*Note:* Under the Crime Victims' Rights Act, 18 U.S.C. § 3771(a)(2) and (3), any victim of the offense has the right to notice of "any public court proceeding . . . involving the crime . . . of the accused," and to attend that proceeding. It may be advisable to ask the prosecutor if there are any victims and, if so, whether the government has fulfilled its duty to notify them.]

Introduction

Fed. R. Crim. P. 44(c)(2) provides as follows in cases of joint representation:

> The court must promptly inquire about the propriety of joint representation and must personally advise each defendant of the right to effective assistance of counsel, including separate representation. Unless there is good cause to believe that no conflict of interest is likely to arise, the court must take appropriate measures to protect each defendant's right to counsel.

When a trial court becomes aware of a potential conflict of interest, it must pursue the matter, even if counsel does not. Judges should strongly recommend to codefendants that they avoid dual representation and should make clear that a court-appointed attorney is available to represent each defendant or to consult with each defendant concerning dual representation. This section is a hearing procedure for so advising defendants and for obtaining a waiver of the right to separate counsel. Note, however, that in certain situations, a district court may disqualify an attorney, despite a defendant's voluntary, knowing, and intelligent waiver of the right to conflict-free counsel. See *Wheat v. United States,* 486 U.S. 153, 163 (1988) ("district court must be allowed substantial latitude in refusing waivers of conflicts of interest not only in those rare cases where an actual conflict may be demonstrated before trial, but in the more common cases where a potential for conflict exists which may or may not burgeon into an actual conflict as the trial progresses").

Procedure

A. Determine if the defendant is competent.

    1. Ask the defendant:

        (a) Mr., Ms., Mrs., Miss _____, how old are you?

        (b) How far did you go in school?

        [If you are not sure the defendant can understand English, ask:]

        (c) Are you able to speak and understand English?

[Ask defense counsel if he or she has been able to communicate with the defendant in English. If you doubt the defendant's capacity to understand English, use a certified interpreter. See 28 U.S.C. § 1827.]

(d) Have you taken any drugs, medicine, or pills or drunk any alcoholic beverage in the past twenty-four hours? Do you understand what is happening today?

2. Then ask defense counsel and prosecutor:

Do either of you have any doubt as to the defendant's competence at this time?

3. State your finding on the record of the defendant's competence.

B. Emphasize the seriousness of the charges. Tell the defendant the maximum punishment for each count.

C. Tell the defendant:

1. If at any time you do not understand something or have a question, consult your lawyer or ask me any questions.

2. This proceeding can be continued to another day if you wish to consult another lawyer.

D. Advise the defendant about the apparent conflict of interest in his or her lawyer's representation. For example, state:

The United States Constitution gives every defendant the right to effective assistance of counsel. When one lawyer represents two or more defendants in a case, the lawyer may have trouble representing all of the defendants with the same fairness. This is a conflict of interest that denies the defendant the right to effective assistance of counsel. Such conflicts are always a potential problem because different defendants may have different degrees of involvement. Each defendant has the right to a lawyer who represents only him or her.

E. Point out the various ways in which dual representation might work to the defendant's disadvantage. This may be done by giving the defendant a form to read or by advising the defendant in the following way:

1. Dual representation may inhibit or prevent counsel from conducting an independent investigation in support of each defendant's case. For example, the attorney–client privilege may prevent your lawyer from communicating to you information gathered from another defendant.

2. The government may offer immunity or offer to recommend a lesser sentence to one defendant for cooperating with the government. Should you receive such an offer, your lawyer ought to

advise you whether or not to accept it. But if your lawyer advises you to accept the offer, it may harm the cases of the other defendants represented by that lawyer.

3. The government may let a defendant who is not as involved as other defendants plead guilty to lesser charges than the other defendants. After the guilty plea, however, the government may require the defendant to testify. A lawyer who represents more than one defendant might recommend that the first defendant not plead guilty in order to protect the other defendants that the lawyer represents. On the other hand, the lawyer might recommend that the first defendant plead guilty, which might harm the cases of the other defendants.

4. Dual representation may affect how your lawyer exercises peremptory challenges or challenges for cause during jury selection. Potential jurors who may be perceived as favorable to you may be perceived as harmful to another defendant, or jurors who may be perceived as favorable to other defendants may be harmful to you.

5. Sometimes one of the defendants represented by a lawyer will take the stand to testify in his or her own behalf. In order to represent the other defendants fairly, the lawyer should question the defendant on the stand as completely as possible. However, the lawyer may not be able to do that because he or she cannot ask the defendant as a witness about anything that the defendant has told the lawyer in confidence.

6. The best defense for a single defendant often is the argument that while the other defendants may be guilty, he or she is not. A lawyer representing two or more defendants cannot effectively make such an argument.

7. Evidence that helps one defendant might harm another defendant's case. When one lawyer represents two or more defendants, the lawyer might offer or object to evidence that could help one defendant but harm another.

8. Regarding sentencing, dual representation would prohibit the lawyer from engaging in post-trial negotiations with the government as to full disclosure by one defendant against the other. It would also prohibit the lawyer from arguing the relative culpability of the defendants to the sentencing judge.

F. An attorney proposing to represent codefendants should be required to assure the court that there will be no conflict that could result in a lack of effective assistance of counsel or other prejudice to any defendant.

G. Consider recommending that the defendant consult with other, independent counsel about the wisdom of waiving the right to separate counsel. Offer to make CJA counsel available (if appropriate) and allow adjournment for that purpose.

H. If the defendant wants to waive the right to separate counsel, get a clear, on-the-record oral waiver by him or her of the right to separate counsel. In addition, you may want the defendant to sign a written waiver.

1.09 Waiver of jury trial (suggested procedures, questions, and statements)

Fed. R. Crim. P. 23

[*Note:* Under the Crime Victims' Rights Act, 18 U.S.C. § 3771(a)(2) and (3), any victim of the offense has the right to notice of "any public court proceeding . . . involving the crime . . . of the accused," and to attend that proceeding. It may be advisable to ask the prosecutor if there are any victims and, if so, whether the government has fulfilled its duty to notify them.]

Introduction

Trial by jury is a fundamental constitutional right, and waiver of the right to a jury trial should be accepted by a trial judge only when three requirements are satisfied:

1. the procedures of Fed. R. Crim. P. 23(a) have been followed;
2. the waiver is knowing and voluntary; and
3. the defendant is competent to waive a constitutional right.

Fed. R. Crim. P. 23(a) requires that the accused's waiver of the right to trial by jury be

1. made in writing;
2. consented to by the government; and
3. approved by the court.

Following this rule alone does not satisfy the requirement that the waiver be knowing and voluntary, however.

The trial judge should ascertain on the record

1. whether the accused understands that he or she has a right to be tried by a jury;
2. whether the accused understands the difference between a jury trial and a nonjury trial; and
3. whether the accused has been made to understand the advantages and disadvantages of a jury trial.

Before approving the waiver, a trial judge must consider a defendant's mental capacity to waive a jury trial. A defendant is not competent to waive a constitutional right if mental incapacity or illness substantially impairs his or her ability to make a reasoned choice among the alternatives presented and to understand the nature and consequences of the waiver.

When information available from any source presents a question as to the defendant's competence to waive a jury trial, sua sponte inquiry into that competence must be made.

In any psychiatric examination ordered under the inherent power of the court or under 18 U.S.C. § 4241, the examining psychiatrist should be directed to give an opinion on the defendant's competence to make an intelligent waiver. Whenever any question as to the defendant's competence arises, a specific finding of competence or incompetence should be made.

Finally, if any doubt of competence exists, the judge should order a jury trial.

Suggested procedures and questions

A. Preliminary questions for the defendant

   1. The court is informed that you desire to waive your right to a jury trial. Is that correct?

   2. Before accepting your waiver to a jury trial, there are a number of questions I will ask you to ensure that it is a valid waiver. If you do not understand any of the questions or at any time wish to interrupt the proceeding to consult further with your attorney, please say so, since it is essential to a valid waiver that you understand each question before you answer. Do you understand?

   3. What is your full name?

   4. How old are you?

   5. How far did you go in school?

      [If you are not sure the defendant understands English, ask:]

   6. Are you able to speak and understand English?

      [Ask defense counsel if he or she has been able to communicate with the defendant in English. If you doubt the defendant's capacity to understand English, use a certified interpreter. See 28 U.S.C. § 1827.]

   7. What is your employment background?

   8. Have you taken any drugs, medicine, or pills, or drunk any alcoholic beverage in the past twenty-four hours?

   9. Do you understand that you are entitled to a trial by jury on the charges filed against you?

   10. Do you understand that a jury trial means that you will be tried by a jury consisting of twelve people and that all of the jurors must agree on the verdict?

   11. Do you understand that you have the right to participate in the selection of the jury?

   12. Do you understand that if I approve your waiver of a jury trial, the court will try the case and determine your innocence or guilt?

   13. Have you discussed with your attorney your right to a jury trial?

    14. Have you discussed with your attorney the advantages and disadvantages of a jury trial? Do you want to discuss this issue further with your attorney?

B. Questions for counsel

In determining whether the accused has made a "knowing and voluntary" waiver and is competent to waive the right to a jury trial, the judge should question both the defense counsel and the prosecutor.

  1. Ask the defense counsel:

    (a) Have you discussed with the defendant the advantages and disadvantages of a jury trial?

    (b) Do you have any doubt that the defendant is making a "knowing and voluntary" waiver of the right to a jury trial?

    (c) Has anything come to your attention suggesting that the defendant may not be competent to waive a jury trial?

  2. Ask the prosecutor:

    Has anything come to your attention suggesting that the defendant may not be competent to waive a jury trial?

C. Form of waiver and oral finding

  1. A written waiver of a jury trial must be signed by the defendant, approved by the defendant's attorney, consented to by the government, and approved by the court.

  2. It is suggested that the judge state orally:

    This court finds that the defendant has knowingly and voluntarily waived his [her] right to a jury trial, and I approve that waiver.

  3. An appropriate written waiver of jury trial may take the form of the one shown on the next page.

Other FJC sources

Manual on Recurring Problems in Criminal Trials 9–10 (Tucker Carrington & Kris Markarian eds., 6th ed. 2010)

In the U.S. District Court
for the District of [   ]

United States of America	)	
	)	No. Cr_____
v.	)	Waiver of trial
	)	by jury
	)	
[Defendant]	)	

I acknowledge that I was fully informed of my right to trial by jury in this cause. I hereby waive that right, request the court to try all issues of fact and law without a jury, and waive my right to special findings.

Dated at _____, this ____ day of _____, 20__ .

_____
Defendant

APPROVED:

_____
Attorney for Defendant

The United States of America consents to the defendant's waiver of a jury trial and waives its right to request special findings.

_____
Assistant U.S. Attorney

I find that the defendant has knowingly and voluntarily waived the right to a jury trial, and I approve the waiver.

_____
Judge

1.10 Speedy Trial Act

18 U.S.C. §§ 3161–3166

Title I of the Speedy Trial Act of 1974 (18 U.S.C. § 3161) imposes time limits within which criminal defendants must be brought to trial. The time limits are expressed as numbers of days from certain events, but the statute provides that certain periods of time be "excluded" in computing these limits, thereby extending the deadlines. The statute applies to offenses other than petty offenses.[1] This section is offered as a general guide to the time limits and exceptions in the Speedy Trial Act. Judges should be aware that circuit law may differ on specific issues.

Judges should also be aware of the possible effect of the Crime Victims' Rights Act. Any victims of the offense have the right to be notified by the government of, and not be excluded from, any public proceeding. They also have a right to "proceedings free from unreasonable delay," which may need to be considered if exceptions to the Speedy Trial Act's time limits are requested. See 18 U.S.C. § 3771(a)(2), (3), and (7).

Dismissal

Failure to comply with the time limits generally requires that a cause be dismissed, although not necessarily with prejudice. In deciding whether to dismiss with or without prejudice, the court should consider the seriousness of the offense, the facts and circumstances that led to the dismissal, and the impact of a reprosecution on the administration of the Speedy Trial Act and the administration of justice. See 18 U.S.C. § 3162(a)(1) and (2). If the defendant may be released, victims should be given an "opportunity to be reasonably heard" at any public proceeding on the issue. 18 U.S.C. § 3771(a)(4).

Waiver by defendant

Although a defendant's failure to make a timely motion for dismissal on speedy trial grounds is deemed a waiver of the right to dismissal,[2] courts should not rely solely on defendants' agreements to delay their trials beyond the statutory time limits. As the Supreme Court concluded,

> § 3161(h) has no provision excluding periods of delay during which a defendant waives the application of the Act, and it is apparent from the terms of the

---

1. "Petty offense" means an offense that is punishable by imprisonment of six months or less and for which the maximum fine (including any "alternative fine" under 18 U.S.C. § 3571(d)) is no more than $5,000 for individuals or $10,000 for organizations. 18 U.S.C. §§ 19 and 3581.

2. *See* 18 U.S.C. § 3162(a)(2) ("Failure of the defendant to move for dismissal prior to trial or entry of a plea of guilty or nolo contendere shall constitute a waiver of the right to dismissal under this section.").

Act that this omission was a considered one. Instead of simply allowing defendants to opt out of the Act, the Act demands that defense continuance requests
fit within one of the specific exclusions set out in subsection (h).

Zedner v. United States, 126 S. Ct. 1976, 1985–87 (2006) (holding that "a defendant may not prospectively waive the application of the Act" and that
"petitioner's waiver 'for all time' was ineffective").

Basic time limits

Indictment or information

An indictment or information must be filed within thirty days after arrest or
service of a summons. However, if a defendant is charged with a felony in a
district in which no grand jury has been in session during the thirty-day period, the time for filing an indictment shall be extended an additional thirty
days. See 18 U.S.C. § 3161(b). If an indictment or information is dismissed or
otherwise dropped and if charges based on or arising from the same conduct
are later refiled, "the provisions of subsections (b) and (c) of this section
shall be applicable with respect to such subsequent complaint, indictment,
or information." 18 U.S.C. § 3161(d)(1).

Trial

A trial must commence within seventy days after the *later* of (a) the date of
the indictment or information or (b) the date of the defendant's initial appearance before a judicial officer in the district in which charges were
brought. See 18 U.S.C. § 3161(c). In some circumstances, the deadline for
trial on a superseding indictment relates back to the original indictment.

Trial, defendant in custody

A trial of a defendant held in pretrial detention must also commence within
ninety days of the beginning of continuous custody. This deadline may in
some cases be earlier than the seventy-day deadline referred to above. See
18 U.S.C. § 3164(b). The sanction is release from custody rather than dismissal of the case. See 18 U.S.C. § 3164(c). If the defendant's release involves a "public hearing," a victim has the right to be heard. See 18 U.S.C.
§ 3771(a)(4).

Retrial

A retrial following a mistrial or order for a new trial must commence within
seventy days after the date the action occasioning the retrial becomes final.
18 U.S.C. § 3161(e). Retrial following a dismissal by the trial court and reinstatement after appeal, or following an appeal or collateral attack, must also
commence within seventy days, but an extension of up to 180 days may be
allowed if trial within seventy days is impractical. 18 U.S.C. § 3161(d) and
(e).

Trial commencement limitations

The Act requires that the trial date be determined at the earliest practicable time, after consultation with counsel. See 18 U.S.C. § 3161(a). A trial may not commence less than thirty days after the defendant first appears through counsel or expressly waives counsel and elects to proceed pro se, unless the defendant consents in writing. See 18 U.S.C. § 3161(c)(2).

Excludable periods

There are several periods of delay that "shall be excluded" from the time limits for filing an indictment or information or for commencing trial. See 18 U.S.C. § 3161(h)(1)–(8). Among these are periods of delay resulting "from other proceedings concerning the defendant,"[3] "from the absence or unavailability of the defendant or an essential witness," and "from the fact that the defendant is mentally incompetent or physically unable to stand trial."

A period of delay resulting from the granting of a continuance may also be excluded if the continuance was granted on the basis of a finding that "the ends of justice served by taking such action outweigh the best interest of the public and the defendant in a speedy trial." The court must put on the record, "either orally or in writing, its reasons for [that] finding."[4] See 18 U.S.C. § 3161(h)(7)(A) & (B) (listing some of the factors a judge should consider in determining whether to grant a continuance).[5] The Supreme Court held that "if a judge fails to make the requisite findings regarding the need for an ends-of-justice continuance, the delay resulting from the continuance

---

3. Section 3161(h)(1)(D) excludes periods of "delay resulting from any pretrial motion, from the filing of the motion through the conclusion of the hearing on, or other prompt disposition of, such motion." However, the Supreme Court has held that any time granted to *prepare* such motions is not automatically excluded, and is only excludable if, following § 3161(h)(7), "the court sets forth, in the record of the case, either orally or in writing, its reasons for finding that the ends of justice served by the granting of such continuance outweigh the best interests of the public and the defendant in a speedy trial." Bloate v. United States, 130 S. Ct. 1345, 1351–58 (2010). Note that once a motion is actually filed, it falls within subsection (D) "irrespective of whether it actually causes, or is expected to cause, delay in starting a trial." United States v. Tinklenberg, 131 S. Ct. 2007, 2011 (2011).

4. Consider asking the U.S. attorney to prepare the form of the order.

5. *See e.g.,* United States v. Sutcliffe, 505 F.3d 944, 956–57 (9th Cir. 2007) ("ends of justice" continuance properly granted "to allow [newly] appointed defense counsel time to prepare for trial given the complexity of the case, the large amount of electronic evidence, and the repeated changes in Defendant's representation"); United States v. Gardner, 488 F.3d 700, 718–19 (6th Cir. 2007) (same, where three codefendants all requested extra time to reconcile trial dates and prepare for trial); United States v. Apperson, 441 F.3d 1162, 1183–84 (10th Cir. 2006) (same, for medical problems of defendant's attorney); United States v. Ruth, 65 F.3d 599, 606 (7th Cir. 1995) (same, for delay caused by defendant's refusal to provide handwriting exemplars); United States v. Drapeau, 978 F.2d 1072, 1072–73 (8th Cir. 1992) (same, to allow time for DNA test that would either exculpate or inculpate defendant); United States v. Sarro, 742 F.2d 1286, 1300 (11th Cir. 1984) (same, where one codefendant's attorney had other trial scheduled at same time and another codefendant's brother had recently died).

must be counted, and if as a result the trial does not begin on time, the indictment or information must be dismissed. . . . [W]e leave it to the District Court to determine in the first instance whether dismissal should be with or without prejudice."[6] *Zedner v. United States*, 547 U.S. 489, 507–09 (2006) (the Court added that "at the very least the Act implies that those findings must be put on the record by the time a district court rules on a defendant's motion to dismiss under § 3162(a)(2)").

Note that a continuance under this section may not be granted "because of general congestion of the court's calendar, or lack of diligent preparation or failure to obtain available witnesses on the part of the attorney for the Government." 18 U.S.C. § 3161(h)(7)(C). The right of crime victims to "proceedings free from unreasonable delay" may also have to be considered. See 18 U.S.C. § 3771(a)(7).

Other aids to interpretation

The speedy trial plan adopted by each district court pursuant to 18 U.S.C. §§ 3165, 3166

Administrative Office of the U.S. Courts, 1 Clerks Manual: United States District Courts § 8.08 (1993)

Judicial Conference Committee on the Administration of the Criminal Law, Guidelines to the Administration of the Speedy Trial Act of 1974 (rev. ed. October 1984), 106 F.R.D. 271 (1984)

Other FJC sources

Anthony Partridge, Legislative History of Title I of the Speedy Trial Act of 1974 (1980)

---

6. *See* § 3162(a)(2) ("In determining whether to dismiss the case with or without prejudice, the court shall consider, among others, each of the following factors: the seriousness of the offense; the facts and circumstances of the case which led to the dismissal; and the impact of a reprosecution on the administration of this chapter and on the administration of justice.").

1.11 Delinquency proceedings

18 U.S.C. §§ 5031 et seq.

A. Proceeding as an adult or a juvenile

  1. Jurisdiction

     (a) The district court has jurisdiction over a juvenile who is alleged to have committed a violation of law in the court's special maritime and territorial jurisdiction for which the maximum authorized term of imprisonment is six months or less.

     (b) In other cases, the district court has jurisdiction only if the Attorney General, after investigation, certifies one of the following:

         (i)   that a juvenile court or other appropriate state court does not have jurisdiction or refuses to assume jurisdiction over a juvenile with respect to the alleged act of juvenile delinquency;

         (ii) that the state does not have available programs and services adequate for the needs of juveniles; or

         (iii) that the offense charged is a crime of violence that is a felony, or is an offense described in certain sections of title 21, *and* that there is a substantial federal interest in the case or the offense.

     If jurisdiction is not established under paragraph (a) or (b) above, the juvenile must be surrendered to appropriate state authorities. If jurisdiction is established, the prosecution proceeds by information or by violation notice or complaint under 18 U.S.C. § 3401(g). See 18 U.S.C. § 5032. See also the Calendar of Events at the end of this section.

  2. Preliminary procedures

     (a) Clear the courtroom of all persons except those associated with the case. Close the outside and inside doors and instruct the marshal not to open them during the proceedings.

     (b) Take the appearances of counsel.

     (c) Explain to the parties that the hearing will be divided into two parts as follows:

         (i) the court determines if the juvenile should proceed as an adult or a juvenile;

         (ii) the juvenile admits or denies the charges against him or her (see *infra* subsection B of this section).

     (d) Ensure that the juvenile can speak and understand English and that defense counsel has been able to communicate with the juvenile in English. If there is any doubt about the juvenile's ability to understand English, use a certified interpreter. See 28 U.S.C. § 1827.

3. Explain the rights of an adult:
   (a) to an initial appearance before the magistrate judge;
   (b) to counsel;
   (c) to a bail hearing;
   (d) to an indictment, if applicable;
   (e) to a preliminary examination to determine probable cause if the defendant is not indicted; and
   (f) to a trial by jury (explain composition of jury) in which the government will have to prove that the defendant is guilty beyond a reasonable doubt and in which the defendant has the right
      (i) to confront and cross-examine witnesses; and
      (ii) to remain silent, testify, or call witnesses.

4. Explain the rights of a juvenile:
   (a) to an initial appearance before the magistrate judge;
   (b) to counsel;
   (c) to an information, violation notice, or complaint, as opposed to an indictment by grand jury;[1]
   (d) to a hearing before the court to determine delinquency,[2] during which the defendant has the right
      (i) to confront and cross-examine witnesses;[3]
      (ii) to remain silent, testify, or call witnesses;[4] and
      (iii) to have the government prove guilt beyond a reasonable doubt;[5]
   and
   (e) to have his or her name and picture withheld from the media.[6]

---

1. 18 U.S.C. § 5032; United States v. Hill, 538 F.2d 1072 (4th Cir. 1976).

2. McKeiver v. Pennsylvania, 403 U.S. 528 (1971); United States v. Hill, 538 F.2d 1072 (4th Cir. 1976).

3. *In re* Gault, 387 U.S. 1 (1967); United States v. Costanzo, 395 F.2d 441 (4th Cir. 1968).

4. *In re* Gault, 387 U.S. 1 (1967); United States v. Hill, 538 F.2d 1072 (4th Cir. 1976); West v. United States, 399 F.2d 467 (5th Cir. 1968) (factors in deciding if juvenile has waived privilege against self-incrimination.

5. *In re* Gault, 387 U.S. 1 (1967); United States v. Hill, 538 F.2d 1072 (4th Cir. 1976); United States v. Costanzo, 395 F.2d 441 (4th Cir. 1968).

6. 18 U.S.C. § 5038(e).

5. Election to proceed as an adult or a juvenile
    (a) Explain the maximum penalties under the applicable statute if the juvenile elects to proceed as an adult.
    (b) Explain the disposition under the Federal Juvenile Delinquency Act (FJDA), which gives the court the following options:
        (i)   to suspend the findings of delinquency;
        (ii)   to require that the juvenile make restitution to the victim(s) of the delinquent conduct;
        (iii)   to place the juvenile on probation; or
        (iv)   to commit the juvenile to official detention.
        18 U.S.C. § 5037(a)
    (c) Explain that if the juvenile elects to proceed as an adult,
        (i)   the request must be in writing and upon the advice of counsel.[7]
        (ii)   the juvenile may plead not guilty and force the government to trial by jury under an indictment, if applicable.
        (iii)   the juvenile may plead guilty and forgo trial.
    (d) Explain that if the juvenile elects to proceed as a juvenile,
        (i)   the request may be oral.
        (ii)   the juvenile may deny the charges against him or her and force the government to try the case before the judge.
        (iii)   the juvenile may admit the charges filed in the information, violation notice, or complaint, forgoing trial.
    (e) Ask counsel
        (i)   if proceeding as a juvenile is in the individual's best interests; and
        (ii)   if family members present in the courtroom have discussed the individual's election with counsel.
    (f) Ask the juvenile:

    Do you elect to proceed as an adult or as a juvenile?

        (i)   If the juvenile elects to proceed as an adult, proceed to arraignment as an adult (see *infra* section 2.01: Taking pleas of guilty or nolo contendere).
        (ii)   If the juvenile elects to proceed as a juvenile, proceed to arraignment of a juvenile (see *infra* subsection B of this section).

---

7. 18 U.S.C. § 5032.

6. Motion by Attorney General to proceed against the juvenile as an adult
   (a) The Attorney General may make a motion to transfer the juvenile to adult prosecution if the juvenile
       (i) committed an act that if committed by an adult would be a felony that is a crime of violence or a specified drug offense from title 21; and
       (ii) committed the act after his or her fifteenth birthday.
   (b) The court may grant the motion if, after a hearing and after considering and making findings in the record on the factors listed in the statute, it finds that the transfer would be "in the interest of justice."
   (c) The age limit for committing the act is lowered to after the thirteenth birthday for certain crimes of violence or if the juvenile possessed a firearm during the offense.
   (d) Reasonable notice of a transfer hearing must be given to the juvenile; the juvenile's parents, guardian, or custodian; and counsel. The juvenile shall be assisted by counsel, and any statements the juvenile makes before or during the transfer hearing are not admissible at subsequent criminal prosecutions.
   See 18 U.S.C. § 5032.
7. Mandatory proceeding as an adult
   The juvenile shall be transferred to district court for prosecution as an adult if the juvenile
   (a) committed an act after his or her sixteenth birthday that if committed by an adult would be a felony offense that is a crime of violence, or a drug offense or other serious crime as described in the statute; and
   (b) has been previously found guilty of an act that if committed by an adult would have been one of the offenses described above or in paragraph 6 above, or found guilty of a violation of a state felony statute that would have been such an offense if committed under federal jurisdiction.
   See 18 U.S.C. § 5032.
B. Arraignment of a juvenile
   1. Administer oath and make sure the juvenile understands that to lie under oath is to commit the crime of perjury.
   2. Direct the U.S. attorney to read the charge(s) against the juvenile.
      (a) The charge(s) must
          (i) reflect that the individual committed an act of juvenile delinquency;

(ii)   cite the statute allegedly violated; and

(iii)   cite 18 U.S.C. § 5032.

(b) The court should direct the following questions to the juvenile:

(1) Have you been given a copy of the charge(s)?

(2) Have you talked to counsel about the charge(s) filed against you?

[Explain the charge(s) and inquire:]

(3) Do you understand the charge(s) against you?

[Explain the penalty and inquire:]

(4) Do you understand the maximum penalty that could be assessed against you if you are found guilty of the charge(s)?

(5) Do you understand that you are entitled to have counsel present with you at all times during these proceedings?

(6) Are you satisfied with your representation (counsel)?

(7) Do you understand that you have a right to deny the charge(s) that has (have) just been read?

(8) Do you understand that if you deny the charge(s), the government will have to bring witnesses that your counsel can cross-examine, and the government will have to convince the court beyond a reasonable doubt

(a) that you committed the crime with which you have been charged; and

(b) that you committed this crime before you reached the age of eighteen?

3. Read the elements of the offense that the government will have to prove.

4. Determine the competence of the juvenile to understand the proceedings and to enter an admission or denial.

(a) The court should ask the following questions:

(1) Have you taken any drugs, medicines, or pills or drunk any alcoholic beverages in the past twenty-four hours?

(2) Do you understand what is happening today?

(b) The court should also ask the juvenile's counsel and the prosecutor this question:

> Do either of you have any doubt as to the juvenile's competence to admit or deny the charge(s) against him [her] at this time?

(c) If, after further interrogation of the juvenile and counsel, there is any question of the juvenile's understanding of the proceedings and of his or her competence to plead, continue the taking of the admission or denial to a later date.

5. Determine the juvenile's awareness of the consequences of an admission. Ask:

   (a) Are you aware that, if you admit the charge(s) against you, you are giving up your right:

      (1) to trial by the court?

      (2) to confront and cross-examine witnesses?

      (3) to remain silent, testify, and call witnesses?

      (4) to require the government to prove guilt beyond a reasonable doubt?

   (b) Are you aware that if you admit the charge(s) against you, you will lose the right to elect to proceed as an adult with the following rights:[8]

      (1) to an indictment, if applicable?

      (2) to a trial by jury?

      [See *supra* subsection A.3(f) of this section.]

6. Explain to the juvenile that if he or she admits to the act with which he or she has been charged, the government will then tell the court what it believes the facts to be and what it could prove if the case were to go to trial. Next, explain that the court would then ask the juvenile

   (a) if what the government says is true as far as he or she knows;

   (b) if any part of what the government says is not true, and if so, what is not true;

   (c) if he or she believes that the government can prove what it says it can prove; and

   (d) if he or she committed [here, go through the elements of the offense].

---

8. *Cf.* United States v. Doe, 627 F.2d 181 (9th Cir. 1980) (discussing timing requirement for making request to proceed as an adult).

7. Determine the voluntariness of the admission:

   The court must be satisfied that if the juvenile admits to the charge(s) against him or her, this admission is voluntary and not the result of any force or threat or inducement. Suggested questions to ask the juvenile include the following:

   (a) Has anyone threatened you or anyone else or forced you in any way to admit to the charge(s)?

   [If the answer is yes, ascertain the facts and recess if necessary to permit the juvenile and his or her counsel to confer, or postpone taking the admission.]

   (b) Do you understand that no one can compel you to admit anything?

8. Take the admission or denial. Ask the juvenile:

   Do you admit or deny that you are a juvenile delinquent as charged in the information?

   (a) If the juvenile denies the charge(s), set the case for trial.

   (b) If the juvenile admits to the charge(s):

   (1) Ask the U.S. attorney to state what he or she can prove at trial.

   (2) Ask the juvenile the following questions:

   (a) So far as you know, is what the government says true?

   (b) Is any part of what the government says not true, and if so, what is not true?

   (c) Do you believe that the government can prove what it says it can prove?

   (d) Did you [here, go through the elements of the offense]?

   NOTE
   Consider asking the juvenile to tell, in his or her own words, what he or she did.

   (3) Ask counsel for the juvenile if counsel is satisfied that the government can prove what it says it can prove.

9. Make findings for the record:

   (a) Find that all laws (18 U.S.C. § 5031 et seq.) have been complied with and that a basis for federal jurisdiction exists (see *supra* subsection A.1 of this section).

   (b) Find that the juvenile is competent.

   (c) Find that the juvenile understands his or her rights and has elected to give them up, except the right to counsel.

   (d) Find that the juvenile has voluntarily admitted to the charge(s) against him or her after fully knowing and understanding his or her constitutional rights as a juvenile.

     (e) Find that the juvenile is aware of the maximum penalty that could be imposed against him or her.

     (f) Find that the juvenile is aware that the government has sufficient facts to support an adjudication of juvenile delinquency.

     (g) Ask the juvenile if he or she wants to change his or her mind and not proceed as a juvenile or not admit to the charge(s) against him or her.

     (h) Adjudge that the juvenile is a juvenile delinquent.

10. Inform the juvenile and his or her parents or guardian, in writing, of the juvenile's rights relating to the confidentiality of juvenile records.[9]

C. Disposition (18 U.S.C. § 5037)[10]

   1. Detention prior to disposition (18 U.S.C. § 5035)

     (a) A juvenile alleged to be delinquent may be detained only in a juvenile facility or other suitable place designated by the Attorney General.

     (b) Detention shall be in a foster home or community-based facility located in or near the juvenile's home community whenever possible.

     (c) The juvenile shall not be detained or confined in any institution in which he or she would have regular contact with adults convicted of crimes or awaiting trial on criminal charges. Also, insofar as possible, *alleged* delinquents shall be kept separate from *adjudicated* delinquents.

     (d) Every juvenile in custody should be provided with adequate food, heat, light, sanitary facilities, bedding, clothing, recreation, education, and medical care, including necessary psychiatric, psychological, or other care and treatment.

   2. Timing of hearing (18 U.S.C. § 5037(a))

   If the juvenile is adjudicated to be delinquent, the court must have a hearing disposing of the case within twenty court days after said adjudication unless the court has ordered further studies in accordance with 18 U.S.C. § 5037(d). (See *infra* paragraph C.5 of this section.)

   3. Judgment following disposition hearing

   After the disposition hearing, the court may

     (a) suspend the findings of delinquency;

---

9. 18 U.S.C. § 5038(b). See 18 U.S.C. § 5038(a), (c), (d), and (f) for authority to release juvenile records.

10. The following outline is not intended as a procedure for conducting a dispositional hearing, but as supplemental material to be used in setting the dispositional hearing.

    (b) require the juvenile to make restitution pursuant to 18 U.S.C. § 3556;

    (c) place the juvenile on probation; or

    (d) commit the juvenile to official detention in the custody of the Attorney General.

4. Sentence

A juvenile may not be placed on probation or committed for a term longer than the maximum probation or prison term that would have been authorized had the juvenile been sentenced as an adult under the Sentencing Guidelines. *United States v. R.L.C.,* 112 S. Ct. 1329, 1339 (1992). Subject to that limitation, the maximum terms applicable are as follows:

    (a) For a juvenile under eighteen at the time of disposition, neither the probation term nor the detention term may extend beyond the juvenile's twenty-first birthday. 18 U.S.C. § 5037(b)(1), (c)(1).

    (b) For a juvenile between eighteen and twenty-one at the time of disposition, the probation term may not exceed three years. 18 U.S.C. § 5037(b)(2). The detention term may not exceed five years if the act of delinquency was a Class A, B, or C felony; it may not exceed three years in other cases. 18 U.S.C. § 5037(c)(2).

5. Observation and study (§ 5037(d))

An alleged or adjudicated delinquent may be committed, after notice and a hearing at which the juvenile is represented by counsel, to the custody of the Attorney General for observation and study by an appropriate agency. This observation and study shall be conducted on an outpatient basis unless the court determines that inpatient observation and study are necessary to obtain the desired information. If the juvenile is only an alleged juvenile delinquent, inpatient study may be ordered only with the consent of the juvenile and his or her attorney. The agency shall make a complete study of the alleged or adjudicated delinquent to ascertain his or her personal traits, capabilities, and background; any previous delinquency or criminal experience; any mental or physical defects; and any other relevant factors.

The Attorney General must submit a report on the observation and study to the court and "to the attorneys for the juvenile and the government" within thirty days after commitment unless the court grants additional time.

Calendar of events

Juvenile in custody

The juvenile must be brought to trial within thirty days from the date detention was begun. 18 U.S.C. § 5036.

The dispositional hearing must occur within twenty court days after a juvenile is adjudicated delinquent. 18 U.S.C. § 5037(a).

Juvenile not in custody

The juvenile must be tried within seventy days from the date of filing of the charging information or from the date the juvenile appeared before a judicial officer of the court in which such charge is pending, whichever date occurs last. 18 U.S.C. §§ 3161 et seq.[11]

The dispositional hearing must occur within twenty court days after a juvenile is adjudicated delinquent. 18 U.S.C. § 5037(a).

---

11. *But see* Model Statement of the Time Limits and Procedures for Achieving Prompt Disposition of Criminal Cases (Committee on the Administration of the Criminal Law of the Judicial Conference of the United States) (1979) (except as specifically provided, the time limits are not applicable to proceedings under the FJDA).

1.12 Mental competency in criminal matters

18 U.S.C. §§ 4241–4248; Fed. R. Crim. P. 12.2

[*Note:* Under the Crime Victims' Rights Act, 18 U.S.C. § 3771(a)(2) and (3), any victim of the offense has the right to notice of "any public court proceeding . . . involving the crime . . . of the accused," and to attend that proceeding. It may be advisable to ask the prosecutor if there are any victims and, if so, whether the government has fulfilled its duty to notify them.]

The mental competency of a the defendant may come before the court in a number of different contexts. The most important are

- competency to stand trial;
- competency to plead guilty;
- competency to commit the crime with which the defendant is charged (e.g., ability to form the requisite intent);
- competency after acquittal by reason of insanity;
- competency to be sentenced;
- mental condition as it bears on the sentence to be imposed; and
- civil commitment of a convicted offender in need of care or treatment for a mental condition.

The Insanity Defense Reform Act of 1984, 18 U.S.C. §§ 4241–4248, is now controlling with respect to most situations involving the mental competency of a defendant. It is a complex enactment, the provisions of which are spelled out in great detail. Its provisions must be read with care and complied with meticulously.

A. Competency to stand trial (18 U.S.C. § 4241)

1. Section 4241(a) provides that after the commencement of a prosecution and prior to sentencing, either the U.S. attorney or defense counsel may move for a hearing to determine the defendant's mental competency. The court shall grant the motion, or shall order a hearing on its own motion, if there is reasonable cause to believe that the defendant is not mentally competent

    (a) to understand the nature and consequences of the proceedings against him or her; or

    (b) to assist properly in his or her defense.

2. Prior to the hearing the court may (and probably should) order that a psychiatric or psychological examination be conducted and that a report be filed with the court. 18 U.S.C. § 4241(b).

    (a) The examiner should be asked for his or her opinion as to whether the defendant is suffering from a mental disease or defect rendering the defendant mentally incompetent to understand the nature and consequences of the proceedings against him or her or to assist properly in his or her defense. The examiner's report must include all of the information required by 18 U.S.C. § 4247(c)(1) through (c)(4).

(b) The psychiatrist or psychologist should not be asked to determine the defendant's mental competency at the time the alleged offense was committed.

(c) To secure a § 4241 examination, the court may, if necessary, order the defendant committed to a suitable hospital or facility for a reasonable period not to exceed thirty days, even if the defendant is not otherwise confined. For just cause this commitment may be extended by fifteen days. 18 U.S.C. § 4247(b).

3. The court shall then hold an evidentiary hearing, to be conducted pursuant to the provisions of 18 U.S.C. § 4247(d). The defendant "shall be represented by counsel." *Id.*

4. At the conclusion of the evidentiary hearing, the court shall make a finding by a preponderance of the evidence as to the accused's mental competency to stand trial. 18 U.S.C. § 4241(d).

(a) A finding of mental competency to stand trial does not prejudice a plea of not guilty by reason of insanity, because the court's finding is not admissible in evidence on the issue of guilt or innocence. 18 U.S.C. § 4241(f).

(b) If the defendant is found to be incompetent to stand trial, the court shall commit the defendant to the custody of the Attorney General. 18 U.S.C. § 4241(d). The trial court should receive periodic reports as to the defendant's mental condition.

(c) The Attorney General shall hospitalize the defendant for a reasonable period not to exceed four months, to determine whether there is a substantial probability that the defendant will in the foreseeable future become competent to stand trial. 18 U.S.C. § 4241(d)(l).

(d) The Attorney General may hospitalize the defendant for an additional reasonable period of time if the court finds that within that additional period there is a substantial probability that the defendant will become competent to stand trial. 18 U.S.C. § 4241(d)(2).

(e) If, at the end of the time provided for by 18 U.S.C. § 4241(d), the defendant is still not competent to be tried, he or she is subject to further commitment under the provisions of § 4246 if the court finds by *clear and convincing evidence* that releasing the defendant would create a substantial risk of bodily injury to another or of serious damage to another's property. The provisions of § 4246 are detailed and complex. To avoid error the court must refer to those provisions and follow them with great care. The report of any § 4246 psychiatric or psychological examination must comply with the requirements of § 4247(c). Any hearing must be held pursuant to the provisions of § 4247(d).

(f) When the director of the facility certifies to the court that the defendant is competent to stand trial, the court must hold a hearing, conducted pursuant to the requirements of 18 U.S.C. § 4247(d). If the court determines that the defendant is competent to stand trial, it shall order the defendant's discharge from the facility and set the matter for trial. 18 U.S.C. § 4241(e).

B. Competency to plead guilty

Because a defendant is required to make a knowing and voluntary waiver of certain constitutional rights in entering a guilty plea, the court must, in accepting a Fed. R. Crim. P. 11 plea, be satisfied that the defendant has sufficient mental competency to waive those rights, to make a reasoned choice among the alternatives presented to him or her, and to understand the nature and consequences of the guilty plea (see the plea colloquy in *infra* section 2.01: Taking pleas of guilty or nolo contendere).

If there is any question as to the defendant's mental competency to enter a guilty plea, an 18 U.S.C. § 4241 examination should be ordered and a hearing held prior to acceptance of the plea. In requesting such an examination, the court should spell out for the examiner the criteria that the examiner is to apply in determining whether the defendant is competent to enter a guilty plea. The examiner should be requested to furnish the information required by § 4247(c), along with an opinion as to the defendant's competency to enter a guilty plea.

C. Competency to commit the crime with which the defendant is charged (Fed. R. Crim. P. 12.2; 18 U.S.C. §§ 17, 4242):

1. If the defendant intends to rely on the insanity defense or to introduce expert testimony relating to his or her mental condition, the defendant must notify the government attorney in writing of that intention within the time provided for filing pretrial motions or at a later time if so ordered by the court. The court may allow late filing of the notice if good cause is shown. Fed. R. Crim. P. 12.2(a) and (b).

2. The court may order the defendant to submit to a competency examination under 18 U.S.C. § 4241. If the defendant has provided notice of a defense of insanity under Fed. R. Crim. P. 12(a), the court must order an examination under 18 U.S.C. § 4242 upon motion of the government. If the defendant provides notice of an intent to introduce expert evidence relating to the defendant's mental condition

under Fed. R. Crim. P. 12(b), the court may, upon motion of the government, order the defendant examined under procedures ordered by the court. Fed. R. Crim. P. 12.2(c)(1).

The examiner should be asked to give his or her opinion as to whether, at the time of the acts constituting the offense, the defendant was unable to appreciate the nature and quality or the wrongfulness of his or her acts as a result of a severe mental disease or defect. See 18 U.S.C. § 17(a). The examiner should be requested to include in his or her report all of the information required by § 4247(c).

3. The defendant bears the burden of proving the defense of insanity by clear and convincing evidence. 18 U.S.C. § 17(b).

4. No statement made by the defendant during a court-ordered mental examination (whether the examination was with or without the defendant's consent), no testimony by the expert based on that statement, and no fruit of that statement may be admitted against the defendant in any criminal proceeding except with regard to an issue concerning mental condition on which the defendant has introduced testimony or, in a capital sentencing proceeding, has introduced expert evidence. Fed. R. Crim. P. 12.2(b)(2) and (c)(4).

5. Results and reports of any examination conducted for a capital sentencing hearing after notice under Fed. R. Crim. P. 12.2(b)(2) must be sealed and not disclosed to either party unless the defendant is found guilty of a capital crime and intends to offer at sentencing expert evidence on mental condition. Once the results and reports of the government's examination have been disclosed, the defendant must disclose to the government the results and reports of any examination on mental condition conducted by the defendant's expert about which the defendant intends to introduce expert evidence. Fed. R. Crim. P. 12.2(c)(2) and (3).

6. If the defendant fails to provide timely notice to the government attorney of his or her intent to introduce expert testimony relating to an insanity defense, or if he or she fails to submit to an examination, the court may exclude the testimony of any expert witness offered by the defendant on the issue of the defendant's mental condition at the time of the alleged criminal offense or on the issue of punishment in a capital case. Fed. R. Crim. P. 12.2(d).

NOTE

Serious due process and compulsory process issues may arise the court excludes expert testimony concerning an insanity defense when a continuance of the trial would be feasible. See *Taliaferro v. Maryland*, 456 A.2d cert. denied, 461 U.S. 948 (1983) (White, dissenting).

D. Competency after acquittal by reason of insanity (18 U.S.C. § 4243)
If a defendant is found not guilty only by reason of insanity, he or she shall be committed to a suitable facility until such time as he or she is eligible for release under 18 U.S.C. § 4243(f). The provisions of § 4243(e) relating to the confinement and release of a defendant acquitted by rea-

son of insanity are detailed and complex. Those provisions must be followed with meticulous care. Any hearing must comply with the provisions of § 4247(d). Any report of a psychiatric or psychological examination must comply with the requirements of § 4247(c).

E. Competency to be sentenced

Because the defendant has the right of allocution at sentencing and must be able to understand the nature of the proceedings, the defendant cannot be sentenced if he or she does not have the mental capacity to exercise the right of allocution or to understand the nature of the proceedings.

If there is any question as to the defendant's mental competency to be sentenced, an 18 U.S.C. § 4241 examination should be ordered and a hearing held before sentencing. The court should provide the examiner with the criteria the examiner is to apply in determining whether the defendant is competent to be sentenced. The court should request the examiner to include in his or her report all of the information required by § 4247(c). Any hearing must be held pursuant to the requirements of § 4247(d).

F. Mental condition as it bears on sentence imposed

1. Adult offenders (18 U.S.C. § 3552(b))[1]

    (a) If the court determines that it needs more detailed information about the defendant's mental condition as a basis for determining the sentence to be imposed, the court may order a study of the defendant.

    (b) The study should be conducted by a qualified consultant in the local community, unless the court finds that there is a compelling reason to have the study done by the Bureau of Prisons or that there are no adequate professional resources in the local community to perform the study.

        (i) If the study is to be done in the local community, the court should designate a consultant, usually a psychiatrist or psychologist, to conduct the study and order the defendant to submit to the examination. The probation office will assist in identifying people who are qualified and willing to perform such studies; the probation office can also provide funds for this purpose.

        (ii) If the study is to be done by the Bureau of Prisons, the defendant should be committed under 18 U.S.C. § 3552(b) to

---

1. Subsections (b) and (c) of § 3552 both authorize studies in aid of sentencing. Subsection (c) specifically authorizes a psychiatric or psychological exam, but it appears preferable to rely on the more flexible general authority of § 3552(b).

the custody of the bureau to be studied. Imposing a provisional sentence is not necessary.

(c) The court order should specify the additional information the court needs before determining the sentence to be imposed and should inform the examiner of any guideline or policy statement that should be addressed by the study.

(d) The court order should specify a period for the study, not to exceed sixty days. The period may be extended, at the discretion of the court, for up to sixty more days.[2]

(e) To minimize delay if the study is to be done by the Bureau of Prisons, the court should consider directing the probation officer to secure immediate designation of the institution at which the study will be performed, and directing the marshal to transport the defendant to that institution by the most expeditious means available.

(f) After receiving the report of the study, the court should proceed to sentencing. The report must be included in the presentence report. See Fed. R. Crim. P. 32(d)(2)(E).

(g) See also U.S.S.G. §§ 5H1.3 and 5K2.13, which delineate the extent to which a defendant's mental or emotional condition may be taken into account under the Sentencing Guidelines.

2. Juvenile offenders (18 U.S.C. § 5037(d))

(a) If the court determines that it needs additional information concerning an alleged or adjudicated juvenile delinquent's mental condition, the court may commit the juvenile to the Attorney General's custody for observation and study after notice and a hearing at which the juvenile is represented by counsel.

(b) The observation and study of the juvenile must be performed on an outpatient basis, unless the court determines that inpatient observation is necessary to obtain the desired information. If the juvenile has not been adjudicated delinquent, inpatient study can be ordered only with the consent of the juvenile and his or her attorney.

(c) The agency selected by the Attorney General shall make a complete study of the juvenile's mental health.

(d) The Attorney General shall submit to the court and to the juvenile's attorney the results of the study. That report shall be submitted within thirty days of the juvenile's commitment, unless the time for reporting is extended by the court.

---

2. A court may also have to consider that, if there are victims of the offense, they have a right "to proceedings free from unreasonable delay." 18 U.S.C. § 3771(a)(7).

G. Civil commitment of convicted offender in need of care or treatment for mental condition (18 U.S.C. § 4244)[3]

1. Upon motion of the defendant or the government or on its own motion, the court may, before sentencing, determine that there is reasonable cause to believe that the defendant may be suffering from a mental disease or defect that requires custody for treatment in a suitable facility. In that event the court shall order a hearing. 18 U.S.C. § 4244(a).

2. Before the hearing the court may order that a psychiatric or psychological examination of the defendant be conducted and that a report be filed with the court, pursuant to § 4247(b) and (c). If it is the opinion of the examiner that the defendant is suffering from a mental disease or defect but that the condition is not such as to require the defendant's custody for care or treatment, the examiner shall give his or her opinion concerning the sentencing alternatives that could best accord the defendant the kind of treatment he or she does need. 18 U.S.C. § 4244(b).

3. The hearing shall be conducted pursuant to the provisions of § 4247(d).

4. If, after the hearing, the court finds by a preponderance of the evidence that the defendant is suffering from a mental disease or defect and that, in lieu of being sentenced to imprisonment, he or she should be committed to a suitable facility for care or treatment, the court shall commit the defendant to the custody of the Attorney General for care or treatment in a suitable facility. Such commitment shall constitute a provisional sentence of imprisonment to the maximum term authorized by law for the offense of which the defendant was found guilty. 18 U.S.C. § 4244(d).

5. When the director of the facility to which the defendant is sent certifies that the defendant is no longer in need of custody for care or treatment, the court shall proceed to sentencing, provided that the provisional sentence has not yet expired. 18 U.S.C. § 4244(e).

Other FJC sources

David N. Adair, Jr., The Bail Reform Act of 1984, at 25 (3d ed. 2006)

Pattern Criminal Jury Instructions 67 (1987)

---

3. If the civil commitment hearing is considered a "public proceeding in the district court involving . . . sentencing," any victims of the offense have the rights to notification and attendance, plus the right "to be reasonably heard." 18 U.S.C. § 3771(a)(2)–(4).

1.13 Referrals to magistrate judges (criminal matters)

Fed. R. Crim. P. 58 and 59; 28 U.S.C. § 636

Procedure

The general procedure for referring matters to magistrate judges is set forth in Fed. R. Crim. P. 59, which became effective December 1, 2005:

> **(a) Nondispositive Matters.** A district judge may refer to a magistrate judge for determination any matter that does not dispose of a charge or defense. The magistrate judge must promptly conduct the required proceedings and, when appropriate, enter on the record an oral or written order stating the determination. . . .
>
> **(b) Dispositive Matters.**
>
> (1) . . . A district judge may refer to a magistrate judge for recommendation a defendant's motion to dismiss or quash an indictment or information, a motion to suppress evidence, or any matter that may dispose of a charge or defense. The magistrate judge must promptly conduct the required proceedings. A record must be made of any evidentiary proceeding and of any proceeding if the magistrate judge considers it necessary. The magistrate judge must enter on the record a recommendation for disposing of the matter, including any proposed findings of fact.

In either case, the parties have ten days to object to the order or recommendation, unless the court sets a longer period. "Failure to object in accordance with this rule waives a party's right to review," Fed. R. Crim. P. 59(a) and (b)(2), although the district court retains discretion to review the decision. The Advisory Committee Notes to Rule 59 emphasize that, "[a]lthough the rule distinguishes between 'dispositive' and 'nondispositive' matters, it does not attempt to define or otherwise catalog motions that may fall within either category. Instead, that task is left to the case law."

Specific proceedings

Listed below are duties in criminal matters that are covered in sections 1, 2, and 4 of this *Benchbook* and that may be referred to magistrate judges. See also 28 U.S.C. § 636. Most districts have local rules or standing orders governing referrals to magistrate judges.

For a more comprehensive listing of the duties magistrate judges may perform, see *Inventory of United States Magistrate Judge Duties* (December 1999), available from the Magistrate Judges Division of the Administrative Office of the U.S. Courts.[1] This information also appears in Chapter 3, "Juris-

---

1. The online version of the *Inventory* was updated in July 2009. *See* http://jnet.ao.dcn/ Judges/Magistrate_Judges/Authority/Inventory_of_United_States_Magistrate_Judge_Dutie s_July_2009.html. The Administrative Office also provides an online web page summarizing

diction," of the *Legal Manual for U.S. Magistrate Judges*, published by the Administrative Office.

A magistrate judge may conduct

1. bail proceedings and detention hearings. 18 U.S.C. §§ 3041, 3141–3148; 28 U.S.C. § 636(a)(2). (See *supra* section 1.03: Release or detention pending trial.)

2. arraignments, and may take not guilty pleas in felony cases.[2] 28 U.S.C. § 636(b)(1)(A). (See *supra* section 1.07: Arraignment and plea.)

3. trial, judgment, and sentencing in a petty offense case; for other misdemeanors, the defendant's express consent to be tried before a magistrate judge in writing or orally on the record is required. The defendant must also specifically waive trial, judgment, and sentencing by a district judge. See Fed. R. Crim. P. 58(b)(2)(E) and (3)(A); 18 U.S.C. § 3401(b); 28 U.S.C. § 636(a)(3)–(5). A judgment of conviction or sentence by a magistrate judge may be appealed to the district court. 18 U.S.C. § 3402. Fed. R. Crim. P. 58 governs trials and appeals of misdemeanors and petty offenses. (See generally *infra* section 2.03: Trial outline—criminal.)

4. pretrial matters:

    (a) A magistrate judge may hear and determine non-dispositive pretrial matters in felony cases,[3] including discovery and appointment of counsel. A district court may reconsider a magistrate judge's ruling on a non-dispositive matter if it is "clearly erroneous or contrary to law." 28 U.S.C. § 636(b)(1)(A) and Fed. R. Crim. P. 59(a).

    (b) A magistrate judge may hear and submit to the district court proposed findings of fact and recommended determinations of dispositive pretrial matters, such as a motion to suppress evidence or to dismiss an indictment. 28 U.S.C. § 636(b)(1)(B) and Fed. R. Crim. P. 58(b)(1). A district court must make a de novo determination of those portions of proposed findings and recommenda-

---

more recent decisions and articles relating to the duties and authority of magistrate judges at http://jnet.ao.dcn/Judges/Magistrate_Judges/Authority/Decisions.html.

2. Note that your circuit may allow a magistrate judge to take a plea of guilty in a felony case if the defendant consents. See Inventory of United States Magistrate Judge Duties 124–26. It is recommended that this consent be in writing and expressly waive the right to enter the plea before an Article III judge. It is also advisable for the district court, at the start of the sentencing hearing, to state on the record that it, too, accepts the defendant's plea of guilty, based upon information provided at the plea hearing and contained in the presentence report.

3. The Supreme Court held that decisions touching the core trial features of a felony case may be delegated to a magistrate judge only if expressly authorized by statute. Gomez v. United States, 490 U.S. 858 (1989).

tions to which the parties object, 28 U.S.C. § 636(b)(1)(C) and Fed. R. Crim. P. 58(b)(3), but need not hold a de novo hearing of all the evidence, *United States v. Raddatz,* 447 U.S. 667 (1980).

See generally *infra* section 2.03: Trial outline—criminal.

5. voir dire in a felony case, if the parties consent. *Peretz v. United States,* 111 S. Ct. 2661 (1991). Note that "express consent by counsel suffices to permit a magistrate judge to preside over jury selection in a felony trial"—express consent by the defendant is not required. *Gonzalez v. United States,* 553 U.S. 242, 250 (2008). A magistrate judge may not conduct voir dire in a felony trial if the defendant objects. *Gomez v. United States,* 490 U.S. 858 (1989). (See *infra* section 2.06: Standard voir dire questions—criminal.)

6. probation and supervised release modification hearings:

    (a) A magistrate judge may revoke, modify, or reinstate probation and modify, revoke, or terminate supervised release if any magistrate judge imposed the probation or supervised release in a misdemeanor case. 18 U.S.C. § 3401(d), (h).

    (b) In other cases, a district court judge may designate a magistrate judge to conduct hearings to modify, revoke, or terminate supervised release, and to submit to the district judge proposed findings of fact and recommend disposition under 18 U.S.C. § 3583(e). 18 U.S.C. § 3401(i).[4]

    See generally *infra* section 4.02: Revocation of probation or supervised release.

7. an omnibus hearing, subject to any right of review before a district court of dispositive matters. 28 U.S.C. § 636(b)(1)(A) and (B).

---

4. The Ninth Circuit held that neither 28 U.S.C. § 636 nor 18 U.S.C. § 3401 authorizes a magistrate judge to conduct probation revocation hearings in a *felony* case without the defendant's consent. *See* United States v. Colacurcio, 84 F.3d 326, 329–34 (9th Cir. 1996) (reversed). *See also* United States v. Curry, 767 F.2d 328, 331 (7th Cir. 1985) (magistrate judge not authorized by 28 U.S.C. § 636(b)(3) to conduct probation revocation hearings without the defendant's consent); Banks v. United States, 614 F.2d 95, 97–98 (6th Cir. 1980) (same). However, the Sixth Circuit held that § 3401(i) does not require a defendant's consent when a magistrate judge is designated to conduct a hearing to revoke *supervised release* in a felony case. United States v. Waters, 158 F.3d 933, 938–39 (6th Cir. 1998) (declining to extend holding of *Colacurcio* to revocation of supervised release). *Cf.* United States v. Azure, 539 F.3d 904, 907–10 (8th Cir. 2008) (record must reflect that district court "designated" magistrate judge to conduct revocation hearings pursuant to § 3401(i), but defendant may waive right to challenge designation by failing to object); United States v. Sanchez-Sanchez, 333 F.3d 1065, 1069 (9th Cir. 2003) (section 3401(i) "must be strictly adhered to" and requires order from district court).

8. extradition hearings. 18 U.S.C. § 3184; *Ward v. Rutherford,* 921 F.2d 286 (D.C. Cir. 1990), *cert. dismissed,* 111 S. Ct. 2844 (1991). (See *supra* section 7.05: Foreign extradition proceedings.)

9. "additional duties [that] are not inconsistent with the Constitution and laws of the United States." 28 U.S.C. § 636(b)(3). For examples of additional duties and case law on § 636(b)(3), see *Inventory of United States Magistrate Judge Duties* 112–40 (December 1999).

2.01 Taking pleas of guilty or nolo contendere

Fed. R. Crim. P. 11

Introduction

This section is intended to serve as a guide to district judges, and to magistrate judges who are authorized to conduct change of plea hearings by consent,[1] when they conduct the formal plea taking, whether it occurs before or after review of the presentence report. It is important to emphasize that, while the plea of guilty is entered at the Rule 11 proceeding, the court may defer deciding whether to accept the terms of a plea agreement until after review of the presentence report.[2] If after review of the report the district court rejects an agreement made pursuant to Rule 11(c)(1)(A) or (C), the court shall give the defendant the option to withdraw the plea. In either event, the judge's goal in taking the plea must be to establish that the defendant is competent, that the plea is free and voluntary, that the defendant understands the charges and penalties, and that there is a factual basis for the plea.

This section is not intended to be all-inclusive. Circumstances may require that additional matters be established of record. In some cases, moreover, the court may find it necessary to resolve disputes about the presentence report before determining whether a plea agreement is acceptable. See *infra* section 4.01: Sentencing procedure.

Taking pleas from defendants who do not speak English raises problems beyond the obvious language barrier. Judges should be mindful not only of the need to avoid using legalisms and other terms that interpreters may have difficulty translating, but also of the need to explain such concepts as the right not to testify and the right to question witnesses, which may not be familiar to persons from different cultures. See 28 U.S.C. § 1827 regarding use of certified interpreters.

Some courts have developed Application for Permission to Enter Plea of Guilty forms and Written Plea Agreement forms. If used, such forms do not obviate the need for complete oral proceedings in open court that meet the requirements of Fed. R. Crim. P. 11.

Outline

[*Note:* Before proceeding with the hearing, the court may want to ask the prosecutor if there are any victims of the offense and, if so, whether the government has fulfilled its duty to notify them of the hearing and their right to

---

1. If the defendant consents to entering a plea of guilty before a magistrate judge, it is recommended that the consent be in writing and expressly waive the defendant's right to enter the plea before an Article III judge.

2. Fed. R. Crim. P. 11(c)(3)(A); U.S.S.G. § 6B1.1(c), p.s.

attend, and whether any victims want to be "reasonably heard." 18 U.S.C. § 3771(a)(2)–(4).[3]]

A. Determine, on the record, the purpose of the defendant's appearance, that is, obtain a statement from defense counsel[4] that the defendant wishes to enter a plea of guilty (or nolo contendere).

B. If it has not previously been established, determine whether the plea is being made pursuant to a plea agreement of any kind. If so, require disclosure of the terms of the agreement (or if the agreement is in writing, require that a copy be produced for your inspection and filing). See Fed. R. Crim. P. 11(c)(2).

C. Have the clerk administer the oath to the defendant.[5]

    [*Note:* If you have any doubts about the defendant's ability to speak and understand English, consider appointing a certified interpreter in accordance with 28 U.S.C. § 1827.]

D. Ask the defendant:

    1. Do you understand that you are now under oath and if you answer any of my questions falsely, your answers may later be used against you in another prosecution for perjury or making a false statement?

        [See Fed. R. Crim. P. 11(b)(1)(A)]

    2. What is your full name?

    3. Where were you born?

        [If the answer is not the United States or one of its territories, ask if the defendant is a United States citizen.]

    4. How old are you?

    5. How far did you go in school?

    6. Have you been treated recently for any mental illness or addiction to narcotic drugs of any kind?

        [*Note:* If the answer to this question is yes, pursue the subject with the defendant and with counsel in order to determine whether the defendant is currently competent to plead.]

---

3. If there are many victims who want to be heard, the court may need to "fashion a reasonable procedure to give effect to [their right to be heard] that does not unduly complicate or prolong the proceedings." 18 U.S.C. § 3771(d)(2).

4. If the defendant lacks counsel, you must advise the defendant of the right to an attorney. *See supra* section 1.02: Assignment of counsel or pro se representation; Fed. R. Crim. P. 11(b)(1)(D).

5. An oath (or affirmation) is not required by Fed. R. Crim. P. 11, but is strongly recommended to avoid any subsequent contention in a proceeding under 28 U.S.C. § 2255 that the defendant did not answer truthfully at the taking of the plea because he or she was not sworn.

7. Are you currently under the influence of any drug, medication, or alcoholic beverage of any kind?

   [*Note:* Again, if the answer is yes, pursue the subject with the defendant and with counsel to determine whether the defendant is currently competent to plead.]

8. Have you received a copy of the indictment (information)[6] pending against you—that is, the written charges made against you in this case—and have you fully discussed those charges, and the case in general, with Mr./Ms. _____ as your counsel?

9. Are you fully satisfied with the counsel, representation, and advice given to you in this case by your attorney, Mr./Ms. _____?

E. *If there is a plea agreement of any kind,* ask the defendant:

   1. [If the agreement is written:]

      Did you have an opportunity to read and discuss the plea agreement with your lawyer before you signed it?

   2. Does the plea agreement represent in its entirety any understanding you have with the government?

   3. Do you understand the terms of the plea agreement?

   4. Has anyone made any promise or assurance that is not in the plea agreement to persuade you to accept this agreement? Has anyone threatened you in any way to persuade you to accept this agreement?

   5. [If the terms of the plea agreement are nonbinding recommendations pursuant to Rule 11(c)(1)(B):[7]]

      Do you understand that the terms of the plea agreement are merely recommendations to the court—that I can reject the recommendations without permitting you to withdraw your plea of

---

6. If the case involves a felony offense being prosecuted by information rather than indictment, and if a waiver of indictment has not previously been obtained in open court (see Fed. R. Crim. P. 7(b)), refer to *supra* section 1.06: Waiver of indictment.

7. Note that a plea agreement may contain factual stipulations which, unless part of a Rule 11(c)(1)(C) agreement, are not binding under the Rules or the Guidelines. However, some cases have held that a factual stipulation that directly affected the severity of the sentence should have been construed as a Rule 11(e)(1)(C) agreement, or that the stipulation was otherwise relied on by the parties so that it should have been followed or the defendant allowed to withdraw the plea. *See, e.g.,* United States v. Bohn, 959 F.2d 389 (2d Cir. 1992); United States v. Torres, 926 F.2d 321 (3d Cir. 1991); United States v. Kemper, 908 F.2d 33 (6th Cir. 1990); United States v. Jeffries, 908 F.2d 1520 (11th Cir. 1990); United States v. Mandell, 905 F.2d 970 (6th Cir. 1990). *See also* Guideline Sentencing: An Outline of Appellate Case Law § IX.A.4 (Federal Judicial Center 2002). Courts are advised to discuss any such stipulations before accepting the plea and to warn the defendant that the court might not follow them and that the defendant will not be allowed to withdraw the plea.

guilty and impose a sentence that is more severe than you may anticipate?

6. [If any or all of the terms of the plea agreement are pursuant to Rule 11(c)(1)(A) or (C):]

    Do you understand that if I choose not to follow the terms of the plea agreement [if some, but not all, terms are binding, identify those terms], I will give you the opportunity to withdraw your plea of guilty, and that if you choose not to withdraw your plea, I may impose a more severe sentence, without being bound by the plea agreement [or the specific terms rejected by the court]?

7. [Inquire of defense counsel] Were all formal plea offers by the government conveyed to the defendant? [If the answer is no, take a recess to allow time for counsel to consult with the defendant.][8]

F. *If there is no formal plea agreement,* ask the attorneys whether the prosecutor made any formal plea agreement offers and, if so, whether those offers were conveyed to the defendant. [If offers have not been conveyed, take a recess to allow time for counsel to consult with the defendant].[9]

G. Whether or not there is a plea agreement, ask the defendant:

    Has anyone attempted in any way to force you to plead guilty (nolo contendere) or otherwise threatened you? Has anyone made any promises or assurances of any kind to get you to plead guilty (other than those that are in the plea agreement)? Are you pleading guilty of your own free will because you are guilty?

    [See Fed. R. Crim. P. 11(b)(2)].

---

8. *See* Missouri v. Frye, 132 S. Ct. 1399, 1408 (2012) ("defense counsel has the duty to communicate formal offers from the prosecution to accept a plea on terms and conditions that may be favorable to the accused."); Lafler v. Cooper, 132 S. Ct. 1376, 1383–86 (2012) ("when inadequate assistance of counsel caused nonacceptance of a plea offer and further proceedings led to a less favorable outcome," defendant had claim for ineffective assistance of counsel). *See also* Padilla v. Kentucky, 130 S. Ct. 1473, 1486 (2010) ("the negotiation of a plea bargain is a critical phase of litigation for purposes of the Sixth Amendment right to effective assistance of counsel"). If a more favorable plea offer has lapsed, or defense counsel's advice to reject an offer will lead to "a less favorable outcome," defendants may "show prejudice from ineffective assistance of counsel . . . [by] demonstrat[ing] a reasonable probability they would have accepted the earlier plea offer had they been afforded effective assistance of counsel. Defendants must also demonstrate a reasonable probability the plea would have been entered without the prosecution canceling it or the trial court refusing to accept it . . . . To establish prejudice in this instance, it is necessary to show a reasonable probability that the end result of the criminal process would have been more favorable by reason of a plea to a lesser charge or a sentence of less prison time." *Frye,* 132 S. Ct. at 1409.

9. *See supra* note 8 and accompanying text.

H. *If the plea relates to a felony offense,* consider asking the defendant:

Do you understand that the offense to which you are pleading guilty (nolo contendere) is a felony offense, that if your plea is accepted you will be adjudged guilty of that offense, and that such adjudication *may* deprive you of valuable civil rights, such as the right to vote, the right to hold public office, the right to serve on a jury, and the right to possess any kind of firearm?

[If the defendant is not a citizen of the United States, ask:]

1. Have you discussed the possible immigration consequences of a guilty plea with your attorney?

2. Do you understand that if you are not a citizen of the United States, in addition to the other possible penalties you are facing, a plea of guilty may subject you to deportation, exclusion, or voluntary departure, and prevent you from obtaining U.S. citizenship?[10]

[If the defendant is accused of a sex offense, ask:]

Do you understand that a conviction for this offense will likely result in substantial future restrictions on where you may live or work, and with whom you may associate?[11]

---

10. In *Padilla v. Kentucky,* 130 S. Ct. 1473, 1483 (2010), the Supreme Court held that a defense attorney has the duty to advise a defendant of the possible immigration consequences of a guilty plea. Although *Padilla* is directed at advice given by counsel, the Judicial Conference of the United States has approved an amendment to Rule 11(b)(1) to add new subsection (O), which would require a court to warn that, "if convicted, a defendant who is not a United States citizen may be removed from the United States, denied citizenship, and denied admission to the United States in the future." This amendment would take effect on Dec. 1, 2013, if not changed or rejected by the Supreme Court or the U.S. Congress. *Cf.* United States v. Akinsade, 686 F.3d 248, 254 (4th Cir. 2012) (district court's "general and equivocal admonishment [was] insufficient to correct counsel's affirmative misadvice that Akinsade's crime was not categorically a deportable offense. More importantly, the admonishment did not 'properly inform' Akinsade of the consequence he faced by pleading guilty: mandatory deportation. . . . Here, the district court did not elicit a direct response to the deportation admonishment, but instead asked if Akinsade understood a list of generalized warnings of which deportation was a part."); United States v. Bonilla, 637 F.3d 980, 983–86 (9th Cir. 2011) (citing *Padilla,* the court held defense counsel's failure to warn defendant that he faced deportation by pleading guilty until after defendant had done so was a "fair and just reason" under Rule 11(d)(2)(B) that would allow defendant to withdraw plea).

11. In addition to various state and local laws that may place restrictions on convicted sex offenders, the Adam Walsh Child Protection and Safety Act of 2006 ("The Act"), Pub. L. No. 109-248, 120 Stat. 587, established a national sex offender registration system that requires certain sex offenders to register in their jurisdiction of residence after release from prison (or after sentencing if not incarcerated). *See* 42 U.S.C. §§ 16901–16902 & 16911–16929 (the Sex Offender Registration and Notification Act). Failure to register or update registration can result in fines or imprisonment under 18 U.S.C. § 2250. The Act also provided for the possibility that, rather than being released at the conclusion of their sentence, some con-

I. Inform the defendant of the following:

1. The maximum possible penalty provided by law, and any mandatory minimum penalty:

    (a) *For drug offenses:* Determine whether the drug quantity involved or other aggravating factors will trigger application of a mandatory minimum sentence. Because this may not be known at the time the plea is taken, the court is advised to warn the defendant of any *possible* maximum and mandatory minimum sentences that may be imposed after a final determination of quantity and other aggravating factors.

    (b) Determine whether the defendant faces a mandatory minimum sentence or an increase in the statutory maximum sentence because of one or more prior firearms offenses, violent felonies, or drug offenses. If this is not known at the time of the plea, advise the defendant of the *possible* maximum sentence.

    (c) Include the duration of any authorized or mandatory term of supervised release, and ask the defendant:

    > **Do you understand that if you violate the conditions of supervised release, you can be given additional time in prison?**

    (d) *If the offense carries a maximum sentence of twenty-five years or more, or the statute specifically prohibits probation,* include a reference to the unavailability of a probation sentence under 18 U.S.C. § 3561(a)(1) or (2).

    (e) Inform the defendant of the maximum possible fine, if any.

2. *If applicable,* that the court may also order, or may be required to order under the Mandatory Victims Restitution Act, that the defendant make restitution to any victim of the offense. See 18 U.S.C. § 3663A. See also 18 U.S.C. § 3771(a)(6) (giving victims the right "to full and timely restitution as provided in law").

---

victed sex offenders could be subject to civil commitment as a "sexually dangerous person" under 18 U.S.C. § 4248.

Although not required to do so by Rule 11, in light of *Padilla,* courts should consider providing some warning to defendants of the possible collateral consequences of a conviction for a sexual offense. *See, e.g.,* United States v. Youngs, 687 F.3d 56, 61–63 & n.6 (2d Cir. 2012) (although due process and Rule 11 do not require warning defendants about the possibility of civil commitment as a sexually dangerous person, "it is a potential consequence that could affect defendants' assessment of the costs and benefits of a guilty plea, and alerting defendants to it on the record could forestall later claims by defendants that they were misadvised by counsel concerning the relative costs and benefits of the plea."). *Cf.* Bauder v. Dept. of Corrections, State of Fla., 619 F.3d 1272, 1274-75 (11th Cir. 2010) (citing *Padilla* in holding that defense counsel's affirmative misrepresentation that defendant would not be exposed to state's civil commitment law after his sentence ended was ineffective assistance of counsel that warranted postconviction relief).

3. *If applicable,* that the court may require the defendant to forfeit certain property to the government.

4. *If the offense involved fraud or other intentionally deceptive practices,* that the court may order the defendant to provide notice of the conviction to victims of the offense. See 18 U.S.C. § 3555.

5. That for each offense, the defendant must pay a special assessment of $100 ($25 for a Class A misdemeanor, $10 for Class B, $5 for Class C or infraction) required by 18 U.S.C. § 3013.

   Fed. R. Crim. P. 11(b)(1).

J. Ask the defendant:

   Do you understand those possible consequences of your plea that I have just gone over with you?

K. Inform the defendant that his or her sentence will be determined by a combination of advisory Sentencing Guidelines, possible authorized departures from those guidelines, and other statutory sentencing factors. Fed. R. Crim. P. 11(b)(1)(M).

L. Ask the defendant:

   1. Have you and your attorney talked about how these advisory Sentencing Guidelines might apply to your case?

      [*Note: If there is a plea agreement that a specific sentence will be imposed* (Fed. R. Crim. P. 11(c)(1)(C)), skip to question 4.]

   2. Do you understand that the court will not be able to determine the advisory guideline range for your case until after the presentence report has been completed and you and the government have had an opportunity to challenge the reported facts and the application of the guidelines recommended by the probation officer, and that the sentence ultimately imposed may be different from any estimate your attorney may have given you?

   3. Do you also understand that, after your initial advisory guideline range has been determined, the court has the authority in some circumstances to depart upward or downward from that range, and will also examine other statutory sentencing factors, under 18 U.S.C. § 3553(a), that may result in the imposition of a sentence that is either greater or lesser than the advisory guideline sentence?

   4. Do you also understand that parole has been abolished and that if you are sentenced to prison you will not be released on parole?

M. Ask the defendant:

   1. Do you also understand that under some circumstances you or the government may have the right to appeal any sentence that I impose?

[*If the plea agreement involves a waiver of the right to appeal the sentence,* ask the defendant:]

2. Do you understand that by entering into this plea agreement and entering a plea of guilty, you will have waived, or given up, your right to appeal or collaterally attack all or part of this sentence?

(The court should discuss the specific terms of the waiver with the defendant to ensure that the waiver is knowingly and voluntarily entered into and that the defendant understands the consequences. Fed. R. Crim. P 11(b)(1)(N).[12])

N. Ask the defendant:

1. Do you understand

   (a) that you have a right to plead not guilty to any offense charged against you and to persist in that plea;

   (b) that you would then have the right to a trial by jury;

   (c) that at trial you would be presumed to be innocent and the government would have to prove your guilt beyond a reasonable doubt;

   (d) that you would have the right to the assistance of counsel for your defense—appointed by the court if necessary—at trial and every other stage of the proceeding, the right to see and hear all the witnesses and have them cross-examined in your defense, the right on your own part to decline to testify unless you voluntarily elected to do so in your own defense, and the right to compel the attendance of witnesses to testify in your defense?[13]

   Do you understand that should you decide not to testify or put on any evidence, these facts cannot be used against you?

2. Do you further understand that by entering a plea of guilty (nolo contendere), if that plea is accepted by the court, there will be no trial and you will have waived, or given up, your right to a trial as well as those other rights associated with a trial as I just described them?

See Fed. R. Crim. P. 11(b(1)(B) to (F).

O. Inform the defendant of the nature of the charge(s) to which he or she is pleading guilty (nolo contendere) by reading or summarizing the indictment (information). Then

---

12. Note that the waiver may not be enforceable if the sentence is not in accordance with the terms of the plea agreement.

13. Although it is not required as part of the Rule 11 colloquy, the court may inform the defendant of the right under Rule 17(c)(1)to compel the production of documents from witnesses by subpoena.

1. further explain the essential elements of the offense, i.e., what the government would be required to prove at trial;[14] and/or (except in pleas of nolo contendere)

2. have the defendant explain and assent to the facts constituting the crime(s) charged.

See Fed. R. Crim. P. 11(b)(1)(G).

P. *In the case of a plea of guilty (including an Alford plea[15]),* have the government counsel make a representation concerning the facts the government would be prepared to prove at trial (to establish an independent factual basis for the plea). See Fed. R. Crim. P. 11(b)(3)].

   If the defendant's plea is nolo contendere, he or she is neither admitting nor denying guilt.[16] Fed. R. Crim P. 11(b)(3) is therefore not applicable. The court may wish to consider having the government make a representation concerning the facts of the case.

Q. If there is a plea agreement involving dismissal of other charges, or an agreement that a specific sentence will be imposed, and if consideration of the agreement is to be deferred, ask the defendant:

   Do you understand that if you plead guilty, a presentence report will be prepared, and I will then consider whether to accept the plea agreement, and that if I decide to reject the plea agreement, you will then have an opportunity to withdraw your plea and change it to not guilty?

R. Ask the defendant:

   How do you now plead to the charge: guilty or not guilty?

S. Before accepting the defendant's plea, if there are victims of the offense present, allow them the opportunity "to be reasonably heard." 18 U.S.C. § 3771(a)(4).

T. If you are satisfied with the responses given during the hearing, make the following finding on the record:

   It is the finding of the court in the case of United States v. _____ that the defendant is fully competent and capable of entering an

---

14. Reference may be made to the standard or pattern jury instructions normally used in your court.

15. North Carolina v. Alford, 400 U.S. 25 (1970). *See also* United States v. Tunning, 69 F.3d 107, 110–14 (6th Cir. 1995) (discussing establishment of factual basis for *Alford* plea and difference between *Alford* plea and plea of nolo contendere).

16. The plea of nolo contendere is never entertained as a matter of course. Fed. R. Crim. P. 11(a)(1) provides that the plea may be entered "with the court's consent." Rule 11(a)(3) provides further that before accepting the plea "the court must consider the parties' views and the public interest in the effective administration of justice." In general, courts accept a plea of nolo contendere only in certain types of cases involving nonviolent crimes where civil implications may arise from a guilty plea.

informed plea, that the defendant is aware of the nature of the charges and the consequences of the plea, and that the plea of guilty [nolo contendere] is a knowing and voluntary plea supported by an independent basis in fact containing each of the essential elements of the offense. The plea is therefore accepted, and the defendant is now adjudged guilty of that offense.

U. If a presentence report has been reviewed before plea taking or is not required (see Fed. R. Crim. P. 32(c)(1)(A)), proceed to disposition. (See *infra* section 4.01: Sentencing procedure.) Otherwise, inform the defendant

1. that a written presentence report will be prepared by the probation office to assist the judge in sentencing;

2. that the defendant will be asked to give information for the report, and that his or her attorney may be present if the defendant wishes;

3. that the court shall permit the defendant and counsel to read the presentence report and file any objections to the report before the sentencing hearing (Fed. R. Crim. P. 32(e)(2) and (f));

4. that the defendant and his or her counsel shall have an opportunity to speak on behalf of the defendant at the sentencing hearing (Fed. R. Crim. P. 32(i)(4)(A)); and

5. that, if there are any victims of the offense, the victims shall be afforded an opportunity to be heard at the sentencing hearing. 18 U.S.C. § 3771(a)(4).

V. Refer the defendant to the probation officer for a presentence investigation and report (pursuant to Fed. R. Crim. P. 32(c)(1)), set the disposition date for sentencing, and determine bail or conditions of release pending sentencing. See *infra* section 2.11: Release or detention pending sentence or appeal.

1. If the defendant has been at liberty on bond or personal recognizance, invite defense counsel to argue for release pending sentencing. See 18 U.S.C. § 3143(a). Give the U.S. attorney an opportunity to respond. If any victims of the offense are present, allow them an opportunity "to be reasonably heard." 18 U.S.C. § 3771(a)(4).

2. If the defendant is to be released pending sentencing, advise the defendant

   (a) when and where he or she is required to appear for sentencing;

   (b) that failure to appear as required is a criminal offense for which he or she could be sentenced to imprisonment;

   (c) that all the conditions on which he or she was released up to now continue to apply; and

   (d) that the penalties for violating those conditions can be severe.

W. If appropriate, enter a preliminary order of forfeiture under Fed. R. Crim. P. 32.2(b). The preliminary order must be entered "sufficiently in advance of sentencing to allow the parties to suggest revisions or modifications before the order becomes final." Fed. R. Crim. P. 32.2(b)(2)(B). Note that the defendant must be provided notice and a reasonable opportunity to be heard on the timing and form of the order.

2.02 Taking pleas of guilty or nolo contendere (organization[1])

Fed. R. Crim. P. 11

[*Note:* Under the Crime Victims' Rights Act, 18 U.S.C. § 3771(a)(2) and (3), any victim of the offense has the right to notice of "any public court proceeding . . . involving the crime . . . of the accused," and to attend that proceeding. It may be advisable to ask the prosecutor if there are any victims and, if so, whether the government has fulfilled its duty to notify them. Also, any victims who are present at the plea hearing have a right "to be reasonably heard." § 3771(a)(4).][2]

A. Before accepting a plea of guilty or nolo contendere from the representative of an organization, the court should be satisfied that

1. the person appearing before the court is an officer or authorized employee of the organization;

2. the board of directors is empowered to authorize a person to enter a plea of guilty or nolo contendere to a charge brought against the organization;

3. the person before the court is authorized by a valid resolution to enter a plea of guilty or nolo contendere to the charge before the court; and

4. the organization is financially able to pay a substantial fine that could be imposed by the court for the charge involved in the plea of guilty or nolo contendere.

B. After the court receives the information set out above and ascertains that the plea can be taken from the person before the court, the person should be placed under oath and informed of the following:

1. the nature of the charge(s) to which the plea is offered;

2. the mandatory minimum penalty provided by law, if any;

3. the special assessment for each offense of $400 ($125 for a Class A misdemeanor, $50 for Class B, $25 for Class C or infraction) required by 18 U.S.C. § 3013;

4. the maximum possible penalty provided by law;

5. *if applicable,* that the court may also order the organization to make restitution to any victim of the offense;

---

1. Effective December 1, 1999, Fed. R. Crim. P. 11(a) substituted "organization" for "corporation." Organization is defined in 18 U.S.C. § 18 as "a person other than an individual."

2. If there are many victims who want to be heard, the court may need to "fashion a reasonable procedure to give effect to [their right to be heard] that does not unduly complicate or prolong the proceedings." 18 U.S.C. § 3771(d)(2).

6. *if applicable,* that the court may require the organization to forfeit certain property to the government;
7. *if the offense involved fraud or other intentionally deceptive practices,* that the court may order the organization to provide notice of the conviction to victims of the offense (see 18 U.S.C. § 3555);
8. if appropriate, the right to be represented by an attorney;
9. that the organization has the right to plead not guilty or to persist in that plea if it has already been made;
10. that the organization has a right to be tried by a jury and at that trial has the right to
    (a) the assistance of counsel;
    (b) confront and cross-examine witnesses against the organization;
11. that if the organization pleads guilty, there will be no further trial of any kind;
12. that by pleading guilty for the organization, the representative of the organization waives the organization's right to trial;
13. that the court will ask the representative of the organization questions about the offense before the court and that if he or she answers these questions, under oath, on the record, and in the presence of counsel, the answers may later be used against the representative in a prosecution for perjury or false statement; and
14. the essential elements of the offense that are involved, and whether the representative understands what the government must prove.

C. The court will then inquire
1. whether the plea is voluntarily made on behalf of the organization and not as a result of force, threats, or promises apart from a plea agreement; and
2. whether there is a plea agreement and, if so, what the agreement is.

D. If the court is satisfied with the representative's responses, ask how he or she pleads: guilty, not guilty, or nolo contendere.

E. If the plea is guilty, follow your normal Fed. R. Crim. P. 11 procedure for establishing the factual basis in the case. If the plea is nolo contendere, the court may wish to consider having the government make a representation concerning the facts of the case.

F. Make the required findings concerning the establishment of the plea, which should include findings concerning items A.1, A.2, A.3, and A.4 above, relating to the propriety of taking the plea from the representative of the organization. Allow any victims of the offense who are present to be "reasonably heard." 18 U.S.C. § 3771(a)(4).

G. Make a finding on the guilt of the organization after the guilty or nolo contendere plea.

H. Inform the representative
   1. that a written presentence report will be prepared by the probation office to assist the court in sentencing;
   2. that the organization, the representative, or both will be required to give information for the report and that the organization's attorney may be present;
   3. that the representative and the organization's counsel shall be afforded the opportunity to speak on behalf of the organization at the sentencing hearing (Fed. R. Crim. P. 32(i)(4)(A));
   4. that if there are any victims of the offense, the victims shall be afforded an opportunity to be heard at the sentencing hearing (18 U.S.C. § 3771(a)(4)); and
   5. that the court shall permit the representative and counsel to read the presentence report before the sentencing hearing (Fed. R. Crim. P. 32(e)(2)).
I. Advise the representative of the date, time, and place of the sentencing hearing, and order him or her to appear.

2.03 Trial outline—criminal

1. Have the case called for trial.[1]
2. Jury is selected (see *infra* section 2.05: Jury selection—criminal).
3. Give preliminary instructions to the jury (see *infra* section 2.07: Preliminary jury instructions—criminal case).
4. Ascertain whether any party wishes to invoke the rule to exclude from the courtroom witnesses scheduled to testify in the case. [But see 18 U.S.C. § 3510, stating that victims of the offense may not be excluded from trial merely because they may speak at the sentencing hearing. See also 18 U.S.C. § 3771(a)(3) and (b), giving any victim of the offense the right to attend "any public court proceeding ... involving the crime" unless the court finds that "testimony by the victim would be materially altered if the victim heard other testimony at that proceeding." The court "shall make every effort to permit the fullest attendance possible by the victim."[2]]
5. Government counsel makes an opening statement.
6. Defense counsel makes an opening statement (unless counsel asked to reserve).
7. Government counsel calls witnesses. [*Note:* If there may be testimony by child victims or child witnesses, judges should be aware of the special procedures and safeguards in 18 U.S.C. § 3509 that may apply.]
8. Government rests.
9. Motion for judgment of acquittal. Fed. R. Crim. P. 29(a) (see *infra* section 2.10: Trial and post-trial motions).
10. Defense counsel makes an opening statement if he or she has asked to reserve.
11. Defense counsel calls witnesses for the defense.
12. Defense rests.
13. Counsel call rebuttal witnesses.
14. Government rests on its entire case.
15. Defense rests on its entire case.
16. Motion for judgment of acquittal. Fed. R. Crim. P. 29(a), (b) (see *infra* section 2.10: Trial and post-trial motions).

---

1. Fed. R. Crim. P. 43 prohibits trial in absentia of a defendant who is not present at the beginning of trial. Crosby v. United States, 506 U.S. 255 (1993).

2. Note also that Fed. R. Evid. 615 does not authorize the exclusion of "a person authorized by statute to be present."

17. Out of hearing of the jury, rule on counsel's requests for instructions and inform counsel as to the substance of the court's charge. Fed. R. Crim. P. 30(b).

18. Closing argument by prosecution, closing argument by defense, rebuttal by prosecution. Fed. R. Crim. P. 29.1.

19. Charge the jury (see *infra* section 2.08: General instructions to jury at end of criminal case). In the court's discretion, the jury may be instructed before closing arguments. Fed. R. Crim. P. 30(c).

20. Rule on objections to the charge and make any appropriate additional charge. Provide an opportunity for counsel to object out of the jury's hearing and, on request, out of the jury's presence. Fed. R. Crim. P. 30(d).

21. If you are going to discharge the alternate jurors, excuse and thank them.[3] If you plan to retain the alternate jurors, ensure that they do not discuss the case with any other person unless they replace a regular juror. If an alternate juror replaces a juror after deliberations have begun, instruct the jury to begin its deliberations anew. Fed. R. Crim. P. 24(c)(3).

22. Instruct the jury to go to the jury room and commence its deliberations.

23. Determine which exhibits are to be sent to the jury room.

24. Have the clerk give the exhibits and the verdict forms to the jury.

25. Recess court during the jury deliberations.

26. Before responding to any communications from the jury, consult with counsel on the record (see *infra* section 2.08: General instructions to jury at end of criminal case).

27. If the jury fails to arrive at a verdict before the conclusion of the first day's deliberations, either provide for their overnight sequestration or permit them to separate after instructing them as to their conduct and fixing the time for their return to resume deliberations. Provide for safekeeping of exhibits.

28. If the jury reports that they cannot agree on a verdict, determine by questioning whether they are hopelessly deadlocked. Do not inquire as to the numerical split of the jury. If you are convinced that the jury is hopelessly deadlocked, declare a mistrial. If you are not so convinced, direct them to resume their deliberations. Consider giving your circuit's approved *Allen*-type charge to the jury before declaring a mistrial.

---

3. In a case involving potentially lengthy jury deliberations, judges may wish to consider retaining at least one alternate juror.

29. When the jury has agreed on a verdict, reconvene court and take the verdict (see *infra* section 2.09: Verdict—criminal).

30. Poll the jurors individually on the request of either party, or on your own motion (see *infra* section 2.09: Verdict—criminal). Fed. R. Crim. P. 31(d).

31. Thank and discharge the jury.

32. If the verdict is "not guilty," discharge the defendant.

33. If the defendant has been found guilty, determine whether the defendant should be committed to the custody of the U.S. marshal or released on bail (see *infra* section 2.11: Release or detention pending sentence or appeal).

34. Fix a time for post-trial motions.

35. Adjourn or recess court.

Other FJC sources

Manual on Recurring Problems in Criminal Trials (Tucker Carrington & Kris Markarian eds., 6th ed. 2010)

For a discussion of case-management techniques in civil trials, some of which may also be helpful in the management of criminal trials, see Civil Litigation Management Manual 87–90 (Judicial Conference of the United States 2001)

For a discussion of trial management in complex civil litigation, some of which may be applicable to management of a criminal trial, see Manual for Complex Litigation, Fourth 131–66 (2004)

2.04 Findings of fact and conclusions of law in criminal cases and motions

Fed. R. Crim. P. 12 and 23

A. When required

    1. Fed. R. Crim. P. 23(c):

    In all cases tried without a jury, "the court must find the defendant guilty or not guilty. If a party requests before the finding of guilty or not guilty, the court must state its specific findings of fact in open court or in a written decision or opinion."

    2. Fed. R. Crim. P. 12(d) and (f)—Ruling upon Motions:

    "When factual issues are involved in deciding a motion, the court must state its essential *findings* on the record." (Emphasis added.)

B. Form

    1. Fed. R. Crim. P. 23(c) provides that, after a trial without a jury, "the court must state its specific findings of fact in open court or in a written decision or opinion."

    2. Fed. R. Crim. P. 12(d) provides that "[w]hen factual issues are involved in deciding a motion, the court must state its essential findings on the record."

    3. Fed. R. Crim. P. 12(f) provides that "[a]ll proceedings at a motion hearing, including any findings of fact or conclusions of law made orally by the court, must be recorded by a court reporter or a suitable recording device."

2.05 Jury selection—criminal

The *Benchbook* Committee recognizes that there is no uniform recommended procedure for selecting jurors to serve in criminal or civil cases and that judges will develop the patterns or procedures most appropriate for their districts and their courts. Section 2.06 *infra*, however, provides an outline of standard voir dire questions. For a sample juror questionnaire, see Sample Forms 42 and 43 in Appendix A of the *Civil Litigation Management Manual* (Judicial Conference of the United States, 2d ed. 2010) (the forms are available only online at http://cwn.fjc.dcn/fjconline/home.nsf/pages/1245). A discussion of *Batson* cases and anonymous juries is included below.

The 1982 Federal Judicial Center publication *Jury Selection Procedures in United States District Courts*, by Gordon Bermant, contains a detailed discussion of several different methods of jury selection. Copies are available from the Federal Judicial Center library on request. See also the section on jury selection and composition (pp. 580–82) in Judge William W Schwarzer's article "Reforming Jury Trials" in volume 132 of *Federal Rules Decisions* (1990).

Note that any victims of the offense are entitled to be notified of and to attend "any public court proceeding . . . involving the crime," which would include jury selection. See 18 U.S.C. § 3771(a)(2) and (3).

Peremptory challenges

Judges should be aware of the cases, beginning with *Batson v. Kentucky*, 476 U.S. 79 (1986), that prohibit peremptory challenges based on race. *Batson* has been extended to cover a criminal defendant's peremptory challenges, *Georgia v. McCollum*, 505 U.S. 42 (1992), and a defendant may object to race-based exclusions whether or not he or she is the same race as the challenged juror, *Powers v. Ohio*, 499 U.S. 400 (1991). Peremptory strikes based on gender are also prohibited. *J.E.B. v. Alabama ex rel. T.B.*, 511 U.S. 127 (1994).

The Supreme Court has left it to the trial courts to develop rules of procedure and evidence for implementing these decisions. It has, however, set out a three-step inquiry for resolving a *Batson* challenge (see *Purkett v. Elem*, 514 U.S. 765, 767 (1995)):

1. At the first step of the *Batson* inquiry, the burden is on the opponent of a peremptory challenge to make out a prima facie case of discrimination. A prima facie case may be shown where (1) the prospective juror is a member of a cognizable group, (2) the prosecutor used a peremptory strike to remove the juror, and (3) the totality of the circumstances raises an inference that the strike was motivated by the

juror's membership in the cognizable group. *Johnson v. California,* 545 U.S. 162, 170 (2005). The burden at this stage is low.[1]

2. If the opponent of the peremptory challenge satisfies the step one prima facie showing, the burden then shifts to the proponent of the strike, who must come forward with a nondiscriminatory explanation of the strike.

3. If the court is satisfied with the neutral explanation offered, it must then proceed to the third step, to determine the ultimate question of intentional discrimination. *Hernandez v. New York,* 500 U.S. 352 (1991). The opponent of the strike has the ultimate burden to show purposeful discrimination. The court may not rest solely upon the neutral explanation offered by the proponent of the strike. Instead, the court must undertake a sensitive inquiry into the circumstantial and direct evidence of intent, *Batson,* 476 U.S. at 93, and evaluate the "persuasiveness of the justification" offered by the proponent of the strike. *Purkett,* 514 U.S. at 768. One method of undertaking such an inquiry is to make a "side-by-side comparison" of the reasons given for striking panelists and the reasons for not striking those who were allowed to serve. *Miller-El v. Dretke,* 545 U.S. 231, 241 (2005).

The *Benchbook* Committee suggests that judges

- conduct the above inquiry on the record but outside of the venire's hearing, to avoid "tainting" the venire by discussions of race, gender, or other characteristics of potential jurors; and

- use a method of jury selection which requires litigants to exercise challenges at sidebar or otherwise outside the venire's hearing and in which no venire members are dismissed until all of the challenges have been exercised. See *Jury Selection Procedures in United States District Courts, supra.*

These procedures should ensure that prospective jurors are never aware of *Batson* discussions or arguments about challenges and therefore can draw no adverse inferences by being temporarily dismissed from the venire and then recalled.[2]

---

1. "[A] defendant satisfies the requirements of *Batson*'s first step by producing evidence sufficient to permit the trial judge to draw an inference that discrimination has occurred." The defendant does not have to show that it was "more likely than not" that discrimination occurred. *Johnson,* 545 U.S. at 170.

2. For a summary of procedures that courts developed for criminal cases in the first two years after *Batson,* see *Bench Comment,* nos. 3 & 4 (1988). For a discussion of voir dire practices in light of *Batson,* see *Chambers to Chambers,* vol. 5, no. 2 (Federal Judicial Center 1987).

Anonymous juries[3]

In rare cases, a district court may determine that a jury should be impaneled anonymously because of concerns about juror safety or tampering. The court may enter an order to prevent disclosure of names, addresses, places of employment, and other facts that might reveal the identity of jurors.[4] The *Benchbook* Committee neither advocates nor discourages use of an anonymous jury but notes that courts must be careful to take steps to minimize potential prejudice to defendants from this procedure. Listed below are the main "rules" that may be summarized from circuit court decisions on this issue.[5]

1. There must be a strong reason to believe the jury needs protection. For example, anonymous juries have been approved in cases involving organized crime figures who, currently or previously, attempted to or did influence, intimidate, or harm witnesses, jurors, or judges. Extensive media coverage may be considered in combination with other factors.

2. The court must take reasonable precautions to minimize any prejudicial effects on the defendant and ensure that fundamental rights to an impartial jury and fair trial are not infringed. For example, the court should

    (a) ensure that the voir dire allows the defendant to adequately assess the prospective jurors and uncover possible bias as to the defendant or the issues in the case. The court should conduct a thorough and searching voir dire, which could include use of written questionnaires.

---

3. Note that, with one exception, anonymous juries are not allowed in capital cases. *See* 18 U.S.C. § 3432 (defendant charged with capital offense must be given list of potential jurors and witnesses three days before trial, "except that such list of the veniremen and witnesses need not be furnished if the court finds by a preponderance of the evidence that providing the list may jeopardize the life or safety of any person") (exception added Sept. 13, 1994).

4. The Third Circuit held that it is within the trial court's discretion to hold an evidentiary hearing on whether the facts warrant an anonymous jury. It also held that the court is not required to make findings and give reasons on the record for using an anonymous jury, but suggested that doing so is the "better practice." *See* United States v. Eufrasio, 935 F.2d 553 (3d Cir. 1991).

5. Most circuits have now ruled on this issue and approved the use of anonymous juries under appropriate circumstances. *See* United States v. Shryock, 342 F.3d 948, 971 (9th Cir. 2003); United States v. Talley, 164 F.3d 989, 1001–02 (6th Cir. 1999); United States v. DeLuca, 137 F.3d 24 (1st Cir. 1998); United States v. Darden, 70 F.3d 1507 (8th Cir. 1995); United States v. Krout, 66 F.3d 1420 (5th Cir. 1995); United States v. Edmond, 52 F.3d 1080 (D.C. Cir. 1995) (per curiam); United States v. Ross, 33 F.3d 1507 (11th Cir. 1994); United States v. Crockett, 979 F.2d 1204 (7th Cir. 1992); United States v. Paccione, 949 F.2d 1183 (2d Cir. 1991) (also discussing several prior Second Circuit cases); United States v. Scarfo, 850 F.2d 1015 (3d Cir. 1988).

(b) give plausible and nonprejudicial reasons to ensure that the explanation for jury anonymity does not adversely reflect on the defendant. The court may, for example, assure jurors that this is a common practice or that it is to protect them from unwanted media attention.[6] It may be advisable to repeat the explanation during jury instructions and before jury deliberation, to stress that the need for anonymity should have no effect on the verdict.

Other FJC sources

For a discussion of techniques for selecting and assisting the jury in civil trials, some of which may also be helpful in criminal trials, see *Civil Litigation Management Manual* 106–07, 110–12 (Judicial Conference of the United States, 2d ed. 2010) and *Manual for Complex Litigation,* Fourth 150–53 (2004)

Gordon Bermant, Jury Selection Procedures in United States District Courts (1982)

Manual on Recurring Problems in Criminal Trials 19–22 (Tucker Carrington & Kris Markarian eds., 6th ed. 2010)

---

6. For examples of explanations, *see Ross*, 33 F.3d 1507, at n.27; United States v. Tutino, 883 F.2d 1125 (2d Cir. 1989); *Scarfo*, 850 F.2d 1015, at Appendix; United States v. Barnes, 604 F.2d 121 (2d Cir. 1979).

2.06 Standard voir dire questions—criminal

[*Note:* Under the Crime Victims' Rights Act, 18 U.S.C. §3771(a)(2) and (3), any victim of the offense has the right to notice of "any public court proceeding ... involving the crime ... of the accused," and to attend that proceeding. It may be advisable to ask the prosecutor if there are any victims and, if so, whether the government has fulfilled its duty to notify them.]

A. The following outline for an initial in-depth voir dire examination of the entire panel by the court assumes that

1. if there are affirmative responses to any questions, follow-up questions will be addressed to the juror(s) (at sidebar, if such questions concern private or potentially embarrassing matters); and

2. the court and counsel have been furnished with the name, address, age, and occupation of each prospective juror.

B. If the court conducts the entire examination, it should require counsel to submit proposed voir dire questions before trial to permit the court to incorporate additional questions at the appropriate places in this outline.

1. Have the jury panel sworn.

2. Explain to the jury panel that the purpose of the voir dire examination is

    (a) to enable the court to determine whether any prospective juror should be excused for cause; and

    (b) to enable counsel for the parties to exercise their individual judgment with respect to peremptory challenges—that is, challenges for which no reason need be given.

3. Explain to prospective jurors that presenting the evidence is expected to take _____ days, and ask if this presents a special problem for any of them.

4. Read or summarize the indictment.

5. Ask if any member of the panel has heard or read anything about the case.

6. Ask counsel for the government to introduce himself or herself and counsel associated with the trial, as well as all the witnesses who will testify in the government's presentation of its case in chief. Ask if the jurors

    (a) know any of these persons;

NOTE

Fed. R. Crim P. 24(a)(1) provides that the court "may examine prospective jurors or may permit the attorneys for the parties to do so."

    (b) had any business dealings with them or were represented by them or members of their firms; and

    (c) had any other similar relationship or business connection with any of them.

7. Ask counsel for each defendant to introduce himself or herself and indicate any witnesses that the defendant may choose to call. Ask if the jurors

    (a) know any of these persons;

    (b) had any business dealings with them or were represented by them or members of their firms; and

    (c) had any other similar relationship or business connection with any of them.

8. Ask prospective jurors:

    (a) Have you ever served as a juror in a criminal or civil case or as a member of a grand jury in either a federal or state court?

    (b) Have you, any member of your family, or any close friend ever been employed by a law enforcement agency?

    (c) If you answer yes to [either of] the following question[s], or if you do not understand the question[s], please come forward, be seated in the well of the courtroom, and be prepared to discuss your answer with the court and counsel at the bench.

        (1) Have you ever been involved, in any court, in a criminal matter that concerned yourself, any member of your family, or a close friend either as a defendant, a witness, or a victim?

        (2) [Only if the charged crime relates to illegal drugs or narcotics, ask:]

        Have you yourself, any member of your family, or any close friend had any experience involving the use or possession of illegal drugs or narcotics?

    (d) If you are selected to sit on this case, will you be able to render a verdict solely on the evidence presented at the trial and in the context of the law as I will give it to you in my instructions, disregarding any other ideas, notions, or beliefs about the law that you may have encountered in reaching your verdict?

    (e) Is there any member of the panel who has any special disability or problem that would make serving as a member of this jury difficult or impossible?

[At this point, if the court is conducting the entire examination, it should ask those questions suggested by counsel that in the opinion of the court are appropriate.]

(f) Having heard the questions put to you by the court, does any other reason suggest itself to you as to why you could not sit on this jury and render a fair verdict based on the evidence presented to you and in the context of the court's instructions to you on the law?

9. If appropriate, permit counsel to conduct additional direct voir dire examination, subject to such time and subject matter limitations as the court deems proper, or state to counsel that if there are additional questions that should have been asked or were overlooked, counsel may approach the bench and discuss them with the court.

2.07 Preliminary jury instructions— criminal case

These suggested instructions are designed to be given following the swearing of the jury. They are general and may require modification in light of the nature of the particular case. They are intended to give the jury, briefly and in understandable language, information to make the trial more meaningful. Other instructions may be given, as the need arises, at appropriate points during the trial. Many circuits have developed model or pattern jury instructions, and judges should consult the instructions that have been prepared for their circuits.

Members of the jury: Now that you have been sworn, I will give you some preliminary instructions to guide you in your participation in the trial.

Duty of the jury

It will be your duty to find from the evidence what the facts are. You and you alone will be the judges of the facts. You will then have to apply to those facts the law as the court will give it to you. You must follow that law whether you agree with it or not.

Nothing the court may say or do during the course of the trial is intended to indicate, or should be taken by you as indicating, what your verdict should be.

Evidence

The evidence from which you will find the facts will consist of the testimony of witnesses, documents and other things received into the record as exhibits, and any facts that the lawyers agree to or stipulate to or that the court may instruct you to find.

Certain things are not evidence and must not be considered by you. I will list them for you now.

1. Statements, arguments, and questions by lawyers are not evidence.
2. Objections to questions are not evidence. Lawyers have an obligation to their clients to make objections when they believe evidence being offered is improper under the rules of evidence. You should not be influenced by the objection or by the court's ruling on it. If the objection is sustained, ignore the question. If it is overruled, treat the answer like any other. If you are instructed that some item of evidence is received for a limited purpose only, you must follow that instruction.
3. Testimony that the court has excluded or told you to disregard is not evidence and must not be considered.

4. Anything you may have seen or heard outside the courtroom is not evidence and must be disregarded. You are to decide the case solely on the evidence presented here in the courtroom.

There are two kinds of evidence: direct and circumstantial. Direct evidence is direct proof of a fact, such as testimony of an eyewitness. Circumstantial evidence is proof of facts from which you may infer or conclude that other facts exist. I will give you further instructions on these as well as other matters at the end of the case, but keep in mind that you may consider both kinds of evidence.

It will be up to you to decide which witnesses to believe, which witnesses not to believe, and how much of any witness's testimony to accept or reject. I will give you some guidelines for determining the credibility of witnesses at the end of the case.

Rules for criminal cases

As you know, this is a criminal case. There are three basic rules about a criminal case that you must keep in mind.

First, the defendant is presumed innocent until proven guilty. The indictment brought by the government against the defendant is only an accusation, nothing more. It is not proof of guilt or anything else. The defendant therefore starts out with a clean slate.

Second, the burden of proof is on the government until the very end of the case. The defendant has no burden to prove his or her innocence, or to present any evidence, or to testify. Since the defendant has the right to remain silent, the law prohibits you from arriving at your verdict by considering that the defendant may not have testified.

Third, the government must prove the defendant's guilt beyond a reasonable doubt. I will give you further instructions on this point later, but bear in mind that in this respect a criminal case is different from a civil case.

Summary of applicable law

In this case the defendant is charged with _____. I will give you detailed instructions on the law at the end of the case, and those instructions will control your deliberations and decision. But in order to help you follow the evidence, I will now give you a brief summary of the elements of the offense that the government must prove to make its case.

[Summarize the elements of the offense.]

Conduct of the jury

Now, a few words about your conduct as jurors.

You, as jurors, must decide this case based solely on the evidence presented here within the four walls of this courtroom. This means that during the trial you must not conduct any independent research about this case, the matters in the case, and the individuals or corporations involved in the case.

In other words, you should not consult dictionaries or reference materials, search the Internet, websites, or blogs, or use any other electronic tools to obtain information about this case or to help you decide the case. Please do not try to find out information from any source outside the confines of this courtroom.

Until you retire to deliberate, you may not discuss this case with anyone, even your fellow jurors. After you retire to deliberate, you may begin discussing the case with your fellow jurors, but you cannot discuss the case with anyone else until you have returned a verdict and the case is at an end.

I know that many of you use cell phones, Blackberries, the Internet, and other tools of technology. You also must not talk to anyone at any time about this case or use these tools to communicate electronically with anyone about the case. This includes your family and friends. You may not communicate with anyone about the case on your cell phone, through e-mail, Blackberry, iPhone, text messaging, or on Twitter, or through any blog or website, including Facebook, Google+, My Space, LinkedIn, or YouTube. You may not use any similar technology of social media, even if I have not specifically mentioned it here. I expect you will inform me as soon as you become aware of another juror's violation of these instructions.[1] A juror who violates these restrictions jeopardizes the fairness of these proceedings, and a mistrial could result, which would require the entire trial process to start over.

Finally, do not form any opinion until all the evidence is in. Keep an open mind until you start your deliberations at the end of the case.

I hope that for all of you this case is interesting and noteworthy.

[If the court decides to allow note taking, state:]

If you want to take notes during the course of the trial, you may do so. However, it is difficult to take detailed notes and pay attention to what the witnesses are saying at the same time. If you do take notes, be sure that your note taking does not interfere with your listening to and considering all of the evidence. Also, if you do take notes, do not discuss them with anyone before you begin your deliberations. Do not take your notes with you at the end of the day—be sure to leave them in the jury room.

If you choose *not* to take notes, remember that it is your own individual responsibility to listen carefully to the evidence. You cannot give this respon-

---

1. Taken from the "Proposed Model Jury Instructions: The Use of Electronic Technology to Conduct Research on or Communicate about a Case," prepared by the Judicial Conference Committee on Court Administration and Case Management (June 2012). *See* Memorandum, "Juror Use of Social Media" from Judge Julie A. Robinson, Chair, Committee on Court Administration and Case Management to all United States District Court Judges (Aug. 6, 2012). *See also* "Strategies for Preventing Jurors' Use of Social Media During Trials and Deliberations" *in* Jurors' Use of Social Media During Trials and Deliberations: A Report to the Judicial Conference Committee on Court Administration and Case Management 5–10 (Federal Judicial Center Nov. 22, 2011), *available at* http://cwn.fjc.dcn/public/pdf.nsf/lookup/DunnJuror.pdf/$file/DunnJuror.pdf.

sibility to someone who is taking notes. We depend on the judgment of all members of the jury; you all must remember the evidence in this case.[2]

Course of the trial

The trial will now begin. First, the government will make an opening statement, which is simply an outline to help you understand the evidence as it comes in. Next, the defendant's attorney may, but does not have to, make an opening statement. Opening statements are neither evidence nor arguments.

The government will then present its witnesses, and counsel for the defendant may cross-examine them. Following the government's case, the defendant may, if he [she] wishes, present witnesses whom the government may cross-examine. After all the evidence is in, the attorneys will present their closing arguments to summarize and interpret the evidence for you, and the court will instruct you on the law.[3] After that, you will retire to deliberate on your verdict.

Other FJC sources

Pattern Criminal Jury Instructions 1–10 (1987)

For a discussion of techniques for assisting the jury in civil trials, some of which may also be helpful in criminal trials, see Civil Litigation Management Manual 111–12 (Judicial Conference of the United States, 2d ed. 2010) and Manual for Complex Litigation, Fourth 154–60 (2004)

For a discussion of jury-related problems in criminal cases, see Manual on Recurring Problems in Criminal Trials 9–22 (Tucker Carrington & Kris Markarian eds., 6th ed. 2010)

---

2. For another sample instruction on note taking, see Civil Litigation Management Manual 374–75 (Judicial Conference of the United States 2001).

3. Some judges may wish to give some instructions before closing arguments. *See* Fed. R. Crim. P. 30.

2.08 General instructions to jury at end of criminal case

Fed. R. Crim. P. 30

Introductory note

Fed. R. Crim. P. 30 outlines the procedure for the submission and consideration of the parties' requests for specific jury instructions. It requires

1. that the court inform the parties before closing arguments of its proposed action upon the instructions requested by counsel; and

2. that the court give counsel adequate opportunity to object to the court's instructions outside the hearing of the jury or, if requested, outside the presence of the jury.

There is no prescribed method for the court to settle on its final set of instructions. Some courts hold an on-the-record charge conference with counsel during trial. At that conference the tendered instructions are discussed and are accepted, rejected, or modified by the court.

Other courts, without holding a charge conference, prepare a set of proposed instructions from those tendered by counsel. These courts then give a copy of the proposed instructions to all counsel and permit counsel to take exception to the instructions. Thereafter, the court may revise its instructions if convinced by counsel's objections that the instructions should be modified.

Still other courts require counsel to confer during trial and to agree, to the extent that they can, on the instructions that should be given. The court then considers only those instructions upon which the parties cannot agree.

The court may, of course, give an instruction to the jury that neither party has tendered.

While the court is free to ignore tendered instructions and to instruct the jury sua sponte, the usual practice is for the court to formulate the final instructions with the assistance of counsel and principally from the instructions counsel tendered.

Local practice varies as to whether a written copy of the instructions is given to the jury for use during its deliberations. Many courts always give the jury a written copy of the instructions. Some courts have the instructions recorded as they are given in court and permit the jury to play them back in the jury room. Some courts do neither but will repeat some or all of the instructions in response to a request from the jury.

Note that the court may instruct the jury either before or after closing arguments, or at both times. Fed. R. Crim. P. 30(c).

Outline of instructions

Instructions delivered at the end of a case consist of three parts: first, general rules that define and control the jury's duties in a criminal case; second, definitions of the elements of the offenses charged in the indictment (information); third, rules and guidelines for jury deliberation and return of verdict. Many circuits have developed model or pattern jury instructions, and judges should consult the instructions that have been prepared for use in their circuits.

A. General rules
    1. Outline the duty of the jury:
       (a) to find the facts from admitted evidence;
       (b) to apply the law as given by the court to facts as found by the jury; and
       (c) to decide the case on the evidence and the law, regardless of personal opinions and without bias, prejudice, or sympathy.
    2. Clearly enunciate the three basic rules in a criminal case:
       (a) presumption of innocence;
       (b) burden of proof on government; and
       (c) proof beyond a reasonable doubt.
    3. Indicate the evidence to be considered:
       (a) sworn testimony of witnesses;
       (b) exhibits;
       (c) stipulations; and
       (d) facts judicially noticed.
    4. Indicate what is not evidence:
       (a) arguments and statements of counsel;
       (b) questions to witnesses;
       (c) evidence excluded by rulings of the court; and
       (d) indictment (information).
B. Define with precision and with specific consideration of the law of your circuit the elements of each offense to be submitted to the jury and of each defense the jury is to consider.
C. Jury procedure
    1. Explain the selection and duty of the foreperson.
    2. Explain the process of jury deliberation:
       (a) rational discussion of the evidence by all jurors for the purpose of reaching a unanimous verdict;

    (b) each juror is to decide the case for himself or herself in the context of the evidence and the law, with proper consideration of other jurors' views;

    (c) jurors may reconsider their views if persuaded by rational discussion but not solely for the sake of reaching a unanimous verdict.

3. The verdict must be unanimous on each count (explain verdict form if used).[1]

4. The jury's communications with the court during deliberations must be in writing and signed by the foreperson.

5. The jury must not disclose how it stands numerically or otherwise on the question of guilt or innocence.

6. Consider giving the jury the following instruction:

> During your deliberations, you must not communicate with or provide any information to anyone by any means about this case. You may not use any electronic device or media, such as a telephone, cell phone, smart phone, iPhone, Blackberry, or computer, the Internet, any Internet service, or any text or instant messaging service, any Internet chat room, blog, or website such as Facebook, MySpace, LinkedIn, YouTube or Twitter, to communicate to anyone any information about this case or to conduct any research about this case until I accept your verdict. In other words, you cannot talk to anyone on the phone, correspond with anyone, or electronically communicate with anyone about this case. You can only discuss the case in the jury room with your fellow jurors during deliberations. I expect you will inform me as soon as you become aware of another juror's violation of these instructions.
>
> You may not use these electronic means to investigate or communicate about the case because it is important that you decide this case based solely on the evidence presented in this courtroom. Information on the Internet or available through social media might be wrong, incomplete, or inaccurate. You are only permitted to discuss the case with your fellow jurors during deliberations because they have seen and heard the same evidence you have. In our judicial system, it is important that you are not influenced by anything or anyone outside of this courtroom. Otherwise, your decision may be based on information known only by

---

1. If special verdict forms or jury interrogatories are used, instruct the jury on how to answer them. Such devices should be used with caution, but they may be useful in multidefendant or other complex cases, or where jury findings (e.g., drug weights) affect statutory maximums. Note that special verdicts and jury interrogatories in criminal cases are not covered by the criminal rules of procedure or by statute, so the court should be familiar with the law of its circuit.

you and not your fellow jurors or the parties in the case. This would unfairly and adversely impact the judicial process.[2] A juror who violates these restrictions jeopardizes the fairness of these proceedings, and a mistrial could result, which would require the entire trial process to start over.

D. Consider providing the jury with a written copy or transcript of the jury instructions.

Other FJC sources

Pattern Criminal Jury Instructions (1987)

For a discussion of techniques for assisting the jury in civil trials, some of which may also be helpful in criminal trials, see Civil Litigation Management Manual 111–12 (Judicial Conference of the United States 2d ed. 2010) and Manual for Complex Litigation, Fourth 154–60 (2004)

For a discussion of jury-related problems in criminal cases, see Manual on Recurring Problems in Criminal Trials 9–22 (Tucker Carrington & Kris Markarian eds., 6th ed. 2010)

---

2. Taken from the "Proposed Model Jury Instructions: The Use of Electronic Technology to Conduct Research on or Communicate about a Case," prepared by the Judicial Conference Committee on Court Administration and Case Management (June 2012). *See* Memorandum, "Juror Use of Social Media" from Judge Julie A. Robinson, Chair, Committee on Court Administration and Case Management to all United States District Court Judges (Aug. 6, 2012). *See also* "Strategies for Preventing Jurors' Use of Social Media During Trials and Deliberations" *in* Jurors' Use of Social Media During Trials and Deliberations: A Report to the Judicial Conference Committee on Court Administration and Case Management 5–10 (Federal Judicial Center Nov. 22, 2011), *available at* http://cwn.fjc.dcn/public/pdf.nsf/lookup/DunnJuror.pdf/$file/DunnJuror.pdf.

2.09 Verdict—criminal

Fed. R. Crim. P. 31 and 43

A. Reception of unsealed verdict

1. Upon announcement by the jury that it has reached a verdict, have all interested parties convene in open court to receive the verdict. The presence of the defendant(s) is required under Fed. R. Crim. P. 43(a), unless one of the exceptions in Fed. R. Crim. P. 43(b) or (c) applies. Any victims of the offense should be given "reasonable, accurate, and timely notice" of the return of verdict so that they can be present. See 18 U.S.C. § 3771(a)(2) and (3).

2. When court is convened, announce that the jury is ready to return its verdict(s), and instruct the deputy marshal (or bailiff) to have the jurors enter and assume their seats in the jury box.

3. If not already known, inquire of the jury who speaks as its foreperson.

4. Ask the foreperson if the jury has unanimously agreed on its verdict. [*Note:* If the response is anything other than an unqualified yes, the jury should be returned without further inquiry to continue its deliberations.]

5. Instruct the foreperson to hand the verdict form(s) to the clerk to be delivered to you for inspection before publication.

6. Inspect the verdict form(s) to ensure regularity. [*Note:* If the verdict form(s) is (are) not properly completed, take appropriate corrective action before publication.]

7. Explain to the jurors that their verdict(s) will now be "published"—that is, read aloud in open court.

8. Instruct the jury to pay close attention as the verdict(s) is (are) published; explain that, following publication, the jury may be "polled"—that each juror may be asked, individually, whether the verdict(s) as published constituted his or her individual verdict(s) in all respects.

9. Publish the verdict(s) by reading it (them) aloud (or by having the clerk do so).

10. If either party requests, or on your own motion, poll the jury by asking (or by having the clerk ask) each juror, by name or number, whether the verdict(s) as published constituted his or her individual verdict(s) in all respects. (Fed. R. Crim. P. 31(d) requires polling upon request.)

11. If polling verifies unanimity, direct the clerk to file and record the verdict, and discharge the jurors with appropriate instructions concerning their future service, if any.

12. If polling results in any doubt as to unanimity, make no further inquiry and have no further discussions with the jury; rather, confer privately, on the record, with counsel and determine whether the jury should be returned for further deliberations or a mistrial should be declared.

B. Reception of sealed verdict

In some cases a sealed verdict may be delivered to the clerk for subsequent "reception" and publication in open court when the jury, the judge, and all necessary parties are present. For example, on some occasions an indispensable party may not be available to receive a verdict when the jury reaches agreement. This may occur when the jury reaches its verdict late in the evening, a defendant is absent from the courtroom because of illness, or the judge is unavailable. In these instances, the verdict may be sealed and the jurors allowed to return home. A sealed verdict may also be appropriate when the jury reaches a verdict as to one defendant but not as to another or when the jury wishes to return a partial verdict.

1. Upon announcement by the jury that it has reached a verdict, have all interested and available parties convene in open court and on the record. The presence of the defendant(s) is required under Fed. R. Crim. P. 43(a), unless one of the exceptions in Fed. R. Crim. P. 43(b) or (c) applies. Any victims of the offense should be given "reasonable, accurate, and timely notice" of the return of verdict so that they can be present. See 18 U.S.C. § 3771(a)(2) and (3).

2. When court is thus convened, announce that the jury is ready to return its verdict(s) and explain that a sealed verdict will be taken in accordance with the following procedure:

   (a) Instruct the deputy marshal (or bailiff) to usher the jurors into the courtroom to assume their seats in the jury box.

   (b) If not already known, inquire of the jury who speaks for it as its foreperson.

   (c) Ask the foreperson if the jury has unanimously agreed on its verdict.

   [*Note:* If the response is anything other than an unqualified yes, the jury should be returned without further inquiry to continue its deliberations.]

   (d) Poll the jurors individually on the record.

   (e) Explain to the jury that a sealed verdict will be taken, and further explain why that procedure has become necessary in the case.

   (f) Direct the clerk to hand a suitable envelope to the foreperson. Instruct the foreperson to place the verdict form(s) in the envelope, to seal the envelope, and to hand it to the clerk for safekeeping.

[*Note:* In the event the jury will not be present at the opening of the verdict, it is recommended that each juror sign the verdict form(s).]

(g) Recess the proceedings, instructing the jury and all interested parties to return at a fixed time for the opening and formal reception of the verdict. Instruct that, in the interim, no member of the jury should have any conversation with any other person, including any other juror, concerning the verdict or any other aspect of the case.

(h) When court is again convened for reception of the verdict, have the clerk hand the sealed envelope to the jury foreperson.

(i) Instruct the foreperson to open the envelope and verify that the contents consist of the jury's verdict form(s) without modification or alteration of any kind.

(j) Follow the steps or procedures outlined in paragraphs A.5 through A.12, *supra.*

Other FJC sources

Manual on Recurring Problems in Criminal Trials 72–74 (Tucker Carrington & Kris Markarian eds., 6th ed. 2010)

2.10 Trial and post-trial motions

Fed. R. Crim. P. 29, 33, 34, and 45(b)

Effective December 1, 2005, Fed. R. Crim. P. 29, 33, and 34 were amended to eliminate the restriction that a court may extend the time to make a motion under these rules only if it acts within the seven-day period the defendant has to file the motion or seek an extension. Motions for extending time to file under these rules are now covered by Rule 45(b).

Also note that if the motion occurs during a "public court proceeding," any victims of the offense must be notified and allowed to attend. If the motion is granted and the defendant might be released, victims would have the right to "be reasonably heard." See 18 U.S.C. § 3771(a)(2)–(4).

The case law on this subject will vary from circuit to circuit. The suggested procedure may be varied to conform with the law of the circuit, the practice of the district, and the preferences of the individual judge.

A. Fed. R. Crim. P. 29—Motion for Judgment of Acquittal
   1. Timing
      (a) The motion may be made by the defendant or the court before submission to the jury, after the evidence on either side is closed. Fed. R. Crim. P. 29(a).
      (b) The motion may also be made or renewed (if the court earlier reserved decision under Fed. R. Crim. P. 29(b)) within seven days of a guilty verdict or discharge of the jury, whichever is later, or within such further time as the court may fix. Fed. R. Crim. P. 29(c)(1) and 45(b); *Carlisle v. United States,* 517 U.S. 416 (1996).
      (c) Failure to make a Fed. R. Crim. P. 29 motion prior to submission of the case to the jury does not waive the defendant's right to move after the jury returns a guilty verdict or is discharged without reaching a verdict. Fed. R. Crim. P. 32(c)(3).
   2. Procedure
      (a) The motion should be heard out of the presence of the jury. Whether an oral hearing will be held or the motion will be decided on written submissions alone is a matter within the court's discretion. If the court reserved decision on a motion that is later renewed, "it must decide the motion on the basis of the evidence at the time the ruling was reserved." Fed. R. Crim. P. 29(b).
      (b) If the defendant moves for a judgment of acquittal, but not for a new trial under Fed. R. Crim. P. 33, the district court may not grant a new trial in lieu of granting the motion for judgment of acquittal. If the motion for acquittal is granted and the defendant has moved for a new trial, the court must conditionally determine

whether any motion for new trial should be granted in case the judgment of acquittal is vacated or reversed on appeal. The reasons for that determination must be specified. See Fed. R. Crim. P. 29(d)(1).

(c) When the court grants a motion for judgment of acquittal, it should consider whether the evidence was sufficient to sustain conviction of a lesser offense necessarily included in the offense charged.

3. Standard

(a) The motion shall be granted for "any offense for which the evidence is insufficient to sustain a conviction." Fed. R. Crim. P. 29(a).

(b) In resolving the motion, the court should not assess the credibility of witnesses, weigh the evidence, or draw inferences of fact from the evidence.[1] The role of the court is simply to decide whether the evidence viewed in the light most favorable to the government was sufficient for any rational trier of fact to find guilt beyond a reasonable doubt.

Caution: Consult your circuit's law for any special rules governing consideration of the evidence.

B. Fed. R. Crim. P. 33—Motion for New Trial

1. Timing

Except as noted below with respect to newly discovered evidence, the motion must be made within seven days after a verdict or finding of guilty, *unless* the court fixes a longer period.

Exception: A motion for a new trial based on newly discovered evidence may be made only within three years after the verdict or finding of guilty. If made during the pendency of an appeal, the motion may be granted only if the case is remanded.

2. Procedure

Whether an oral hearing will be held or the motion will be decided on written submissions alone is a matter within the discretion of the court. The propriety of holding a hearing will depend necessarily on the grounds invoked. This motion may be made only by the defendant and cannot be granted by the court sua sponte. Fed. R. Crim. P. 33(b).

3. Standard

(a) Any alleged error in the trial that could be raised on appeal may be raised on a motion for a new trial, and the motion may be

---

1. Of course, these restrictions do not apply in a bench trial. However, the standard for deciding the motion remains the same.

granted "if the interest of justice so requires," that is, if letting the verdict stand would result in a miscarriage of justice. Fed. R. Crim. P. 33(a).

(b) When the motion for a new trial is made on the ground that the verdict is contrary to the weight of the evidence, the motion should be granted only in exceptional cases where the evidence preponderates heavily against the verdict. Unlike a motion for judgment of acquittal, a motion for a new trial does not require the court to view the evidence in the light most favorable to the government. Some circuits hold that the court has broad power to weigh the evidence and consider the credibility of witnesses. However, other circuits reject the idea of the court as a "thirteenth juror" and limit the extent to which courts may reweigh the evidence. Courts should look to the law of their circuit on this issue.

(c) For a motion based on newly discovered evidence, a defendant must show that the evidence is newly discovered and was unknown to the defendant at the time of trial; failure to discover the evidence sooner was not due to lack of diligence by the defendant; the evidence is material, not merely cumulative or impeaching; and the new evidence would likely lead to acquittal at a new trial. Many circuits have held that such motions are disfavored and should be granted with caution.

4. Findings and conclusions

The court's findings and conclusions should be placed on the record. An order denying a new trial is appealable as a final decision under 28 U.S.C. § 1291. An order granting a new trial may be appealed by the government under 18 U.S.C. § 3731.

C. Fed. R. Crim. P. 34—Motion for Arrest of Judgment

1. Timing

The motion must be made within seven days after a verdict or finding of guilty, or after a plea of guilty or nolo contendere, *unless* the court fixes a longer period.

2. Procedure

Whether an oral hearing will be held or the motion will be decided on written submissions alone is a matter within the discretion of the court. Despite the fact that this motion raises jurisdictional issues, after trial it cannot be granted by the court sua sponte but may only be made by the defendant. Compare Fed. R. Crim. P. 12(b)(2) (same issues raised here may be raised pretrial by either the defendant *or* the court).

3. Standard

   The motion is resolved upon examination of the "record" (i.e., the indictment or information, the plea or the verdict, and the sentence). The court does not consider the evidence produced at trial. A motion for arrest of judgment is based only on one or both of the following contentions: (i) the indictment or information does not charge an offense or (ii) the court was without jurisdiction over the offense charged. Fed. R. Crim. P. 34(a)(1) and (2).

Other FJC sources

For a discussion of techniques in managing motions in civil trials, some of which may be helpful in criminal trials, see Civil Litigation Management Manual 51–67 (Judicial Conference of the United States, 2d ed. 2010)

Manual on Recurring Problems in Criminal Trials 73 (Tucker Carrington & Kris Markarian eds., 6th ed. 2010)

2.11 Release or detention pending sentence or appeal

18 U.S.C. §§ 3142, 3143, 3145; Fed. R. Crim. P. 46;
Fed. R. App. P. 9

A. Release or detention pending imposition or execution of sentence

1. If the defendant was in custody at the time of sentencing, there will ordinarily be no question of release after sentencing to a term of imprisonment.

2. If the defendant was at liberty at the time of sentencing, invite counsel for the defendant to address the question of whether continued release is appropriate. Invite counsel for the government to respond. If any victims of the offense are present, give them the opportunity "to be reasonably heard." 18 U.S.C. § 3771(a)(4).

3. Except for those individuals subject to paragraph 4 below, a person may be released while awaiting imposition or execution of sentence only if the judge finds "by clear and convincing evidence that the person is not likely to flee or pose a danger to the safety of any other person or the community." 18 U.S.C. § 3143(a)(1). "The burden of establishing that the defendant will not flee or pose a danger to any other person or to the community rests with the defendant." Fed. R. Crim. P. 46(c).

    Release shall be in accordance with the provisions of 18 U.S.C. § 3142(b) or (c) (governing release pending trial). This authority may be used to permit an offender to surrender at a Bureau of Prisons institution as well as to permit a delay before a defendant begins to serve the sentence.

4. Persons convicted of a crime of violence, an offense punishable by life imprisonment or death, or a drug offense for which the maximum term of imprisonment is ten years or more shall not be released pending imposition or execution of sentence unless the judge finds by clear and convincing evidence that the person is not likely to flee or to pose a danger to any other person or the community, *and* (i) there is a substantial likelihood that a motion for acquittal or new trial will be granted or (ii) an attorney for the government has recommended that no sentence of imprisonment be imposed upon the person. 18 U.S.C. § 3143(a)(2). Release may also be authorized "if it is clearly shown that there are exceptional reasons why such person's detention would not be appropriate." See 18 U.S.C. § 3145(c).

B. Release or detention pending appeal by the defendant

  1. Except for those individuals subject to paragraph 2 below, if the defendant appeals, he or she may be released pending appeal *only* if the judge finds

    (A) by clear and convincing evidence that the person is not likely to flee or pose a danger to the safety of any other person or the community if released under section 3142(b) or (c) of this title; and

    (B) that the appeal is not for purpose of delay and raises a substantial question[1] of law or fact likely to result[22] in—

      (i) reversal,

      (ii) an order for a new trial,

      (iii) a sentence that does not include a term of imprisonment, or

      (iv) a reduced sentence to a term of imprisonment less than the total of the time already served plus the expected duration of the appeal process.

18 U.S.C. § 3143(b).

Release under § 3143(b) shall be in accordance with the provisions of 18 U.S.C. § 3142(b) or (c) (governing release pending trial). If the defendant is to be released because of the likelihood of a reduced sentence under § 3143(b)(1)(B)(iv), "the judicial officer shall order the

---

1. A "substantial question" has been defined differently by different circuits. *Compare* United States v. Giancola, 754 F.2d 898, 900–01 (11th Cir. 1985) (per curiam) ("a 'close' question or one that very well could be decided the other way"), *with* United States v. Handy, 761 F.2d 1279, 1281–83 (9th Cir. 1985) ("fairly debatable"). Most circuits that have considered the issue have followed *Giancola:* United States v. Steinhorn, 927 F.2d 195, 196 (4th Cir. 1991); United States v. Perholtz, 836 F.2d 554, 555 (D.C. Cir. 1987) (per curiam); United States v. Shoffner, 791 F.2d 586, 589–90 (7th Cir. 1986) (per curiam); United States v. Pollard, 778 F.2d 1177, 1182 (6th Cir. 1985); United States v. Bayko, 774 F.2d 516, 523 (1st Cir. 1985); United States v. Powell, 761 F.2d 1227, 1231–34 (8th Cir. 1985) (en banc); United States v. Valera-Elizondo, 761 F.2d 1020, 1024–25 (5th Cir. 1985); United States v. Affleck, 765 F.2d 944, 952 (10th Cir. 1985) (en banc). The Third Circuit has followed *Handy,* which is generally regarded as posing less of a barrier to the appellant seeking release. United States v. Smith, 793 F.2d 85, 89–90 (3d Cir. 1986). The Second Circuit has expressed the view that the two standards are not significantly different but has indicated a preference for the *Giancola* formulation. United States v. Randell, 761 F.2d 122, 125 (2d Cir. 1985).

2. "Likely to result" means likely to result if the defendant prevails on the substantial question. United States v. Miller, 753 F.2d 19, 23 (3d Cir. 1985), and cases cited *supra* note 1. A substantial question concerning only harmless error would not meet this requirement. "Likely" has been defined by some circuits as "more probable than not." United States v. Bayko, 774 F.2d 516, 522 (1st Cir. 1985); United States v. Valera-Elizondo, 761 F.2d 1020, 1024–25 (5th Cir. 1985); United States v. Pollard, 778 F.2d 1177, 1182 (6th Cir. 1985); United States v. Bilanzich, 771 F.2d 292, 299 (7th Cir. 1985); United States v. Powell, 761 F.2d 1227, 1232–34 (8th Cir. 1985) (en banc).

detention terminated at the expiration of the likely reduced sentence."

If any victims of the offense are present, they must be given the opportunity "to be reasonably heard" regarding the release of the defendant. 18 U.S.C. § 3771(a)(4).

2. Detention is mandatory for persons appealing from a sentence to a term of imprisonment for a crime of violence, an offense punishable by life imprisonment or death, or a drug offense for which the maximum term of imprisonment is ten years or more. 18 U.S.C. § 3143(b)(2). Release may be authorized, however, in "exceptional cases." See 18 U.S.C. § 3145(c).

C. Government appeal of sentence

1. After sentence of imprisonment: If the defendant does not appeal and the government appeals a sentence pursuant to 18 U.S.C. § 3742(b), release pending appeal may not be granted. 18 U.S.C. § 3143(c)(1).

2. After sentence not including imprisonment: If the government appeals pursuant to 18 U.S.C. § 3742(b) from a nonprison sentence, the government should move for a redetermination of the defendant's status. Release or detention is to be determined in accordance with 18 U.S.C. § 3142 (governing release or detention pending trial). 18 U.S.C. § 3143(c)(2); see *supra* section 1.03: Release or detention pending trial. Place the reasons for the determination on the record. If any victims of the offense are in the courtroom, they must be given the opportunity "to be reasonably heard" regarding the release of the defendant. 18 U.S.C. § 3771(a)(4).

3. Note that, except for a sentence imposed by a magistrate judge, the government's appeal must be approved personally by the Attorney General, the Solicitor General, or a deputy solicitor general designated by the Solicitor General. 18 U.S.C. § 3742(b) and (g).

D. Burden of proof

"The burden of establishing that the defendant will not flee or pose a danger to any other person or to the community rests with the defendant." Fed. R. Crim. P. 46(c). The rules of evidence do not apply. Fed. R. Evid. 1101(d)(3). A testimonial hearing may be required. If there are any victims of the offense, they must be provided notice of such a hearing and allowed to attend, and be given an opportunity "to be reasonably heard." 18 U.S.C. § 3771(a)(2)–(4).

E. Written order required

If the defendant is detained or conditions of release are imposed, the reasons must be stated in writing or on the record. Fed. R. App. P. 9(b). If the defendant is released over the government's objection, reasons should be placed on the record to facilitate appellate review.

Other FJC sources

David N. Adair, Jr., The Bail Reform Act of 1984, at 36–43 (3d ed. 2006)

3.01 Death penalty procedures

18 U.S.C. §§ 3591–3595; 21 U.S.C. § 848(e)–(q)

[*Note:* The Crime Victims' Rights Act, 18 U.S.C. § 3771(e), specifies that when the victim of a crime is deceased, "the representatives of the crime victim's estate, family members, or any other persons appointed as suitable by the court, may assume the crime victim's rights." Those rights include notification of and attendance at "any public court proceeding . . . involving the crime," and the opportunity to be "reasonably heard" at any such proceeding "involving release, plea, [or] sentencing." § 3771(a)(2)–(4). The court may want to consult with the prosecution about who will assume the victim's rights, especially if there are a large number of persons who want to do so.]

This section provides an outline of procedures for imposing the death penalty authorized in various federal statutes. Capital cases can raise complex issues, and a number of problems may arise. This outline is offered to provide basic guidance for consideration.[1]

Effective Sept. 13, 1994, the Federal Death Penalty Act of 1994 established procedures for imposing any death penalty under federal law (except for prosecutions under the Uniform Code of Military Justice). See 18 U.S.C. §§ 3591–3595. These provisions largely duplicate, but did not originally re-

---

1. Judges may want to look at appellate court decisions that have examined various aspects of 18 U.S.C. §§ 3591–3595. *See, e.g.,* Jones v. United States, 119 S. Ct. 2090 (1999), *aff'g* 132 F.3d 232 (5th Cir. 1998); United States v. Rodriguez, 581 F.3d 775 (8th Cir. 2009) (affirmed); *In re* Terrorist Bombings of U.S. Embassies in East Africa, 552 F.3d 93 (2d Cir. 2008) (affirmed in relevant part); United States v. Sampson, 486 F.3d 13 (1st Cir. 2007) (affirmed); United States v. Fulks, 454 F.3d 410 (4th Cir. 2006) (affirmed); United States v. Paul, 217 F.3d 989 (8th Cir. 2000) (affirmed); United States v. Battle, 173 F.3d 1343 (11th Cir. 1999) (affirmed); United States v. Webster, 162 F.3d 308 (5th Cir. 1998) (affirmed); United States v. McVeigh, 153 F.3d 1166 (10th Cir. 1998) (affirmed). It may also be useful to examine decisions on death penalty procedures under 21 U.S.C. § 848. *See* United States v. Tipton, 90 F.3d 861 (4th Cir. 1996) (affirmed); United States v. McCullah, 76 F.3d 1087 (10th Cir. 1996) (remanded); United States v. Flores, 63 F.3d 1342 (5th Cir. 1995) (affirmed); United States v. Chandler, 996 F.2d 1073 (11th Cir. 1993), *vacated in part,* 193 F.3d 1297 (1999).

The Federal Judicial Center has prepared a "Resource Guide for Managing Capital Cases, Volume I: Federal Death Penalty Trials," by Molly Treadway Johnson and Laurel L. Hooper. The guide contains information on many more aspects of handling a capital case than can be covered here, is available on the Center's website (www.fjc.gov or http://cwn.fjc.dcn/library/fjc_catalog.nsf), and is periodically updated. The website also includes a large collection of orders and other selected case materials from judges who have handled capital cases. Additional resource materials are added as they become available. *See* "Managing Federal Death Penalty Trials" in the FJC Resource Catalog at http://cwn.fjc.dcn/library/fjc_catalog.nsf. The Center also issued a series of *Chambers to Chambers* in 1995 and 1996 that discussed legal and practical issues unique to capital cases. The series drew upon the experiences of district court judges who have handled death penalty cases under section 848; the first issue includes the names of judges who have tried capital cases and may be contacted.

place,[2] the authorization and procedure for imposing the death penalty for certain drug-related killings in 21 U.S.C. § 848(e). However, effective March 9, 2006, the procedural sections in § 848(g)–(r) were deleted, and capital offenses under § 848(e) will now be prosecuted under §§ 3591–3595. The information provided in this outline applies to capital cases under both statutes unless noted otherwise.

Killing someone in the course of a drug-related offense under 21 U.S.C. § 848(e) appears to be a separate offense that must be charged and proved, not merely an aggravating factor to be considered in sentencing on the underlying drug offense.[3] When the death penalty is sought for an offense under 18 U.S.C. § 3591, the court should determine whether the relevant activity is a separate offense—or an element of the offense—that must be charged and proved.

A. Pretrial

   1. Pursuant to 18 U.S.C. § 3005, when a defendant has been indicted for a capital offense, the court "shall promptly,[4] upon the defendant's request," assign two counsel to the defendant, "of whom at least one shall be learned in the law applicable to capital cases."[5]

---

2. Nothing in the Federal Death Penalty Act of 1994 specifically repealed or superseded any part of section 848, and there are some differences in the statutes' procedures and requirements.

3. Subsection (e) was added to 21 U.S.C. § 848 by the Anti-Drug Abuse Act of 1988, Pub. L. No. 10-690, § 7001(a), 102 Stat. 4181, 4387–88. The catch line of § 7001(a) was "Elements of Offense." Moreover, other subsections refer to being found guilty of or pleading guilty to "an offense under subsection (e)." 21 U.S.C. § 848(i)(1), (j), (n).

4. The Judicial Conference of the United States recommends that the court appoint qualified counsel "at the outset" of a capital case, rather than waiting for the government to provide written notice that it intends to seek the death penalty. *See* Recommendation 1(b) in Federal Death Penalty Cases: Recommendations Concerning the Cost and Quality of Defense Representation, May 1998 (prepared by the Subcommittee on Federal Death Penalty Cases, Committee on Defendant Services and adopted by the Judicial Conference September 15, 1998). *See also In re* Sterling-Suarez, 306 F.3d 1170, 1173 (1st Cir. 2002) ("learned counsel is to be appointed reasonably soon after the indictment and prior to the time that submissions are to be made to persuade the Attorney General not to seek the death penalty"); United States v. Boone, 245 F.3d 352, 359 (4th Cir. 2001) (right to two counsel "becomes available upon *indictment* for a capital crime and not upon the later decision by the government to seek or not to seek the death penalty"). *Cf.* United States v. Waggoner, 339 F.3d 915, 917 (9th Cir. 2003) (agreeing in dicta that right commences "promptly upon the defendant's request after the defendant is indicted for a capital crime"). *But cf.* United States v. Casseus, 282 F.3d 253, 256 (3d Cir. 2002) (finding harmless error where defendants' requests for second counsel made promptly after indictment were not acted upon until after government decided not to seek death penalty a month and a half later).

5. *See Chambers to Chambers,* vol. 10, no. 1 (Federal Judicial Center 1995), for a discussion of whether more than two attorneys may be appointed under § 3005. *See also McCullah,* 76 F.3d at 1098 (no abuse of discretion to refuse to appoint additional counsel where district court found that two were adequate). For a discussion of compensation of counsel, investigators, and expert witnesses, see *Chambers to Chambers,* vol. 10, no. 1. Note that 21 U.S.C.

2. The government must provide written notice to the court and the defendant that it will seek the death penalty, and it must identify which statutory and nonstatutory aggravating factors it intends to prove at "a reasonable time" before trial or acceptance by the court of a guilty plea.[6] 18 U.S.C. § 3593(a); 21 U.S.C. § 848(h)(1).

3. At least three days before commencement of trial, the defendant must receive a copy of the indictment and a list of the names and addresses of venire members and witnesses, unless the court finds by a preponderance of the evidence that providing the list may endanger any person. 18 U.S.C. § 3432.

4. Arrange for a jury venire large enough to accommodate additional peremptory challenges (twenty for each side, see Fed. R. Crim. P. 24(b)(1)), the length of time required for trial and penalty phases, and the likelihood that alternate jurors will be needed.[7]

5. Consider having venire members complete a juror questionnaire, and consider providing attorneys with the responses prior to jury selection.

6. After familiarizing the venire members with jury service, explain the two-stage decision process. The following is a suggested explanation.

---

§ 848(q)(10) was amended by the Antiterrorism and Effective Death Penalty Act of 1996 (effective April 24, 1996) to limit attorneys' fees and costs for other services. In cases not affected by the Act, compensation for appointed counsel is not limited by Criminal Justice Act maximums. Effective March 9, 2006, § 848(q) has effectively been replaced by new 18 U.S.C. § 3599 ("Counsel for financially unable defendants").

6. For § 848(e) offenses prior to March 9, 2006, the government must identify and prove one aggravating factor from § 848(n)(1) plus at least one factor from § 848(n)(2)–(12). Section 3591 contains three groups of offenses for which death is authorized, and each group has a separate list of aggravating factors from which the government must identify and prove at least one. Additional factors from any list may be used, but only the one is required to impose the death penalty. See § 3593(e). The Fourth and Tenth Circuits have held that allowing the jury to find duplicative aggravating factors is prohibited and would require a new penalty phase. *See Tipton,* 90 F.3d at 898–901 (but affirming sentence because error was harmless in this case); *McCullah,* 76 F.3d at 1111–12 (remanded: prosecution submitted both § 841(n)(1)(C) and § 841(n)(1)(D), which substantially overlap, and a nonstatutory aggravating factor that overlapped § 841(n)(1)(C)). *See also* United States v. McCullah, 87 F.3d 1136, 1137–38 (10th Cir. 1996) (upon denial of rehearing and rehearing en banc, clarifying that overlapping aggravating factors are improper if supported by same underlying conduct, thus distinguishing *Flores*). *But cf. Flores,* 63 F.3d at 1372–73 (defendant's conduct supported finding of both n(1)(A) (intentionally killed the victim) and n(1)(C) (intentionally engaged in conduct intending that the victim be killed) factors—defendant personally participated in the killings and hired others to help). The Fourth and Tenth Circuits rejected the claim that allowing the government to introduce nonstatutory aggravating factors violated separation of powers principles.

7. *See Chambers to Chambers,* vol. 10, no. 1 (Federal Judicial Center 1995), for discussion of this issue and of the juror questionnaire mentioned in the next paragraph.

Before we continue with the jury selection process, I will explain to you how a capital case proceeds. Potentially this case has two stages. The first requires the jury to consider whether or not the government has proved the charges brought against the defendant, _____, beyond a reasonable doubt. In this stage of the proceeding, the jury shall not consider any possible punishment that might be imposed.

If, at the conclusion of the first stage, the jury reports that it does not find the defendant, _____, guilty of the capital charge, then the jury's responsibilities are at an end. This is so regardless of how the jury finds as to any other charges because the court decides the punishment for noncapital crimes.

If the jury reports that it finds the defendant, _____, guilty of the capital charge, then we proceed to a second stage: a sentencing hearing, at which the jury considers whether the death penalty should be imposed.[8]

Now, during the sentencing hearing, the government has the opportunity to introduce evidence of aggravating factors that might make the conduct alleged in the capital count so serious as to merit imposition of the death penalty. The defendant has the opportunity to present mitigating factors about the crime or about himself [herself] that might suggest that the death penalty is not appropriate in this case.

No aggravating factor may be considered by the jury unless all jurors agree on that factor unanimously. Nor can the jury find in favor of the death penalty unless it also unanimously agrees that the unanimously-agreed-upon aggravating factors sufficiently outweigh any mitigating factors that one or more jurors believe exist.

Even if no one on the jury finds that any mitigating factors exist, the jury cannot find in favor of the death penalty unless everyone on the jury finds that the aggravating factors that the jurors have unanimously found to exist are sufficiently serious to justify a death sentence. Even if the jury unanimously makes such findings, it is not required under law to find in favor of the death penalty; that is a matter for the jury to decide.

[For § 3591 offenses, add:] If a jury does not unanimously find in favor of the death penalty, it may consider whether a sentence of

---

8. The term "recommend," used in the statutes, should be avoided as potentially misleading. *See* Caldwell v. Mississippi, 472 U.S. 320 (1985). The court is without authority to reject the recommendation. *See* 18 U.S.C. § 3594; 21 U.S.C. § 848(*l*).

life imprisonment without the possibility of release should be imposed, a decision that must also be unanimous.[9]

If a jury unanimously finds in favor of the death penalty, this court is required to sentence the defendant to death. [*For § 3591 offenses, add:*] If a jury unanimously finds in favor of a sentence of life imprisonment without the possibility of release, the court is required to impose that sentence.

7. During voir dire, question the venire members as to their views on the death penalty.[10] It is recommended that this be done by questioning individual venire members at side-bar. A juror may not be excused for cause simply because the juror voices "general objections to the death penalty or express[es] conscientious or religious scruples against its infliction."[11] "The standard is whether the juror's views would 'prevent or substantially impair the performance of his duties as a juror in accordance with his instructions and his oath.'"[12] Excuse the juror for cause if the juror answers yes to either of the following questions:

   (a) Would you never find, under any circumstances, in favor of the death penalty under the law as I will explain it?[13]

   (b) If the defendant is found guilty of conduct that is a capital offense, beyond a reasonable doubt, would you always find in favor of the death penalty?[14]

Note that the harmless error analysis does not apply to *Witherspoon* violations.[15]

---

9. The option of a jury-imposed sentence of life without release is not available under § 848. Section 3593(e) allows the jury to "recommend" such a sentence, and under § 3594 "the court shall sentence defendant accordingly." *See also infra* note 21.

10. *See Chambers to Chambers,* vol. 10, no. 1 (Federal Judicial Center 1995), for a discussion of jury selection, including "death-qualifying" the jury. *See also* United States v. Purkey, 428 F.3d 738, 750–52 (8th Cir. 2005) (discussing use of juror questionnaire and affirming exclusion of three potential jurors); United States v. McVeigh, 153 F.3d 1166, 1205–11 (10th Cir. 1998) (discussing voir dire issues regarding "death-qualifying" and pretrial publicity); United States v. Tipton, 90 F.3d 861, 870–81 (4th Cir. 1996) (affirming district court's method of voir dire and the dismissal for cause of some jurors who opposed the death penalty); United States v. Flores, 63 F.3d 1342, 1353–56 (5th Cir. 1995) (same).

11. Witherspoon v. Illinois, 391 U.S. 510, 521–22 (1968).

12. Wainwright v. Witt, 469 U.S. 412, 424 (1985), *quoting* Adams v. Texas, 448 U.S. 38, 45 (1980). *See also* Lockhart v. McCree, 476 U.S. 162 (1986) (allowing a juror who could not perform in the penalty phase to be excluded from the guilt/innocence phase).

13. *See Witherspoon,* 391 U.S. 510.

14. *See* Morgan v. Illinois, 504 U.S. 719 (1992).

15. Gray v. Mississippi, 481 U.S. 648 (1987).

8. When the jury retires to consider its verdict, do not discharge the alternate jurors.[16] Instruct the alternates to avoid discussing the case with anyone. If an alternate juror replaces a juror after deliberations have begun, instruct the jury to begin its deliberations anew. Fed. R. Crim. P. 24(c)(3).

B. After verdict or plea

1. No presentence report should be prepared. 18 U.S.C. § 3593(c); 21 U.S.C. § 848(j).

2. Unless the defendant moves for a hearing without a jury and the government consents, the hearing must be before a jury.

   (a) If the defendant was convicted after a jury trial, the hearing should be before the jury that determined guilt, unless such jury has been discharged for good cause.

   (b) If the defendant was convicted upon a plea or after a bench trial, a jury and alternates should be impaneled in accordance with Fed. R. Crim. P. 24(c).

   18 U.S.C. § 3593(b); 21 U.S.C. § 848(i)(1).

3. Instruct the jury about the purpose of the hearing.[17]

   (a) Inform the jurors that they will be required to make specific findings about possible aggravating circumstances, that any or all of them may make a finding regarding any mitigating circumstances,[18] and that if certain findings are made, they will be required to decide whether the defendant should be sentenced to death (or, if the offense is under § 3591, to life imprisonment without the possibility of release).

---

16. Fed. R. Crim. P. 24(c)(3) gives district courts the discretion to retain alternate jurors when the jury retires. Note that §§ 3593(b) and 848(i) do not allow a jury of fewer than twelve members unless the parties stipulate to a lesser hearing before the conclusion of the sentencing hearing. See *Chambers to Chambers*, vol. 10, no. 1 (Federal Judicial Center 1995), for a discussion of retaining the alternate jurors.

17. Samples of jury instructions that have been used in death penalty cases are available from the Federal Judicial Center's Information Services Office.

18. Under §§ 3593(d) and 848(k), specific findings about mitigating factors are not required. However, both sections state that such findings "may be made by one or more members of the jury," and the Eleventh Circuit held that "[s]ection 848(k) requires that the jury be instructed that it has the option to return written findings of mitigating factors." United States v. Chandler, 996 F.2d 1073, 1087 (11th Cir. 1993), *vacated in part*, 193 F.3d 1297 (1999). The court also noted that under § 848(q)(3)(B), the reviewing court is to consider whether such findings, or any failure to find a mitigating factor, are supported by the record, but held that this section requires only "that if the jury exercises its option, we must review those findings." 996 F.2d at 1087. There is no similar provision regarding appellate review of mitigating circumstances in § 3595(c)(2). Nevertheless, it is recommended that the trial judge require such findings.

(b) Instruct the jurors that, in considering whether a sentence of death is justified, they shall not consider the race, color, religious beliefs, national origin, or sex of the defendant or of any victim; that the jury is not to recommend a sentence of death unless it has concluded that it would recommend a sentence of death for the crime in question no matter what the race, color, religious beliefs, national origin, or sex of the defendant or of any victim may be; and that each of the jurors will be required to certify that he or she has not been influenced by such factors. 18 U.S.C. § 3593(f); 21 U.S.C. § 848(o)(1).

4. Proceed with the hearing in the manner set forth in 18 U.S.C. § 3593(c) or 21 U.S.C. § 848(j). Note that

   (a) the government may seek to prove only those aggravating factors of which it gave notice;

   (b) the rules of evidence do not apply, but information may be excluded if its probative value is outweighed (§ 3593(c)) or "substantially outweighed" (§ 848(j)) by the danger of unfair prejudice, confusion of the issues, or misleading the jury;[19]

   (c) the trial transcript and exhibits may be used, particularly if a new jury has been impaneled for the sentencing stage;

   (d) the order of argument is prescribed by the statute; and

   (e) the representative(s) of any victim must be provided an opportunity "to be reasonably heard" during the sentencing hearing. 18 U.S.C. § 3771(a)(4) and (e).

5. Instruct the jury and provide it with a form for findings relative to sentencing. (See the suggested form for sentencing findings at the end of this section.[20]) Be sure to cover the following points:

   (a) The jury should first consider the aggravating factors that the government has sought to establish.

   (b) The aggravating factors must be proved beyond a reasonable doubt, and the jury can find that an aggravating factor exists only by unanimous vote. If the jury is not unanimous in finding that an aggravating factor has been proved, it must treat it as not proved.[21]

---

19. *See, e.g.,* United States v. McVeigh, 153 F.3d 1166, 1211–16 (10th Cir. 1998) (discussing standards for admission of mitigating evidence).

20. Sample jury instructions and forms are available from the Federal Judicial Center's website (www.fjc.gov). Follow the links for the "Resource Guide for Managing Capital Cases, Volume I: Federal Death Penalty Trials."

21. This outline and the accompanying form are based on the understanding that, if the jurors disagree about the findings required for a death sentence, a sentence other than death will be imposed. 18 U.S.C. § 3594; 21 U.S.C. § 848(*l*). For § 3591 offenses, the jury is specifically instructed that it may choose a sentence of life imprisonment without release or

(c) For the jurors even to consider the death penalty, they must
   (i) *for § 3591 offenses:* answer yes to the required § 3592(b), (c), or (d) question (question 1 on the suggested form);
   (ii) *for § 848(e) offenses (committed before March 9, 2006):* answer yes to the § 848(n)(1) question (question 1 on the suggested form) and to at least one of the § 848(n)(2)–(12) questions (question 2 on the suggested form).

(d) If the jury's findings about aggravating factors permit consideration of a death sentence, the jury should then consider the defendant's evidence of mitigating factors.

(e) A mitigating factor should be taken as true if it has been established by a preponderance of the evidence. Distinguish between the reasonable doubt and preponderance tests.

(f) The jurors should discuss the evidence about mitigating factors but are not required to reach a unanimous decision. A finding of a mitigating factor may be made by one or more jurors, and any member of the jury who finds the existence of a mitigating factor by a preponderance of the evidence may consider such a factor established, regardless of whether any other juror agrees.

(g) In considering whether the death penalty should be imposed, each juror should consider only those aggravating factors that have been found to exist beyond a reasonable doubt by unanimous vote, but each juror should consider any mitigating factors that have been proved by a preponderance of the evidence to his or her own satisfaction.

---

a lesser sentence. However, there is no similar choice for the jury in § 848, and no requirement that the jurors be told the consequences of failure to unanimously agree on a sentence of death. *See Chandler,* 996 F.2d at 1089 ("district court is not required to instruct the jury on the consequences of the jury's inability to reach a unanimous verdict").

The Supreme Court held that when a defendant's future dangerousness is an issue and the only alternative sentence to death is life with no possibility of parole, due process entitles the defendant to tell the jury that the defendant will never be released from prison. Simmons v. South Carolina, 114 S. Ct. 2187, 2196–201 (1994). The Court later held that such an instruction should have been given where the prosecution introduced evidence of the defendant's future dangerousness, even though the prosecutor did not specifically argue future dangerousness as a reason to impose the death penalty. Kelly v. South Carolina, 534 U.S. 246, 252–57 (2002). *Cf.* United States v. Stitt, 250 F.3d 878, 888–92 (4th Cir. 2001) (distinguishing *Simmons* because, although government used defendant's future dangerousness as an aggravating factor, there was still possibility of departure under the guidelines to less than a life sentence); United States v. Flores, 63 F.3d 1342, 1368–69 (5th Cir. 1995) (affirmed: same, and government focused on danger defendant "would pose *while still in prison,*" not after release). *See also* O'Dell v. Netherland, 521 U.S. 151, 159–67 (1997) (declining to apply *Simmons* retroactively).

(h) The jury should then:
    (i)   for § 3591 offenses:
        (a) consider whether the aggravating factor(s) sufficiently outweigh the mitigating factor(s) to justify a sentence of death, or, in the absence of a mitigating factor, whether the aggravating factor(s) alone are sufficient to justify a sentence of death;
        (b) determine whether the defendant should be sentenced to death, to life imprisonment without possibility of release, or some other sentence, a decision that must be unanimous.[22]

    (ii) *for § 848(e) offenses (committed before March 9, 2006):* determine—based on consideration of whether the aggravating factors sufficiently outweigh any mitigating factors, or in the absence of mitigating factors, whether the aggravating factors alone are sufficient to justify a sentence of death—whether the death penalty should be imposed. The jury may find in favor of the death penalty only by unanimous vote.

(i) Regardless of its findings about aggravating and mitigating factors, the jury is never required to find in favor of a death sentence.[23]

(j) The jury shall not consider the race, color, religious beliefs, national origin, or sex of the defendant or any victim in considering whether a sentence of death is justified, and must not impose a death sentence unless it would do so no matter what the race, color, religious beliefs, national origin, or sex of the defendant or of any victim. The jurors must sign a certificate to this effect when a death sentence is returned. 18 U.S.C. § 3593(f); 21 U.S.C. § 848(o)(1).

6. Consider retaining the alternates after the jury retires. Fed. R. Crim. P. 24(c)(3). (Note that, although Fed. R. Crim. P. 23(b) permits a court to accept a verdict from eleven jurors if a juror is excused after the jury retires, §§ 3593(b) and 848(i)(2) allow sentencing findings to be accepted from fewer than twelve jurors only if the parties agree to a lesser number before the jury retires.)

---

22. Although § 3593(e) states that the jury may unanimously recommend "some other lesser sentence," § 3594 implies that the court may still impose a sentence of life without release. *See also* Jones v. United States, 119 S. Ct. 2090, 2098–100 (1999) (indicating that "otherwise" clause of § 3594 leaves sentencing determination to court if jury cannot agree unanimously on a sentence).

23. This is explicitly stated in § 848(k) and is implicit in § 3593(e), given the jury's authorization to choose a lesser sanction.

7. If the jury finds in favor of a death sentence, the court must impose such a sentence. Otherwise:

   (a) *For § 3591 offenses:* If the jury unanimously finds in favor of life imprisonment without the possibility of release, the court must impose that sentence; otherwise, the court shall impose any other sentence authorized by law. See 18 U.S.C. § 3594.

   (b) *For § 848(e) offenses (committed before March 9, 2006):* The court may impose any other sentence authorized by law. 21 U.S.C. § 848(*l*).

Suggested form for sentencing findings

1. Do you find unanimously that the government has proved, beyond a reasonable doubt, that the defendant [insert government's claim under § 3592(b), (c), or (d), or § 848(n)(1)(A), (B), (C), *or* (D)]?[24]

    Yes ❑   No ❑

    IF THE ANSWER TO QUESTION 1 IS "NO," STOP HERE. ALL JURORS SHOULD SIGN AT THE END OF THE FORM.

2. [*For § 848(e) offenses (committed before March 9, 2006) only:*] Do you find unanimously that the government has proved, beyond a reasonable doubt, that the defendant [insert government's claim under § 848(n)(2)–(12)]?

    Yes ❑   No ❑

    [Repeat the above for as many separate factors under (n)(2)–(12) as the government alleges.]

    IF THE ANSWER TO QUESTION 2 IS [OR TO QUESTIONS 2 THROUGH __ ARE ALL] "NO," STOP HERE. ALL JURORS SHOULD SIGN AT THE END OF THE FORM.

3. Do you find unanimously that the government has proved, beyond a reasonable doubt, that the defendant [insert government's claim of other aggravating factor]?

    Yes ❑   No ❑

    [Repeat the above for as many additional aggravating factors as the government alleges.]

4. Do any jurors find that the defendant has proved, by a preponderance of the evidence, that [insert the defendant's claim of mitigating factor]?

    Yes ❑   No ❑

---

24. One of the aggravating factors listed in 21 U.S.C. § 848(n)(1) must be found if the death penalty is to be imposed. It is hard to imagine a conviction under § 848(e) that does not subsume a factor under (n)(1). Nevertheless, the statute requires that the existence of an (n)(1) factor be considered at the penalty stage. It appears that subsection (n)(1) was drafted in contemplation of application to a wider range of criminal conduct than § 848(e) encompasses. For the Supreme Court's treatment of a similar statute, see *Lowenfield v. Phelps*, 484 U.S. 231 (1988). *See also* United States v. McCullah, 76 F.3d 1087, 1109–10 (10th Cir. 1996) (recognizing this aspect of § 848(e) but finding it meets requirements of *Lowenfield*); United States v. Flores, 63 F.3d 1342, 1369–72 (5th Cir. 1995) (same); United States v. Chandler, 996 F.2d 1073, 1092–93 (11th Cir. 1993) (same), *vacated in part*, 193 F.3d 1297 (1999). Note that the Fourth and Tenth Circuits have held that it is error to find duplicative (n)(1) factors. *See supra* note 6.

[Repeat the above for as many separate mitigating factors as the defendant alleges.]

5. Do you find unanimously that the aggravating factor(s) to which you have provided a unanimous "yes" answer above sufficiently outweigh(s) the mitigating factor(s) to justify a sentence of death, or in the absence of a mitigating factor, that the aggravating factor(s) alone is (are) sufficient to justify a sentence of death, and that the defendant should be sentenced to death?

    Yes ❑   No ❑

    IF THE ANSWER TO QUESTION 5 IS "NO" AND A § 3591 OFFENSE IS INVOLVED, ASK:

    Do you find unanimously that the defendant should be sentenced to life imprisonment without possibility of release?

    Yes ❑   No ❑

Each of the undersigned jurors hereby certifies that:

1. in reaching my decisions about the sentence in this case, I did not consider the race, color, religious beliefs, national origin, or sex of either the defendant, [defendant's name], or the victim, [victim's name]; and

2. I would have made the same decision about the sentence for this crime no matter what the race, color, religious beliefs, national origin, and sex of the defendant, [defendant's name], and the victim, [victim's name].

(Foreperson)

_____   _____

_____   _____

_____   _____

_____   _____

4.01 Sentencing procedure

Fed. R. Crim. P. 32; 18 U.S.C. § 3553(a)

I. Introduction

Before the promulgation of the Sentencing Guidelines, federal courts sentenced defendants in an indeterminate sentencing regime. Judges had discretion to impose any fair sentence within the bounds of the statutory minimum and maximum. Because of parole, the sentence a judge imposed was often quite different from the time a defendant served. This discretion and indeterminacy led to congressional concern about unwarranted federal sentencing disparity and to the enactment of The Sentencing Reform Act of 1984 (SRA). The SRA was passed with bipartisan and near-unanimous Senate support under the leadership of Senators Kennedy, Thurmond, Hatch, and Biden. Its goals were greater fairness and transparency in federal sentencing. The SRA brought about "truth in sentencing" by eliminating parole, created the Sentencing Commission, and charged the Commission with crafting sentencing guidelines. The Commission, in turn, promulgated guidelines that provide a sentencing range appropriate for the "heartland" of typical cases, based on the defendant's offense level and criminal history. Judges were required to select sentences from within the guidelines range except in unusual circumstances.

In 2005, the Supreme Court issued *United States v. Booker*, 543 U.S. 220 (2005). *Booker*, reinforced by subsequent Supreme Court decisions,[1] changed the sentencing landscape by making the Sentencing Guidelines advisory rather than mandatory. This advisory status notwithstanding, a judge's sentencing calculation must begin with an accurate determination of the applicable sentencing range under the guidelines. The judge must then consider whether any departures from the guidelines would be consistent with guideline policy statements and commentary.[2] *See* 18 U.S.C.

---

1. *See* Dorsey v. United States, 132 S. Ct. 2321 (2012); Setser v. United States, 132 S. Ct. 1463 (2012); Southern Union Co. v. United States, 132 S. Ct. 2344 (2012); Tapia v. United States, 131 S. Ct. 2382 (2011); Pepper v. United States, 131 S. Ct. 1229 (2011); Dillon v. United States, 130 S. Ct. 2683 (2010); Nelson v. United States, 555 U.S. 350 (2009); Spears v. United States, 555 U.S. 261 (2009); Irizarry v. United States, 553 U.S. 708 (2008); Gall v. United States, 552 U.S. 38 (2007); Kimbrough v. United States, 552 U.S. 85 (2007); Rita v. United States, 551 U.S. 338 (2007).

2. *See, e.g.,* United States v. McBride, 434 F.3d 470, 477 (6th Cir. 2006) ("Because Guideline 'departures' are a part of the appropriate Guideline range calculation, we believe that Guideline departures are still a relevant consideration for determining the appropriate Guideline sentence."); United States v. Jordi, 418 F.3d 1212, 1215 (11th Cir. 2005) ("the application of the guidelines is not complete until the departures, if any, that are warranted are appropriately considered"). *See also* United States v. Lofink, 564 F.3d 232, 240–42 (3d Cir. 2009) (failure to rule on defendant's departure motion constitutes procedural error—merits of departure motions must be considered separately from resolution of variance requests). *But see* United States v. Johnson, 427 F.3d 423, 426 (7th Cir. 2005) ("framing of the issue as

§ 3553(a)(4),(5); *see also, e.g.,* USSG § 5K1.1. Finally, the judge should consider the other factors listed in 18 U.S.C. § 3553(a) in order to arrive at the final sentence.[3]

Note that any reference in this section to a "departure" means a departure from the calculated guideline range that is consistent with applicable policy statements and guideline commentary. In contrast, a "variance" refers to a sentence that is outside of the advisory guideline range based on the application of other § 3553(a) factors, as authorized by *Booker.*[4] A final sentence may include both a departure and a variance if warranted by the circumstances.

II. Preliminary matters

A. *Presentence report*

Federal Rule of Criminal Procedure 32(e)(2) requires that the presentence report be disclosed to the defendant, defense counsel, and the attorney for the government not less than thirty-five days before the sentencing hearing, unless this period is waived by the defendant.[5] Each party has fourteen days to provide to the opposing party and the probation officer a written copy of any objections to the presentence report. Fed. R. Crim. P. 32(f)(1)–(2). The probation officer must then submit the presentence report to the court and the parties at least seven days before sentencing, along with "an addendum containing any unresolved objections, the grounds for those ob-

---

one about 'departures' has been rendered obsolete by our recent decisions applying *Booker*"); United States v. Mohamed, 459 F.3d 979, 987 (9th Cir. 2006) (in light of *Booker*, court would "treat such so-called departures as an exercise of post-*Booker* discretion to sentence a defendant outside of the applicable guidelines range" and subject it to a "unitary review for reasonableness, no matter how the district court styles its sentencing decision").

3. The Guidelines provide that courts must follow the three-step sentencing protocol set out in *Booker. See* USSG § 1B1.1 ("[1] The court shall determine the kinds of sentence and the guideline range as set forth in the guidelines . . . . [2] The court shall then consider . . . Specific Offender Characteristics and Departures and any other policy statements or commentary in the guidelines that might warrant consideration . . . . [3] The court shall then consider the applicable factors in 18 U.S.C. § 3553(a) taken as a whole." For a general discussion of the relationship between the manner in which a sentencing hearing is conducted and the interests of the parties involved, see D. Brock Hornby, *Speaking in Sentences*, 14 Green Bag 2D 147 (2011).

4. A court may also base a variance on a disagreement with the policy underpinning a guideline. *See Spears,* 555 U.S. at 264; *Kimbrough,* 552 U.S. at 109–11.

5. Note that the presentence report shall not include any diagnostic opinions that if disclosed may disrupt a program of rehabilitation, sources of information obtained upon a promise of confidentiality, or any other information that may result in harm to the defendant or others if disclosed. Fed. R. Crim. P. 32(d)(3). The probation officer's final recommendation as to sentence, previously withheld, may now be disclosed pursuant to local rule or at the court's discretion. Fed. R. Crim. P. 32(e)(3).

jections, and the probation officer's comments on them." Fed. R. Crim. P. 32(g).

B. *Notice of departure*

If you are contemplating a departure from the advisory guideline range on a ground not identified as such either in the presentence report or in a pre-hearing submission, you must provide "reasonable notice" to the parties and identify the departure grounds. Fed. R. Crim. P. 32(h); *Burns v. United States,* 501 U.S. 129 (1991). Although it is not required, it may be advisable to also provide notice of previously unidentified grounds that may support a non-guidelines sentence.[6]

C. *Concurrent or consecutive sentences*

Determine whether you will need to decide between concurrent, consecutive, or partially consecutive sentences, such as when the defendant was convicted on multiple counts, is subject to an undischarged term of imprisonment, or faces sentencing in a state court. *See* USSG §§ 5G1.2 and 5G1.3 (delineating different circumstances where concurrent or consecutive sentences may be either required or optional); 18 U.S.C. § 3584(a) ("Imposition of concurrent or consecutive terms"). *See also Setser v. United States,* 132 S. Ct. 1463, 1468–70 (2012) (district court has discretion to order federal sentence to run consecutively to anticipated state sentence).

D. *Crime victims' rights*

If there are any victims of the offense, consider asking the government if the victims have been notified of their right to attend the hearing and if any wish to speak. 18 U.S.C. § 3771(a)(2)–(4). *See also* Fed. R. Crim. P. 32(i)(4)(B)–(C) ("Before imposing sentence, the court must address any victim of the crime who is present at sentencing and must permit the victim to be reasonably heard," and the victim may be heard in camera.).

---

6. The Supreme Court held that Rule 32(h)'s notice requirement does not apply to variances. Irizarry v. United States, 553 U.S. 708, 714 (2008). The Court added, however, that "[s]ound practice dictates that judges in all cases should make sure that the information provided to the parties in advance of the hearing, and in the hearing itself, has given them an adequate opportunity to confront and debate the relevant issues. We recognize that there will be some cases in which the factual basis for a particular sentence will come as a surprise to a defendant or the Government. The more appropriate response to such a problem is not to extend the reach of Rule 32(h)'s notice requirement categorically, but rather for a district judge to consider granting a continuance when a party has a legitimate basis for claiming that the surprise was prejudicial." The Court further noted that "at sentencing, the parties must be allowed to comment on 'matters relating to an appropriate sentence,' Rule 32(i)(1)(C), and the defendant must be given an opportunity to speak and present mitigation testimony, Rule 32(i)(4)(A)(ii)." *Id.* at 715–16 & n.2.

E. If guilty plea was before a magistrate judge

At the beginning of the sentencing hearing, if the defendant had previously consented to plead guilty before a magistrate judge, state on the record that, based on the information provided by the defendant at the plea hearing and contained in the presentence report, you accept the defendant's guilty plea. *See supra* section 1.13: Referrals to magistrate judges (criminal matters), at note 2.

III. The sentencing hearing

The following is a suggested outline for the sentencing hearing that is designed to ensure that judges cover the information required by rule or case law. The sentencing hearing does not have to proceed in any particular order, and this outline is only a guide that need not be followed precisely.

A. Opening

1. Ask:

   (a) Will counsel for the government introduce himself/herself?

   (b) Will counsel for the defendant introduce himself/herself?

   (c) Will the probation officer introduce himself/herself?

   (d) [If applicable] Will the interpreter introduce himself/herself?

   The courtroom deputy shall swear in the interpreter.

2. Ask both counsel:

   (a) I have received the following documents submitted by counsel in advance of the hearing: (list the documents: e.g., sentencing memoranda, letters, expert reports).

   (b) Do you have any other documents or letters for the court?

3. Ask the prosecutor:

   (a) Do you have any witnesses or victims present in the courtroom?

   (b) Are you expecting an evidentiary hearing?

   (c) [If applicable] Will the victim(s) be making a statement?

4. Ask the defense counsel:

   (a) Have you and your client read and discussed the presentence report (PSR)?

   (b) Have you discussed the objections?

   (c) Are you expecting an evidentiary hearing?

   (d) Do you have any witnesses present in the courtroom?

B. *Calculation of the advisory guideline range*

1. Ask both counsel:

    (a) I have read the objections to the presentence report. Do counsel want oral argument on the objections?

    (b) If there are fact disputes, do counsel want to make a proffer or is an evidentiary hearing necessary?[7]

2. After hearing, make the following findings:[8]

    (a) I adopt the PSR without objections.

    [or]

    (b) I resolve the objections as follows:[9]

    (i) With respect to [describe issue], the court finds _____.

    (ii) The remaining disputed issues will not affect sentencing, or will not be taken into account at sentencing, so no finding is necessary.

3. [If the government had filed notice under 21 U.S.C. § 851(a)(1)) of increased punishment based on prior convictions, ask the defendant:]

    Do you affirm or deny that you were previously convicted as alleged in the information by the government? If you do not challenge the existence of a previous conviction before I sentence you, you cannot challenge the existence of those previous convictions on appeal or in a post-conviction proceeding. [21 U.S.C. § 851(b).]

4. If, under Rule 11(c)(3)(A), the court had deferred its decision whether to accept a plea agreement that requires dismissal of charges (Rule 11(c)(1)(A)) or that would bind it to a specific sentence or specific sentencing terms (Rule 11(c)(1)(C), state:]

---

7. The court has discretion to permit the introduction of evidence. Fed. R. Crim. P. 32(i)(2). Evidentiary hearings should be reserved for occasions in which there is a disputed issue of fact in the proffer. There is some disagreement among the circuits as to the burden of production with respect to evidence germane to disputed portions of the PSR.

8. If information that will be relied on in determining the sentence has been withheld from the presentence report (PSR) pursuant to Fed. R. Crim. P. 32(d)(3), and the summary has not yet been provided, orally summarize the withheld information (in camera if necessary). *See* Fed. R. Crim. P. 32(i)(1)(B).

9. *See* Fed. R. Crim. P. 32(i)(3)(B). Even if disputed issues will not affect sentencing, it may be important to resolve them and attach the court's findings to the PSR because the Bureau of Prisons bases classification decisions on the PSR.

(a) I accept the provisions of the plea agreement (and upon the motion of the government the following charges are dismissed _____).[10]

[or]

(b) I reject the provisions of the plea agreement, and the defendant may withdraw his/her plea. If you do not withdraw your plea, I may decide the case less favorably than the plea agreement would have required.[11]

5. After making the preceding findings and calculations, state:

(a) After resolving the objections (if any), I calculate the following advisory guideline range: the defendant's offense level is _____, and the defendant's criminal history category is _____. This produces a guidelines range of _____ to _____ months imprisonment (or probation); a supervised release range following imprisonment of ____ to ____ years; and a fine range of _____ to _____. The special assessment is _____.

(b) Are there any objections for the record?

C. *Departure*

1. The court will now consider whether to grant departures from the guidelines range.

(a) [If a motion pursuant to USSG § 5K1.1 has been filed, you may wish to call the parties to sidebar to determine whether to close the courtroom and seal the transcripts, or to consider the motion in chambers. *See* USSG § 5K1.1, comment. (backg'd).]

> The government has filed a motion for a downward departure for substantial assistance to authorities pursuant to USSG § 5K1.1 and/or 18 U.S.C. § 3553(e). Will the government please set forth the facts supporting its motion?
>
> Does the defendant have any comment on the government's statement?

(b) [If applicable] The government has filed a motion for a downward departure for participation in the early disposition program pursuant to section 5K3.1 of the guidelines. What is the government's recommendation?

---

10. Fed. R. Crim. P. 11(c)(4).

11. Fed. R. Crim. P. 11(c)(5)(A)–(C) (the court must "advise the defendant personally" of the right to withdraw the plea and that the sentence may be less favorable than the plea agreement outlined).

> What is the defendant's position regarding the government's recommendation?

(c) [If applicable] The government has moved for an upward departure based on [list all grounds]. Is there any opposition?

(d) [If applicable] The defendant has moved for a downward departure based on [list all grounds]. Is there any opposition?

(e) [If applicable] Although it was not raised by either party, I am considering an upward/downward departure based on [list all grounds]. Is there any opposition?

2. For each departure motion, state as applicable:

(a) I intend to depart downward in accordance with the government's/defendant's motion(s) [and/or the court's own motion]. I believe this departure is consistent with [detail the guidelines provision(s) with which departure(s) is/are consistent].

(b) I intend to depart upward in accordance with the government's motion [and/or the court's own motion]. I believe this departure is consistent with [detail the guidelines provision(s) with which departure(s) is/are consistent].

(c) I do not intend to depart. Although departure is authorized in this case, I believe it is not warranted under the circumstances for the following reasons _____.

(d) I do not intend to depart because departure is not authorized under these facts. [If applicable, add:] Even if departure were authorized under these facts, I would exercise my discretion not to depart.

D. Section 3553(a) factors/variances

1. State: After calculating the guidelines and departures, and hearing argument, I must now consider the relevant factors set out by Congress at 18 U.S.C. § 3553(a) and ensure that I impose a sentence "sufficient, but not greater than necessary, to comply with the purposes" of sentencing. These purposes include the need for the sentence to reflect the seriousness of the crime, to promote respect for the law, and to provide just punishment for the offense. The sentence should also deter criminal conduct, protect the public from future crime by the defendant, and promote rehabilitation. In addition to the guidelines and policy statements, I must consider

(a) "the nature and circumstances of the offense";

(b) "the history and characteristics of the defendant";

> (c) the need to avoid unwarranted sentence disparities among similarly situated defendants; and
>
> (d) the types of sentences available.

2. Does the prosecutor wish to argue about the application of the factors set forth in section 3553(a), request a variance, or otherwise make a sentencing recommendation?

3. Does the defense counsel wish to argue about the application of the factors set forth in section 3553(a), request a variance, or otherwise make a sentencing recommendation?

4. The court is considering a downward [an upward] variance of _____ months for the following reasons [state reasons]. Does either party wish to comment or object?

E. Final statements

(*See* Fed. R. Crim. P. 32(i)(4). Note that, upon motion and for good cause, any statements made under Rule 32(i)(4) may be heard in camera.)

1. [If a victim is present:] Does the victim wish to make a statement?

2. The defendant has the right to make a statement "or present any information to mitigate the sentence." Does the defendant wish to make a statement?

3. Does the defense counsel have anything to add on behalf of the defendant?

4. Does the prosecutor wish to make a final statement?

F. The court's pronouncement of sentence

1. Based on these factors and the Sentencing Guidelines, I sentence the defendant to _____, which is within the guideline range.
    [If the guideline range exceeds 24 months, state the reason for imposing the sentence at that particular point within the range. 18 U.S.C. § 3553(c)(1).]

    [or]

2. Because there are grounds to depart, I sentence the defendant to _____.

    [or]

3. After assessing the particular facts of this case in light of the relevant § 3553(a) factors, including the Sentencing Guidelines, I conclude that a sentence outside of the advisory guideline range is warranted and sentence the defendant to _____, representing a _____ variance from the guidelines range. [Explain the particular factors that influenced your decision and the extent of the variance. 18 U.S.C. § 3553(c)(2). If either party requested a non-

guidelines sentence, explain why you will grant or deny the request and directly address the arguments made by each party.]

4. [If the sentence includes a term of probation, state the length of the term and ask counsel to suggest appropriate conditions. *See* U.S.S.G. § 5B1.1–1.3; 18 U.S.C. §§ 3561–3564.]

5. [If a sentence of imprisonment is imposed:] I must also consider whether to impose a term of supervised release.

    [Ask counsel and probation for appropriate conditions of supervised release. *See* U.S.S.G. § 5D1.3; 18 U.S.C. § 3583(d).]

G. *Imposition of sentence*

State:

I will now impose the sentence.

1. [If sentencing to a term of imprisonment:]

    (a) The defendant is hereby committed to the custody of the Bureau of Prisons for a term of _____ months. [Ask counsel if there is a requested BOP institution.]

    [or]

    (b) The defendant is hereby committed to the custody of the Bureau of Prisons for a term of _____ months and then to community confinement/home detention for a term of _____ months.

    [If applicable, specify whether the sentence imposed on any count should run concurrently with, consecutive to, or partially consecutive to any other sentence that will be imposed, that defendant is already subject to, or that defendant may be facing in another court. *See supra* subsection II.C.]

    (c) [If applicable:] The Court recommends to the Bureau of Prisons that the defendant be placed in an institution with the following programs: [substance abuse treatment, mental health counseling, vocational training, etc.]

2. Upon release from imprisonment, the defendant is to be placed on supervised release for a term of _____ years.[12] While on super-

---

12. Supervised release may be required by specific statute. The guidelines also provide for supervised release if a sentence of more than one year's imprisonment is imposed. *See* USSG § 5D1.1(a); *but cf.* USSG § 5D1.1, comment (n.1) (authorizing departure from § 5D1.1(a) under some circumstances). It may otherwise be imposed at the court's discretion. USSG § 5D1.1(b).

vised release, the defendant is subject to the following standard and special conditions _____ .[13]

3. [If sentencing to probation:[14]]

    The defendant is placed on probation for a term of _____ years. While on probation the defendant is subject to the following conditions _____.

4. [If restitution, a fine, or forfeiture is called for:]

    (a) The defendant must make restitution as follows _____. This restitution is due on the following schedule: _____.[15] If the defendant fails to pay the full restitution owed, each recipient is to receive an approximately proportional allotment of the restitution paid. This restitution obligation is joint and several with any other obligated defendants.[16]

    (b) The court orders that the defendant pay the United States a fine of _____.[17]

    [or]

    The fine (and/or interest on the fine) owed by the defendant is waived/below the guideline range because of the defendant's inability to pay.

    (c) Forfeiture of the property described in count(s) _____ of the indictment/information is hereby ordered.[18]

---

13. *See* permitted conditions of supervised release at USSG § 5D1.3. The court may recommend that the defendant receive residential substance abuse treatment pursuant to the provisions of 18 U.S.C. § 3621(b). Note that the court may suspend the mandatory drug testing provision if the defendant poses a low risk of future substance abuse. 18 U.S.C. § 3583(d).

14. Probation is statutorily prohibited for defendants convicted of certain offenses, e.g., Class A felonies. See USSG § 5B1.3 for the mandatory, recommended, and discretionary conditions of probation.

15. *See* 18 U.S.C. § 3664(f) (outlining the manner and schedule of restitution payments). If restitution is not ordered, or only partial restitution is ordered, the court must state the reasons for that decision. 18 U.S.C. § 3553(c). Note that 18 U.S.C. § 3572 states that any schedule of payments for restitution or fines "shall be set by the court," and some circuits have held that this authority may not be delegated. Fines and restitution of more than $2,500 bear interest if not paid within 15 days after the judgment. 18 U.S.C. § 3612(f)(1). If the court finds that the defendant is unable to pay interest, this requirement may be waived or modified. *Id.* § 3612(f)(3). *See* USSG § 5E1.1.

16. Alternatively, the court may provide a different payment schedule for each victim, 18 U.S.C. § 3664(i), and may apportion liability among the defendants, 18 U.S.C. § 3664(h).

17. 18 U.S.C. § 3572(a); USSG § 5E1.2. *See supra* note 15 regarding interest on fines. Note that the maximum amount of a fine is limited to that which is authorized by the jury's verdict. Southern Union Co. v. United States, 132 S. Ct. 2344, 2350–52 (2012) (rule of *Apprendi* applies to criminal fines).

18. Fed. R. Crim. P. 32.2.

5. It is ordered that the defendant pay to the United States a special assessment in the amount of _____.[19]

H. *Notification of right to appeal*[20]

1. Notify the defendant:

    (a) [If the defendant was convicted after a trial:]

    > You have the right to appeal your conviction(s), and the right to appeal a sentence you believe was illegally or incorrectly imposed.

    (b) [After conviction by guilty plea, advise the defendant:]

    > You can appeal your conviction if you believe that your guilty plea was somehow unlawful or involuntary, or if there is some other fundamental defect in the proceedings that was not waived by your guilty plea.

    (c) [If the defendant has not waived the right to appeal, advise the defendant:]

    > You also have a statutory right to appeal your *sentence* under certain circumstances, particularly if you think the sentence is contrary to law.

    [or]

    [If there is a waiver of the right to appeal, advise the defendant:]

    > Under some circumstances, a defendant also has the right to appeal the sentence. However, a defendant may waive that right as part of a plea agreement, and you have entered into a plea agreement which waives some or all of your rights to appeal the sentence itself. Such waivers are generally enforceable, but if you believe the waiver itself is not valid, you can present that theory to the appellate court.[21]

2. Notify the defendant:

    > Any notice of appeal must be filed within fourteen days of the entry of judgment or within fourteen days of the filing of a notice of appeal by the government. If requested, the clerk will prepare and file a notice

---

19. USSG § 5E1.3 & comment (n.2).

20. In misdemeanor and petty offense trials, magistrate judges must notify defendants of their right to appeal. Fed. R. Crim. P. 58(c)(4). Note also that an appeal from a judgment of conviction or sentence by a magistrate judge is to the district court. Fed. R. Crim. P. 58(g)(2)(B).

21. The specific terms of the waiver should have been reviewed with the defendant during the plea colloquy. If they were not, review them here to ensure that the defendant's waiver is knowing and voluntary. Even if there was a thorough discussion at the plea hearing, it may be advisable to quickly summarize the relevant terms of the agreement and confirm that the defendant is being sentenced in accordance with those terms.

of appeal on your behalf. If you cannot afford to pay the cost of an appeal or for appellate counsel, you have the right to apply for leave to appeal in forma pauperis, which means you can apply to have the court waive the filing fee. On appeal, you may also apply for court-appointed counsel.[22]

I. Conclusion

1. Ask the counselors:

   Are there any other matters to resolve in this case?

2. [If the defendant has been sentenced to a term of imprisonment and was at liberty pending sentencing, ask:]

   (a) Does defense counsel request voluntary surrender?[23]

   (b) Does government counsel oppose voluntary surrender?]

3. State:

   (a) The defendant is remanded to the custody of the marshal;

   [or]

   (b) The defendant is to report for service of sentence in the future. Release conditions previously established continue to apply. Failure to report for service of sentence is a criminal offense.[24]

   Adjourn.

IV. Final matters

A. Entry of judgment

A judgment of the conviction should promptly be prepared on the form required by the Sentencing Commission and issued by the Judicial Conference of the United States, Form AO 245B, "Judgment in a Criminal Case" (as amended September 2011).[25] Include a copy of the final order of forfeiture, if any.

---

22. *See* Fed. R. App. P. 4(b)(1)(A) and 24(a); Fed. R. Crim. P. 32(j)(2); 18 U.S.C. § 3006A.

23. Whether the defendant was permitted to voluntarily surrender affects the defendant's Bureau of Prisons security designation. *See also supra* section 2.11: Release or detention pending sentence or appeal.

24. 18 U.S.C. § 3146(a)(2) ("Whoever … knowingly fails to surrender for service of sentence pursuant to a court order shall be punished as provided" in the statute.).

25. Pursuant to the authority granted in 28 U.S.C. § 994(w)(1), the Sentencing Commission approved Form AO 245B (or 245C for an amended judgment; 245D for revocations; 245E for organizational defendants) as the format courts must use to submit sentencing information. As amended March 9, 2006, § 994(w)(1) states:

The Chief Judge of each district court shall ensure that, within 30 days following entry of judgment in every criminal case, the sentencing court submits to the Commission, in a format approved and required by the Commission, a written report of the sentence, the offense for which it is imposed, the age, race, sex of the of-

B. Statement of reasons

"[A] transcription or other appropriate public record of the court's statement of reasons, together with the order of judgment and commitment," must be provided to the probation office, to the Sentencing Commission, and, if the sentence includes a prison term, to the Bureau of Prisons. 18 U.S.C. § 3553(c). Under 28 U.S.C. § 994(w)(1), as amended March 9, 2006, courts must send to the Sentencing Commission a report containing several documents, including AO Form 245B (Judgment in a Criminal Case), which includes the statement of reasons and satisfies the requirements of § 3553(c). If there was a departure or other non-guidelines sentence, include in the written order of judgment and commitment the specific reasons for sentencing outside of the advisory guideline range.[26]

C. Administrative and research documentation

Order that the U.S. Sentencing Commission be sent copies of the charging documents, plea agreement (if any), written proffer or stipulation of facts or law, presentence report, and judgment of conviction (with statement of reasons), and any other information required under 28 U.S.C. § 994(w)(1).

Other FJC sources

James B. Eaglin, Sentencing Federal Offenders for Crimes Committed Before November 1, 1987 (1991)

Guideline Sentencing: An Outline of Appellate Case Law on Selected Issues (2002)

---

fender, and information regarding factors made relevant by the guidelines. The report shall also include—

(A) the judgment and commitment order;
(B) the written statement of reasons for the sentence imposed (which shall include the reason for any departure from the otherwise applicable guideline range and which shall be stated on the written statement of reasons form issued by the Judicial Conference and approved by the United States Sentencing Commission);
(C) any plea agreement;
(D) the indictment or other charging document;
(E) the presentence report; and
(F) any other information as the Commission finds appropriate.

The information referred to in subparagraphs (A) through (F) shall be submitted by the sentencing court in a format approved and required by the Commission.

26. 18 U.S.C. § 3553(c)(2). As you did with the statement of reasons, be sure to distinguish in the written order between departures and non-guidelines sentences (or "variances") to facilitate appellate review and data collection.

4.02 Revocation of probation or supervised release

Fed. R. Crim. P. 32.1; 18 U.S.C. §§ 3565 and 3583

I. Introduction

Whenever a probationer or a person on supervised release fails to abide by the conditions of supervision or is arrested for another offense, a revocation hearing may be ordered. Revocation is mandatory if a probationer or supervised releasee possesses a firearm (including a destructive device) or a controlled substance, refuses to comply with required drug testing, or fails three drug tests in a year.[1] See 18 U.S.C. §§ 3565(b), 3583(g). Revocation is also called for under the Sentencing Guidelines for conduct that constitutes certain serious offenses. See U.S.S.G. §§ 7B1.1 and 7B1.3, p.s.

Because the proceeding may result in incarceration, particular attention must be given to ensuring that the probationer or releasee receives substantive and procedural due process. The revocation procedure may be initiated by the court or at the request of the probation office or the office of the U.S. attorney. An Order to Show Cause why probation or supervised release should not be revoked is effective for this purpose.

Federal Rule of Criminal Procedure 32.1(a) requires an initial appearance before a magistrate judge, whether the person is held in custody or appears in response to a summons. The Advisory Committee Notes to the 2002 amendments state that, if the initial appearance would not be unnecessarily delayed, it may be combined with the preliminary hearing. Under Rule 32.1(a)(1), the procedures applied at the initial appearance differ depending on whether the district where the person appears is or is not the district where the alleged violation occurred or is one that has jurisdiction to hold the revocation hearing.

At all stages of the proceedings, the probationer or releasee must be informed of the right to retain counsel or to request that one be appointed. Fed. R. Crim. P. 32.1(a)(3)(B), (b)(1)(B)(i), (b)(2)(D), and (c)(1).

[*Note:* It is unclear whether, at a revocation hearing, the rights accorded by the Crime Victims' Rights Act, 18 U.S.C. § 3771, should be accorded to a victim of the conduct that caused the violation of probation or release. If the conduct constituted a federal offense, the CVRA may apply whether or not there is a separate prosecution.[2] Or, if the revocation hearing is considered a

---

1. The mandatory drug testing and revocation for refusal to comply provisions became effective September 13, 1994; revocation for failing three drug tests took effect Nov. 2, 2002. The ex post facto prohibition may prevent the application of those provisions to defendants who committed their offenses before the effective dates of the provisions.

2. Under § 3771(e), *crime victim* is defined as "a person directly and proximately harmed as a result of the commission of a Federal offense." The rights to notification and attendance apply to any public court proceeding "involving the crime," § 3771(a)(1) & (2),

"public court proceeding ... involving the crime or ... any release ... of the accused," the CVRA may apply. If it is determined that the CVRA applies, ensure that any victims receive the required notice of the hearing and the right to attend, as well as the opportunity "to be reasonably heard" at any proceeding involving sentencing or release.]

II. Preliminary hearing

If the probationer or releasee is in custody, Fed. R. Crim. P. 32.1(b)(1) requires a preliminary probable cause hearing before a district judge or magistrate judge. A probable cause hearing is not required if the probationer or releasee is arrested after the issuance of an Order to Show Cause and brought before the court for an immediate revocation hearing without being held in custody, or if he or she appears voluntarily in response to an Order to Show Cause or other notice. Fed. R. Crim. P. 32.1 and Advisory Committee Notes (1979).

III. Suggested procedure at the revocation hearing[3]

A. Establish for the record that the probationer or releasee, defense counsel, a U.S. attorney, and a probation officer are present.

B. Advise the probationer or releasee of the alleged violations by reading or summarizing the revocation motion. If the alleged violation is of a kind that makes revocation mandatory under 18 U.S.C. § 3565(b) or § 3583(g) (possession of a firearm, destructive device, or controlled substance, refusal to comply with a drug test, or testing positive for a controlled substance for the third time in the course of one year[4]), or under U.S.S.G. § 7B1.3(a)(1), p.s., include advice to that effect.

C. Ascertain whether the alleged violations are admitted or denied by the probationer or releasee.

---

and the right to be heard at such a proceeding applies if it "involv[es] release, plea, [or] sentencing," § 3771(a)(4). No provision of the CVRA limits its application to an offense that is prosecuted.

3. Note that under the Federal Courts Administration Act of 1992, a magistrate judge may revoke, modify, or reinstate probation and modify, revoke, or terminate supervised release if any magistrate judge imposed the probation or supervised release. 18 U.S.C. § 3401(d), (h) (effective Jan. 1, 1993).

Also under the Act, a district judge may designate a magistrate judge to conduct hearings to modify, revoke, or terminate supervised release; to submit proposed findings of fact; and to recommend a disposition. 18 U.S.C. § 3401(i) (effective Jan. 1, 1993).

4. The statutory provisions for mandatory revocation for refusal to comply with drug testing and, for supervised releasees, possession of a firearm, were enacted September 13, 1994; mandatory revocation for failing three drug tests was added Nov. 2, 2002. Ex post facto considerations may prohibit the application of those provisions to defendants whose original offenses were committed before the effective dates of the provisions.

1. If the violations are admitted:
   (a) Ask the U.S. attorney to present the factual basis showing the violations of the terms of supervision.
   (b) Permit the probationer or releasee, his or her counsel, the U.S. attorney, and the probation officer to be heard concerning whether supervision should be revoked.
2. If the violations are denied:
   (a) Receive evidence presented by the U.S. attorney and the probationer or releasee.
   (b) The revocation hearing is not a formal trial and the Federal Rules of Evidence need not apply. Fed. R. Evid. 1101(d)(3).[5]
   (c) Proof beyond a reasonable doubt is not required. To revoke probation, the court must be "reasonably satisfied" that the probationer has not met the conditions of probation. *United States v. Francischine,* 512 F.2d 827 (5th Cir. 1975).[6] Revocation of supervised release requires a preponderance of the evidence. 18 U.S.C. § 3583(e)(3).

D. Sentencing options

[*Note:* In a hearing to determine whether to modify or revoke probation or supervised release, the defendant must be given "an opportunity to make a statement and present any information in mitigation." See Fed. R. Crim. P. 32.1(b)(2)(E) and (c)(1).]

1. If a determination is made not to revoke probation or supervised release:
   (a) The original term of probation or supervised release may be extended up to the maximum term of probation or supervised release that could have been imposed originally. 18 U.S.C. §§ 3564(d), 3565(a)(1), 3583(e)(2); U.S.S.G. § 7B1.3(a)(2).
   (b) Conditions of probation or supervised release may be modified, enlarged, or reduced. 18 U.S.C. §§ 3563(c), 3565(a)(1), 3583(e)(2); U.S.S.G. § 7B1.3(a)(2).
2. If a determination is made to revoke probation:
   (a) Resentence the defendant under the provisions of 18 U.S.C. §§ 3551–3559 if the defendant is subject to 18 U.S.C. § 3565(a)(2),

---

5. But note that Fed. R. Crim. P. 32.1(e) requires the production of witness statements pursuant to the terms of Fed. R. Crim. P. 26.2.

6. The Advisory Committee Notes for the creation of Rule 32.1 in 1979 cited *Francischine* for this proposition.

as amended Sept. 13, 1994.[7] The court must also consider the provisions of U.S.S.G. § 7B1.3–1.4, p.s. Otherwise, impose any other sentence that was available under the sentencing provisions "at the time of the initial sentencing."[8] 18 U.S.C. § 3565(a)(2) (before September 13, 1994, amendment). For defendants initially sentenced under the Sentencing Guidelines, consider the provisions of U.S.S.G. § 7B1.3–1.4, p.s.

(b) If probation is revoked for possession of drugs or firearms, for refusal of required drug testing, or for failing three drug tests in one year, sentence the defendant to a term of imprisonment.[9] 18 U.S.C. § 3565(b) (effective Sept. 13, 1994).[10]

3. If a determination is made to revoke supervised release:

(a) Require the person to serve in prison[11] all or part of the term of supervised release without credit for time previously served on post-release supervision, except that the person may not be required to serve more than five years in prison if the person was convicted of a Class A felony, more than three years if convicted of a Class B felony, more than two years if convicted of a Class C or D felony, or more than one year in any other case. 18 U.S.C. § 3583(e)(3). For defendants initially sentenced under the Sentencing Guidelines, consider the provisions of U.S.S.G. § 7B1.3–1.4, p.s.

---

7. Ex post facto considerations may require the use of prior law if the defendant committed the original offense before September 13, 1994.

8. Because of ex post facto considerations, this earlier version of § 3565(a)(2) may be required if the defendant committed the original offense before September 13, 1994. The Third, Fourth, Fifth, Eighth, Ninth, and Eleventh Circuits have held that "any other sentence that was available . . . at the time of the initial sentencing" means the guideline range applicable to the original offense of conviction. Note that some of the sentences in the "Revocation Table," U.S.S.G. § 7B1.4, p.s., may exceed the maximum sentences allowed under this interpretation. *See also* Guideline Sentencing: An Outline of Appellate Case Law on Selected Issues § VII.A.1 (Federal Judicial Center 2002).

9. This amendment to § 3565 removed the requirement to "sentence the defendant to not less than one-third of the original sentence." The Supreme Court resolved a circuit split by ruling that "original sentence" meant the original guideline range, not the term of probation. Thus, defendants sentenced before the 1994 amendment could not be sentenced after revocation to more than the original guideline maximum. United States v. Granderson, 114 S. Ct. 1259, 1263–69 (1994). Ex post facto considerations may limit the length of the sentence that may be imposed in some circuits for defendants who committed their original offenses before September 13, 1994.

10. The provision on revocation for failing three drug tests was not added until Nov. 2, 2002.

11. Home confinement may also be imposed "as an alternative" to incarceration. *See* 18 U.S.C. § 3583(e)(4); U.S.S.G. § 5F1.2.

(b) Require the person to serve a term of imprisonment when revocation is for possession of drugs or firearms, for refusal of required drug testing, or for failing three drug tests in one year. 18 U.S.C. §§ 3583(g) (as amended Sept. 13, 1994)[12] and 3583(e) (before September 13, 1994, amendment).[13]

(c) If the term of imprisonment imposed is less than the statutorily authorized maximum, determine whether to reimpose a term of supervised release. The length of the reimposed term may not exceed the term of supervised release authorized by statute for the original offense, less the term of imprisonment imposed upon revocation of release. 18 U.S.C. § 3583(h) (added Sept. 13, 1994); 18 U.S.C. § 3583(e)(3) (for offenses committed before Sept. 13, 1994).[14]

E. Judgment or order

Enter the appropriate order or judgment. Note that for sentences imposed pursuant to U.S.S.G. § 7B1, p.s., the court should include "the reasons for its imposition of the particular sentence." 18 U.S.C. § 3553(c). For a sentence outside the range resulting from the application of § 7B1, it may be advisable to follow § 3553(c)(2) and state "with specificity in the written order of judgment and commitment" the reasons "for the imposition of a sentence different from" the recommended range.

Other FJC sources

Guideline Sentencing: An Outline of Appellate Case Law on Selected Issues (2002)

---

12. The provision on revocation for failing three drug tests was not added until Nov. 2, 2002.

13. Before September 13, 1994, § 3583 required such defendants "to serve in prison not less than one-third of the term of supervised release" and only applied to revocation for drug possession.

14. Before § 3583(h) was added, § 3583(e) did not specifically authorize reimposition of supervised release after revocation. The circuits disagreed about whether reimposition was allowed and whether § 3583(h) could be applied retroactively. However, the Supreme Court resolved that split by holding that reimposition was authorized under § 3583(e)(3) for offenses committed before enactment of § 3583(h). Johnson v. United States, 120 S. Ct. 1795, 1800–07 (2000).

5.01 Handling a disruptive or dangerous defendant

Fed. R. Crim. P. 43(c)

A. Removal of defendant

> A defendant who was initially present at trial, or who had pleaded guilty or nolo contendere, waives the right to be present . . . when the court warns the defendant that it will remove the defendant from the courtroom for disruptive behavior, but the defendant persists in conduct that justifies removal from the courtroom. . . . If the defendant waives the right to be present, the trial may proceed to completion, including the verdict's return and sentencing, during the defendant's absence.

Fed. R. Crim. P. 43(c)(1)(C) and (2).

The Supreme Court held that a disruptive defendant, after appropriate warning, may be removed from the courtroom. *Illinois v. Allen,* 397 U.S. 337, 344 (1970). (The Court also stated that a defendant may be cited for contempt or, "as a last resort," allowed to remain in the courtroom bound and gagged. See *infra* section B: Restraint of defendant.)

When the court is faced with a disruptive defendant:

1. The court should warn the defendant that continuation of the disruptive conduct will lead to removal of the defendant from the courtroom.[1]

2. If the disruptive conduct continues, the court should determine whether it warrants removal of the defendant.[2]

3. At the beginning of each session, the court should advise the defendant that he or she may return to the courtroom if the defendant assures the court that there will be no further disturbances.

4. The court should consider ways to allow the defendant to communicate with his or her attorney to keep apprised of the progress of the trial. The court may consider making arrangements to allow the defendant to hear or see the proceedings via electronic means, if available.

---

1. One circuit held that, in a multidefendant case, "[n]otice to one defendant is notice to all present in the courtroom for purposes of Rule 43." United States v. West, 877 F.2d 281, 287 (4th Cir. 1989). *Cf.* United States v. Beasley, 72 F.3d 1518, 1530 (11th Cir. 1996) (although district court may not have personally warned defendant that he might be removed, it was sufficient that court warned defense counsel in presence of defendant).

2. Whether the conduct is serious enough to warrant the defendant's removal is generally in the discretion of the trial judge. Rule 43(c)(1)(C) simply states that it must be "conduct that justifies removal from the courtroom," and the Supreme Court described it as conduct that is "so disorderly, disruptive, and disrespectful of the court that [defendant's] trial cannot be carried on with him in the courtroom." Illinois v. Allen, 397 U.S. 337, 343 (1970).

5. The court should consider any other factors required by circuit law.[3]

If the defendant is appearing pro se and standby counsel is present, the court should first warn the defendant that pro se status will be denied and that standby counsel will take over if there is further disruption. If pro se status is denied and standby counsel takes over, the defendant may be removed from the courtroom for any further disruption.

B. Restraint of defendant ("shackling")

As the Supreme Court stated in *Allen*, disruptive defendants may, under certain circumstances, be physically restrained. The Court later expanded upon that holding in reference to defendants who are not merely disruptive but potentially dangerous. "Courts and commentators share close to a consensus that, during the guilt phase of a trial, a criminal defendant has a right to remain free of physical restraints that are visible to the jury; that the right has a constitutional dimension; but that the right may be overcome in a particular instance by essential state interests such as physical security, escape prevention, or courtroom decorum." *Deck v. Missouri*, 544 U.S. 622, 629 (2005). Before a defendant can be visibly restrained in front of the jury, the court must "take account of special circumstances, including security concerns, that may call for shackling. . . . [A]ny such determination must be case specific; that is to say, it should reflect particular concerns, say, special security needs or escape risks, related to the defendant on trial." *Id.* at 632.

When the court is faced with a potentially dangerous defendant:[4]

1. Consider less intrusive protective measures that are less likely to prejudice the jury against the defendant, such as putting extra law enforcement officers in the courtroom.[5]

2. Consider less visible measures, such as draping the defense table so that leg shackles cannot be seen, or using "stun belts" that can be worn underneath a defendant's clothes.[6]

---

3. For example, the Eleventh Circuit requires courts to consider the potential prejudice to the defense of the defendant's absence in addition to the adequacy of the warning and degree of misconduct. *See* Foster v. Wainwright, 686 F.2d 1382, 1388 (11th Cir. 1982).

4. The Court in *Deck* stated that the "[l]ower courts have disagreed about the specific procedural steps a trial court must take prior to shackling [and] about the amount and type of evidence needed to justify restraints," 544 U.S. at 629, but the following common practices may provide guidance to courts that are considering restraining a defendant.

5. Holbrook v. Flynn, 475 U.S. 560, 569 (1986) (although it must be determined on a case-by-case basis, compared with shackling, "the presence of guards at a defendant's trial need not be interpreted as a sign that he is particularly dangerous or culpable").

6. *See, e.g.,* United States v. Wardell, 591 F.3d 1279, 1294 (10th Cir. 2009) ("district court's decision to require a defendant to wear a stun belt during a criminal trial would appear ordinarily to pose no constitutional problem when: (1) the court makes a defendant-specific determination of necessity resulting from security concerns; and (2) it minimizes the risk of prejudice by, for instance, concealing the stun belt from the jury"); United States v. Brazel,

3. Allow defense counsel (or the defendant if pro se) the opportunity to respond to the court's concerns.[7]

4. If the factual basis for restraint is disputed, consider holding an evidentiary hearing and making findings on the record.[8]

5. Make an independent evaluation based on the circumstances of the case and the individual defendant.[9]

6. If the court concludes that physical restraint is advisable, "impose no greater restraints than necessary to secure the courtroom ... [and] take all practical measures, including a cautionary instruction, to minimize the prejudice resulting from a party appearing in physical restraints."[10]

---

102 F.3d 1120, 1158 (11th Cir. 1997) ("The court's use of cloths to cover all counsels' tables so that the leg shackles were not visible significantly reduced the possibility of prejudice."); United States v. Collins, 109 F.3d 1413, 1418 (9th Cir. 1997) (same).

7. *See* Sides v. Cherry, 609 F.3d 576, 586 (10th Cir. 2010) ("district courts should hold a proceeding [outside the presence of the jury] that allows the parties to offer argument bearing on the need for restraints as well as the extent of the restraints deemed necessary (if any)"); United States v. Theriault, 531 F.2d 281, 285 (5th Cir. 1976) ("Counsel, or the defendant himself in appropriate cases, should be given an opportunity both to respond to the reasons presented and to persuade the judge that such measures are unnecessary."); United States v. Samuel, 431 F.2d 610, 615 (4th Cir. 1970) ("Whenever unusual visible security measures in jury cases are to be employed, we will require the district judge to state for the record, out of the presence of the jury, the reasons therefor and give counsel an opportunity to comment thereon, as well as to persuade him that such measures are unnecessary.").

8. *Theriault,* 531 F.2d at 285 ("when unusual visible security measures are utilized before a jury, we will require that the district judge state for the record, outside the jury's presence, the reasons for such action.... A formal evidentiary hearing may not be required, but if the factual basis for the extraordinary security is controverted, the taking of evidence and finding of facts may be necessary." *Accord* United States v. Moore, 651 F.3d 30, 46 (D.C. Cir. 2011) (citing *Theriault* regarding whether evidentiary hearing is required).

9. *See, e.g., Moore,* 651 F.3d at 46 (affirming, in part, because the district court "considered the security concerns presented by the particular defendants at trial before making the determination that stun belts were appropriate. It thoroughly examined factors relevant to each defendant and ... made a determination based on those factors."); United States v. Baker, 432 F.3d 1189, 1244 (11th Cir. 2005) ("if a judge intends to shackle a defendant, he must make a case specific and individualized assessment of each defendant in that particular trial"); United States v. Zuber, 118 F.3d 101, 103 (2d Cir. 1997) ("a presiding judge may not approve the use of physical restraints, in court, on a party to a jury trial unless the judge has first performed an independent evaluation—including an evidentiary hearing, where necessary—of the need to restrain the party"); United States v. Hack, 782 F.2d 862, 868 (10th Cir. 1986) ("The extent to which the security measures are needed should be determined by the trial judge on a case-by-case basis by 'considering the person's record, the crime charged, his physical condition, and other available security measures.'") (citation omitted).

10. *Sides,* 609 F.3d at 586. *See also* Woodard v. Perrin, 692 F.2d 220, 221 (1st Cir. 1982) ("a judge should consider less restrictive measures before deciding that a defendant should be shackled").

Other factors to consider:

1. Do not defer to law enforcement officials—make an independent evaluation.

   Although a court may take into account the recommendation of a U.S. marshal or other law enforcement official in deciding whether shackling is warranted, "trial judges should not blindly defer to the recommendation of law enforcement officials as to the appropriateness of shackling without independently reviewing the facts and circumstances thought to warrant such a security measure and carefully considering the legal ramifications of that decision."[11]

2. Witnesses and civil trials

   Some circuits have concluded that "the concerns expressed [about restraints] are applicable to parties in civil suits as well. . . . The principles consistently applied are that the trial court has discretion to order physical restraints on a party or witness when the court has found those restraints to be necessary to maintain safety or security; but the court must impose no greater restraints than are necessary, and it must take steps to minimize the prejudice resulting from the presence of the restraints."[12]

---

11. United States v. Mays, 158 F.3d 1215, 1226 (11th Cir. 1998). *See also Sides,* 609 F.3d at 582 (agreeing with other circuits that, "though a district court may rely 'heavily' on advice from court security officers, it 'bears the ultimate responsibility' of determining what restraints are necessary") (citation omitted); Lakin v. Stine, 431 F.3d 959, 964 (6th Cir. 2005) (trial court erred when it "simply deferred to the corrections officer's request. Although a trial court might find a corrections officer's opinion highly relevant to answering the ultimate inquiry as to whether shackling is necessary in a particular case, an individualized determination under the due process clause requires more than rubber stamping that request."); Gonzalez v. Pliler, 341 F.3d 897, 902 (9th Cir. 2003) ("It is the duty of the trial court, not correctional officers, to make the affirmative determination, in conformance with constitutional standards, to order the physical restraint of a defendant in the courtroom."); Davidson v. Riley, 44 F.3d 1118, 1124 (2d Cir. 1995) ("If the court has deferred entirely to those guarding the prisoner, . . . it has failed to exercise its discretion."); Woods v. Theiret, 5 F.3d 244, 248 (7th Cir. 1993) ("While the trial court may rely 'heavily' on the marshals in evaluating the appropriate security measures to take with a given prisoner, the court bears the ultimate responsibility for that determination and may not delegate the decision to shackle an inmate to the marshals."); *Samuel,* 431 F.2d at 615 ("We stress that the discretion is that of the district judge. He may not . . . delegate that discretion to the Marshal.").

12. *Davidson,* 44 F.3d at 1122–23. *See also Sides,* 609 F.3d at 581 (agreeing with other circuits "that the concerns expressed in *Allen* also apply in the context of civil trials"); *Woods,* 5 F.3d at 246–47 ("analysis used to determine when restraints are necessary in criminal cases is also applicable in civil cases"); Wilson v. McCarthy, 770 F.2d 1482, 1485 (9th Cir. 1985) ("federal courts use the same standard of review in both defendant shackling and witness shackling cases"); Harrell v. Israel, 672 F.2d 632, 635 (7th Cir. 1982) ("the general rule against the use of physical restraints in the courtroom applies to defense witnesses as well as the defendant himself"). *Cf.* Duckett v. Godinez, 67 F.3d 734, 738 (9th Cir. 1995) ("relying on criminal case precedents, courts have held that when an individual's level of

3. Use of stun belts

   Some circuits have found that, although often concealed and thereby not visible to the jury, "stun belts plainly pose many of the same constitutional concerns as do other physical restraints," and "a decision to use a stun belt must be subjected to at least the same 'close judicial scrutiny' required for the imposition of other physical restraints."[13]

Other FJC sources

Manual on Recurring Problems in Criminal Trials 41–43 (Tucker Carrington & Kris Markarian eds., 6th ed. 2010)

---

dangerousness is a question the jury must decide in a civil proceeding, it is a violation of the right to a fair trial to compel that individual to appear before the jury bound in physical restraints").

13. United States v. Durham, 287 F.3d 1297, 1306 (11th Cir. 2002) (also noting that "[d]ue to the novelty of this technology, a court contemplating its use will likely need to make factual findings about the operation of the stun belt, addressing issues such as the criteria for triggering the belt and the possibility of accidental discharge"). *See also Wardell*, 591 F.3d at 1293–94 (principles that apply to physical restraints "should apply to stun belts because, as numerous circuits have recognized, '[t]he use of stun belts, depending somewhat on their method of deployment, raises all of the traditional concerns about the imposition of physical restraints.' ... If seen or activated, a stun belt 'might have a significant effect on the jury's feelings about the defendant.'") (citations omitted); United States v. Miller, 531 F.3d 340, 344–45 (6th Cir. 2008) (*Deck* applies to use of "stun belt" on defendant during trial); *Gonzalez*, 341 F.3d at 900 ("The use of stun belts, depending somewhat on their method of deployment, raises all of the traditional concerns about the imposition of physical restraints."). *Cf.* Chavez v. Cockrell, 310 F.3d 805, 809 (5th Cir. 2002) (where judge immediately "took steps to mitigate any prejudicial influence on the jury," accidental activation of stun belt on first day of trial did not deny defendant the presumption of innocence).

5.02 Grants of immunity

18 U.S.C. § 6002, 6003; 21 U.S.C. § 884; 28 C.F.R. § 0.175.

The cited statutes provide for the entry of an order requiring an individual to give testimony or provide other information at any proceeding before or ancillary to a court or a grand jury of the United States after the court ensures compliance with the requirements of 18 U.S.C. §§ 6002, 6003, and 28 C.F.R. § 0.175, or, in the case of testimony or information concerning controlled substances, compliance with 21 U.S.C. § 884 and 28 C.F.R. § 0.175.

Procedure

A. Review the motion of the U.S. attorney to satisfy yourself that

1. the motion is made with the approval of the Attorney General, the Deputy Attorney General, or any designated assistant attorney general of the United States Department of Justice;

2. the motion asserts that the testimony or other information from the individual may be necessary to the public interest; and

3. the motion asserts that the individual has refused or is likely to refuse to testify or provide other information on the basis of the privilege against self-incrimination.

B. If the above requirements have been met, enter an order reflecting the court's satisfaction that the prerequisites have been met and ordering, pursuant to 18 U.S.C. § 6003 or 21 U.S.C. § 884, that

1. the person shall give testimony or provide other information as to all matters about which the person may be interrogated before the court or the grand jury, testimony that he or she has refused to give or to provide on the basis of the privilege against self-incrimination;

2. the order shall become effective only if, after the date of the order, the person refuses to testify or provide other information on the basis of his or her privilege against self-incrimination;

3. no testimony or other information compelled from the person under the order, or any information directly or indirectly derived from such testimony or other information, may be used against the person in any criminal case except in a prosecution for perjury, for giving a false statement, or for otherwise failing to comply with the order; and

4. the motion and order are to be sealed, if appropriate.

C. Cause the (sealed) motion and order to be delivered to the clerk of court.

Other FJC sources

Manual for Complex Litigation, Fourth 228 n.683 (2004)
Pattern Criminal Jury Instructions 32 (1987)

5.03   Invoking the Fifth Amendment

The case law on this subject varies from circuit to circuit. The suggested procedure may be varied to conform with the law of the circuit, the practice of the district, and the preferences of the individual judge.

A. If a witness refuses to answer a proper question and invokes the Fifth Amendment privilege to justify that refusal, the trial court must determine whether the privilege has been properly claimed. The Fifth Amendment privilege extends to

   1. answers that would support a conviction of the witness for violating a federal or state criminal statute; or

   2. answers that would furnish a link in the chain of evidence needed to prosecute the witness for violating a federal or state criminal statute.

B. The following suggested procedure may be used when a witness claims the Fifth Amendment privilege:

   1. Excuse the jury.

   2. Explain to the witness the nature of the Fifth Amendment privilege. Ask the witness if he or she wishes to consult counsel. Consider the appointment of counsel.

   3. Have the question repeated to the witness, and ask the witness if he or she still refuses to answer the question.

   4. If the witness still refuses on the ground of the Fifth Amendment, the court should determine whether the claim of the privilege is appropriate. Be careful not to interrogate the witness about the claim in such a way as to force the witness to surrender the privilege in order to claim it.

   5. If the witness makes a prima facie showing of the validity of his or her claim, the party seeking the answer then has the burden to demonstrate that the answer could not possibly tend to incriminate the witness.

   6. Sustain the Fifth Amendment claim if you find that the witness has reasonable cause to believe that answering the particular question might tend to incriminate him or her. The criterion to be applied in making this determination is the *possibility* of prosecution, not the *likelihood* of prosecution.

      As the Supreme Court found in *Hoffman v. United States,* 341 U.S. 479, 486 (1951):

      > To sustain the privilege it need only be evident from the implication of the question, in the setting in which it is asked, that a responsive answer to the question or an explanation of why it cannot be answered

might be dangerous because injurious disclosure could result. The trial judge in appraising the claim must be governed as much by his personal perception of the peculiarities of the case as by the facts actually in evidence.

7. The witness may not assert a blanket claim of the privilege as to all questions. For each question, the witness must assert or not assert the privilege. Out of the jury's presence, the court must rule as to each question whether the witness's claim of privilege is sustained or overruled. The court may sustain a blanket assertion of the privilege only if it concludes, after inquiry, that the witness could legitimately refuse to answer all relevant questions.

Other FJC sources

Manual for Complex Litigation, Fourth 101, 228, 525 (2004)

5.04 Handling the recalcitrant witness

Fed. R. Crim. P. 42

The case law on this subject varies from circuit to circuit. The suggested procedure may be varied to conform with the law of the circuit, the practice of the district, and the preferences of the individual judge.

Refusal by a witness during trial or before a grand jury to answer a proper question, after having been ordered to do so by the court, constitutes contempt of court, and the witness may be subject to both civil and criminal contempt sanctions. See 18 U.S.C. § 401(3); 28 U.S.C. § 1826(a). See also *infra* sections 7.01 and 7.02.

A. Recalcitrant witness during trial

When a witness refuses to answer a proper question during trial, consider the following procedure:

1. Excuse the jury.
2. Determine the reason for the refusal. (If the witness claims the Fifth Amendment privilege, see *supra* section 5.03: Invoking the Fifth Amendment.)
3. If no valid Fifth Amendment claim or other good cause is shown, advise the witness
   (a) that the jury will be recalled and that the witness will be ordered to answer the question.
   (b) that if the witness persists in refusing to answer, he or she will be cited for civil contempt, and if found guilty, will be confined until he or she answers the question or until the trial ends. Advise the witness that he or she may be fined in addition to being confined.
   (c) that if the witness has not answered the question before the trial ends, he or she may then be cited for criminal contempt and, if found guilty, fined *or* imprisoned; that if the witness is found guilty of criminal contempt at a bench trial, he or she may be imprisoned for as much as six months; and that if a jury finds the witness guilty of criminal contempt, he or she may be imprisoned for as long as the judge in his or her discretion determines. (If the witness is currently serving another sentence, advise the witness that if he or she is confined for civil or criminal contempt, the confinement will be in addition to the sentence already being served.)
4. The jury should then be recalled, the question re-asked, and the witness ordered to answer.
5. If the witness refuses to answer, counsel should be permitted to examine the witness concerning other subject matter about which the witness is willing to testify.

6. After the witness has been examined
    (a) direct him or her to remain in court until the next recess; or
    (b) excuse the jury so that a time can be set for a hearing to determine if the witness should be found in civil contempt.

    [*Note:* The witness should be given a reasonable time to prepare for the hearing, but this time depends on the need for prompt action. If the trial is expected to be short, set an early hearing so that effective pressure to testify can be exerted on the witness before the trial ends. If the trial is expected to be lengthy, the hearing need not be held so promptly. (If, but only if, there is need for immediate action, the witness can be held in summary criminal contempt under Fed. R. Crim. P. 42(b) (formerly 42(a)) and committed at once for criminal contempt that occurred in the presence of the court. If committed for criminal contempt, the witness should be committed for a stated period of time but should be advised that the court would reconsider that sentence if the witness decided to testify during the trial. See, e.g., *United States v. Wilson*, 421 U.S. 309 (1975) (summary contempt under former Rule 42(a) appropriate for already imprisoned witnesses who refused to testify despite grant of immunity).[1]) Advise the witness that he or she may be represented by an attorney at the hearing on the civil contempt citation and that if the witness cannot afford an attorney, one will be appointed.]

7. If, at the hearing, the witness fails to show good cause why he or she should not be compelled to answer the question that the court ordered the witness to answer, he or she should be found in civil contempt and remanded into the marshal's custody. Advise the witness that he or she may purge himself or herself of contempt and secure release by answering the question.

8. Direct the marshal to return the witness to the courtroom before court convenes the next day. At that time ask the witness if he or she is prepared to answer the question which was asked of him or her. If the witness is not prepared to answer, again remand the witness into the marshal's custody. Advise the witness to notify the marshal at once if he or she decides to answer the question, so that the witness can be returned to court and permitted to purge himself or herself of contempt.

9. If the witness has not purged himself or herself of contempt by the time the trial ends, have him or her brought back into court.

---

1. Note that *Wilson* applies only to witnesses during a criminal trial. Witnesses before a grand jury should be given notice and a hearing under current Rule 42(a). *See* Harris v. United States, 382 U.S. 162 (1965).

10. Pursuant to the procedure outlined in Fed. R. Crim. P. 42(a), advise the witness that he or she is being cited for criminal contempt for refusing to obey the court's order.

11. Set the matter down for hearing at a certain place and time to determine if the witness is guilty of criminal contempt. (Bear in mind that the maximum prison sentence that can be imposed after a bench trial is six months. For a prison sentence of more than six months, there must be a jury trial.)

12. Advise the witness that he or she has a right to be represented by counsel at that hearing and that if the witness cannot afford counsel, the court will appoint an attorney.

13. Release the witness from custody. Bail may be set to ensure the witness's appearance at the hearing.

B. Recalcitrant witness before grand jury

When a witness refuses to answer a proper question before a grand jury, consider the following procedure:

1. Have the witness appear before the court out of the presence of the grand jury.

2. Determine the reason for the refusal. (If the witness claims the Fifth Amendment privilege, see *supra* section 5.03: Invoking the Fifth Amendment.)

3. If no valid Fifth Amendment claim or other good cause is shown, advise the witness

    (a) that he or she will be returned to the presence of the grand jury and that the court is ordering the witness to answer the question that he or she had previously refused to answer.

    (b) that if the witness persists in refusing, he or she will be cited for civil contempt and, if found guilty, may be confined for the term of the grand jury, including extensions, or for a period of eighteen months, or until the witness answers the question, whichever occurs first. Advise the witness that he or she may be fined in addition to being confined.

    (c) that if the witness has not answered the question before the term of the grand jury and its extensions expire, or after eighteen months have passed, whichever occurs first, the witness will be released from custody but may then be cited for criminal contempt, and if found guilty, may be fined or imprisoned; that if the witness is found guilty of criminal contempt at a bench trial, he or she may be imprisoned for as much as six months; and that if a jury finds the witness guilty of criminal contempt, he or she may be imprisoned for as long as the judge in his or her discretion determines. (If the witness is currently serving another sentence, advise him or her that the confinement for criminal contempt would be in addition to the sentence currently being served.)

4. Return the witness to the grand jury room.[2]

5. If the witness persists in refusing to answer the question before the grand jury, have him or her brought before the court and at that time advise the witness that he or she is being cited for civil contempt. Do not summarily adjudge the witness to be in contempt pursuant to Fed. R. Crim. P. 42(b). Rather, advise the witness when and where a hearing will be held on the civil contempt citation. Advise the witness that he or she may be represented by counsel at that hearing and that if the witness cannot afford counsel, the court will appoint an attorney.

6. If the evidence warrants, adjudge the witness to be in civil contempt and order him or her committed for the term of the grand jury and its extensions, for eighteen months, or until he or she answers the question, whichever occurs first. 28 U.S.C. § 1826(a).

7. Advise the witness that he or she will be released as soon as he or she has purged himself or herself of contempt by answering the question and that the witness should advise the marshal at once if he or she decides to answer the question.

8. If the witness has not purged himself or herself of civil contempt before the term of the grand jury and its extensions expire or eighteen months have passed, whichever occurs first, the witness may be cited for criminal contempt pursuant to Fed. R. Crim. P. 42(a).

9. If you decide to cite the witness for criminal contempt, advise the witness when and where the hearing will be held to determine if he or she should be punished for criminal contempt. (Bear in mind that the maximum prison sentence that can be imposed after a bench trial is six months. For a prison sentence of more than six months, there must be a jury trial.)

10. Advise the witness that he or she has a right to be represented by counsel at the hearing and that if the witness cannot afford counsel, the court will appoint an attorney.

11. Release the witness from custody. If necessary, set bail to ensure that the witness appears at the hearing on the criminal contempt citation.

---

2. This step may be unnecessary if the witness declares during the court proceeding that he or she will persist in refusing and that another opportunity to answer would be pointless.

Other FJC sources

Manual for Complex Litigation, Fourth 20 (2004)

Manual on Recurring Problems in Criminal Trials 38–41 (Tucker Carrington & Kris Markarian eds., 6th ed. 2010)

5.05 Criminal defendant's motion for mistrial

Fed. R. Crim. P. 26.3

General guidelines

When a criminal defendant moves for a mistrial, the general rule is that retrial is not barred by double jeopardy concerns. See *United States v. Scott,* 437 U.S. 82, 93–94 (1978). However, there is one important exception to this rule: Retrial is barred if the motion was provoked by intentional government misconduct.

> Only where the governmental conduct in question is intended to "goad" the defendant into moving for a mistrial may a defendant raise the bar of double jeopardy to a second trial after having successfully aborted the first on his own motion.

Oregon v. Kennedy, 456 U.S. 667, 676 (1982).

The court must find that the *intent* of the government was to deliberately provoke a mistrial, not merely that the conduct was harassing or in bad faith.

> Prosecutorial conduct that might be viewed as harassment or overreaching, even if sufficient to justify a mistrial on defendant's motion, . . . does not bar retrial absent intent on the part of the prosecutor to subvert the protections afforded by the Double Jeopardy Clause.

Id. at 675–76.

Note that mistake or carelessness is not sufficient to support a double jeopardy claim. See, e.g., *United States v. Johnson,* 55 F.3d 976, 978 (4th Cir. 1995); *United States v. Powell,* 982 F.2d 1422, 1429 (10th Cir. 1992). Nor is "[n]egligence, even if gross." *United States v. Huang,* 960 F.2d 1128, 1133 (2d Cir. 1992). Even a deliberate improper act that causes a mistrial does not prevent retrial if it was not *intended* to provoke a mistrial. *United States v. White,* 914 F.2d 747, 752 (6th Cir. 1990) (although prosecutor deliberately attempted to elicit from witness evidence that court had ruled inadmissible, court found that conduct was motivated by "prosecutorial inexperience").

If the defendant moves for a mistrial with jeopardy attached on the specific ground of prosecutorial misconduct, the court should not deny a mistrial on that ground and then declare a mistrial without prejudice over the defendant's objection unless the defendant consents or there is "manifest necessity" for a mistrial. See *Weston v. Kernan,* 50 F.3d 633, 636–38 (9th Cir. 1995). See also *Corey v. District Court of Vermont, Unit #1, Rutland Circuit,* 917 F.2d 88, 90–92 (2d Cir. 1990) (retrial prohibited where the defendant consented to mistrial only if jeopardy attached but court declared mistrial without prejudice).

Before a court may order a mistrial, Fed. R. Crim. P. 26.3 requires it to "give each defendant and the government an opportunity to comment on the propriety of the order, to state whether that party consents or objects, and to suggest alternatives."

Multidefendant cases

If only one or some of the defendants in a multidefendant case move successfully for mistrial, the court should give the other defendants an opportunity to object. Unless the nonmoving defendants join the motion or acquiesce to the decision,[1] the court should sever their cases or must find that there are grounds to declare a mistrial for those defendants, too. *See, e.g., White,* 914 F.2d at 753–55 (conviction must be vacated on double jeopardy grounds where the defendant did not have sufficient opportunity to object to other defendant's mistrial motion at initial trial, the record did not indicate he joined the motion or otherwise consented to mistrial, and "there was no manifest necessity for declaring a mistrial in regard to him").

Courts should be particularly careful in multidefendant cases where some defendants would agree to a mistrial with prejudice but would object to mistrial without prejudice. *See, e.g., United States v. Huang,* 960 F.2d 1128, 1134–36 (2d Cir. 1992) (where all four defendants moved for mistrial, but two specifically moved for mistrial with prejudice and objected to granting of mistrial without prejudice, double jeopardy prevented retrial because there was no manifest necessity to declare mistrial rather than sever the cases and proceed with original trial for them).

Other FJC sources

Manual on Recurring Problems in Criminal Trials 41–43 (Tucker Carrington & Kris Markarian eds., 6th ed. 2010)

---

1. If the defendant has a reasonable opportunity to object to the granting of a mistrial but does not, consent to the mistrial may be implied. *See, e.g.,* United States v. DiPietro, 936 F.2d 6, 10–11 (1st Cir. 1991). *See also* United States v. You, 382 F.3d 958, 965 (9th Cir. 2004) ("Where one defendant moves for a mistrial, and the other defendant, despite adequate opportunity to object, remains silent, the silent defendant impliedly consents by that silence to the mistrial and waives the right to claim a double jeopardy bar to retrial.").

5.06 Duty to disclose information favorable to defendant (*Brady* and *Giglio* material)

Introduction

Federal criminal discovery is governed by Rule 16 of the Federal Rules of Criminal Procedure and for certain specified matters by portions of Rules 12, 12.1, 12.2, and 12.3.[1] The Jencks Act, 18 U.S.C. § 3500, and Rule 26.2 govern the disclosure of witness statements at trial, and the Classified Information Procedures Act, 18 U.S.C. App. 3, governs discovery and disclosure when classified information related to national security is implicated. Prosecutors and defense lawyers should be familiar with these authorities, and judges typically know where to find the relevant law in deciding most discovery issues.

However, it sometimes is more challenging to understand the full scope of a prosecutor's obligations with respect to a defendant's constitutional

---

1. *See also* Rule 15, governing depositions for those limited circumstances in which depositions are permitted in criminal cases, and Rule 17, governing subpoenas.

right to exculpatory information under *Brady v. Maryland,* 373 U.S. 83 (1963), and impeachment material under *Giglio v. United States,* 405 U.S. 150 (1972), and to deal effectively with related disclosure disputes. Applying *Brady* and *Giglio* in particular cases can be difficult; it requires familiarity with Supreme Court precedent, circuit law, and relevant local rules and practices.

This section of the *Benchbook* is intended to give judges general guidance on the requirements of *Brady* and *Giglio* by providing a basic summary of the case law interpreting and applying these decisions. For further reference, the appendices provide three other sources of information: a link to the Federal Judicial Center's recent report summarizing a national survey of Rule 16 and disclosure practices in the district courts; a link to the "Policy Regarding Disclosure of Exculpatory and Impeachment Information" in the *United States Attorneys' Manual* of the Department of Justice; and a list of examples of exculpatory or impeachment information, disclosure of which may be required under *Brady* or *Giglio.*

Because every *Brady* or *Giglio* inquiry is fact-specific, the depth of such an inquiry can vary considerably from case to case. Judges are encouraged, as part of efficient case management, to be mindful of the particular disclosure requirements in each case and to resolve disclosure disputes quickly to avoid unnecessary delay and expense later. The material provided in this section is for informational purposes only; it is not meant to recommend a particular course of action when disclosure issues arise.

Although *Brady* exculpatory material and *Giglio* impeachment material are sometimes distinguished, courts often refer to them together as "*Brady* material" or "exculpatory material," and this section generally follows that practice.

A. Duty to disclose exculpatory information

1. In general

In *Brady,* the Supreme Court held that "suppression by the prosecution of evidence favorable to an accused upon request violates due process where the evidence is material either to guilt or to punishment, irrespective of the good faith or bad faith of the prosecution." 373 U.S. at 87. The Court later held that the prosecution has an obligation to disclose such information even in the absence of a defense request. *See Banks v. Dretke,* 540 U.S. 668, 695–96 (2004); *Kyles v. Whitley,* 514 U.S. 419, 433 (1995); *United States v. Agurs,* 427 U.S. 97, 107, 110–11 (1976).

In *Giglio,* the Supreme Court extended the prosecution's obligations to include the disclosure of information affecting the credibility of a government witness. *See* 405 U.S. at 154–55. As the Court later explained, "[i]mpeachment evidence, . . . as well as exculpatory evidence, falls within the *Brady* rule" because it is "evidence favorable to an accused, . . . so that, if disclosed and used effectively, it may make the difference between conviction and acquittal." *United States v. Bagley,* 473 U.S. 667, 676 (1985) (quotations omitted).

2. Information from law enforcement agencies

Under *Brady,* the prosecutor is required to find and disclose favorable evidence initially known only to law enforcement officers and not to the prosecutor. The individual prosecutor in a specific case has an affirmative "duty to learn of any favorable evidence known to the others acting on the government's behalf in the case, including the police." *Kyles v. Whitley,* 514 U.S. at 437. *See also Youngblood v. West Virginia,* 547 U.S. 867, 869–70 (2006) (per curiam) ("*Brady* suppression occurs when the government fails to turn over even evidence that is 'known only to police investigators and not to the prosecutor'") (quoting *Kyles v. Whitley,* 514 U.S. at 438).

3. Ongoing duty

A prosecutor's disclosure obligations under *Brady* are ongoing: they begin as soon as the case is brought and continue throughout the pretrial and trial phases of the case.[2] *See Pennsylvania v. Ritchie,* 480 U.S. 39, 60 (1987) ("the duty to disclose is ongoing; information that may be deemed immaterial upon original examination may become important as the proceedings progress").[3] If *Brady* information is known to persons on the prosecution team, including law enforcement officers, it should be disclosed to the defendant as soon as reasonably possible after its existence is recognized.

---

2. The Supreme Court has declined to extend *Brady* disclosure obligations to evidence that the government did not possess during the trial but only became available "after the defendant was convicted and the case was closed." *See* District Attorney's Office for Third Judicial District v. Osborne, 557 U.S. 52, 68–69 (2009) ("*Brady* is the wrong framework" for prisoner's post-conviction attempt to retest DNA evidence using a newer test that was not available when he was tried). "[A] post-conviction claim for DNA testing is properly pursued in a [42 U.S.C.] § 1983 action." Skinner v. Switzer, 131 S. Ct. 1289, 1293, 1300 (2011) (also noting that "*Brady* claims have ranked within the traditional core of habeas corpus and outside the province of § 1983"). *Cf.* Whitlock v. Brueggemann, 682 F.3d 567, 587–88 (7th Cir. 2012) (distinguishing *Osborne*: "*Brady* continues to apply [in a post-trial action] to an assertion that one did not receive a fair trial because of the concealment of exculpatory evidence known and in existence at the time of that trial").

3. *See also* Steidl v. Fermon, 494 F.3d 623, 630 (7th Cir. 2007) ("For evidence known to the state at the time of the trial, the duty to disclose extends throughout the legal proceedings that may affect either guilt or punishment, including post-conviction proceedings."); Leka v. Portuondo, 257 F.3d 89, 100 (2d Cir. 2001) ("*Brady* requires disclosure of information that the prosecution acquires during the trial itself, or even afterward"); Smith v. Roberts, 115 F.3d 818, 819–20 (10th Cir. 1997) (same, applying *Brady* to impeachment evidence that prosecutor did not learn of until "[a]fter trial and sentencing but while the conviction was on direct appeal. ... [T]he duty to disclose is ongoing and extends to all stages of the judicial process.").

4. Disclosure favored

When it is uncertain whether information is favorable or useful to a defendant, "the prudent prosecutor will err on the side of transparency, resolving doubtful questions in favor of disclosure." *Cone v. Bell,* 556 U.S. 449, 470 n.15 (2009). *See also Kyles v. Whitley,* 514 U.S. at 439–40; *Agurs,* 427 U.S. at 108.[4]

B. Elements of a violation

There are three elements of a *Brady* violation: (1) the information must be favorable to the accused; (2) the information must be suppressed—that is, not disclosed—by the government, either willfully or inadvertently; and (3) the information must be "material" to guilt or to punishment. *See Strickler v. Greene,* 527 U.S. 263, 281–82 (1999).

1. Favorable to the accused

Information is "favorable to the accused either because it is exculpatory, or because it is impeaching." *Strickler,* 527 U.S. at 281–82. Most circuits have held that information may be favorable even if it is not admissible as evidence itself, as long as it reasonably could lead to admissible evidence. *See, e.g., United States v. Triumph Capital Group, Inc.,* 544 F.3d 149, 162–63 (2d Cir. 2008) (*Brady* information "need not be admissible if it 'could lead to admissible evidence' or 'would be an effective tool in disciplining witnesses during cross-examination by refreshment of recollection or otherwise'") (quoting *United States v. Gil,* 297 F.3d 93, 104 (2d Cir. 2002)).[5]

---

4. *Cf.* United States v. Moore, 651 F.3d 30, 99–100 (D.C. Cir. 2011) ("This is particularly true where the defendant brings the existence of what he believes to be exculpatory or impeaching evidence or information to the attention of the prosecutor and the district court, in contrast to a general request for *Brady* material.").

5. *See also* United States v. Wilson, 605 F.3d 985, 1005 (D.C. Cir. 2010) (no *Brady* violation because undisclosed information was not admissible nor would it have led to admissible evidence or effective impeachment); Ellsworth v. Warden, 333 F.3d 1, 5 (1st Cir. 2003) ("we think it plain that evidence itself inadmissible *could* be so promising a lead to strong exculpatory evidence that there could be no justification for withholding it"); Spence v. Johnson, 80 F.3d 989, 1005 at n.14 (5th Cir. 1996) ("inadmissible evidence may be material under *Brady*"); Spaziano v. Singletary, 36 F.3d 1028, 1044 (11th Cir. 1994) ("A reasonable probability of a different result is possible only if the suppressed information is itself admissible evidence or would have led to admissible evidence."); United States v. Phillip, 948 F.2d 241, 249 (6th Cir. 1991) ("information withheld by the prosecution is not material unless the information consists of, or would lead directly to, evidence admissible at trial for either substantive or impeachment purposes"). *Cf.* Wood v. Bartholomew, 516 U.S. 1, 6 (1995) (per curiam) (where it was "mere speculation" that inadmissible materials might lead to the discovery of admissible exculpatory evidence, those materials are not subject to disclosure under *Brady*); United States v. Velarde, 485 F.3d 553, 560 (10th Cir. 2007) (if defendant "is able to make a showing that further investigation under the court's subpoena power very likely would lead to the discovery of [admissible material] evidence," defendant may "request leave to conduct discovery"); Madsen v. Dormire, 137 F.3d 602, 604 (8th Cir. 1998) (citing *Wood,* there was no *Brady* violation where undisclosed information was not admissible

2. Suppression, willful or inadvertent

Whether exculpatory information has been suppressed by the government is a matter for inquiry first by defense counsel making a request of the prosecutor. If defense counsel remains unsatisfied, the trial court may make its own inquiry and, if appropriate, require the government to produce the undisclosed information for in camera inspection by the court. See also discussion in *infra* section D: Disputed disclosure.

It does not matter whether a failure to disclose is intentional or inadvertent, since "under *Brady* an inadvertent nondisclosure has the same impact on the fairness of the proceedings as deliberate concealment." *Strickler*, 527 U.S. at 288; *Agurs*, 427 U.S. at 110 ("Nor do we believe the constitutional obligation is measured by the moral culpability, or the willfulness, of the prosecutor. ... If the suppression of evidence results in constitutional error, it is because of the character of the evidence, not the character of the prosecutor.").[6]

Information will not be considered "suppressed" for *Brady* purposes if the defendant already knew about it[7] or could have obtained it with reasonable effort.[8] However, suppression still may be found in this situation if a de-

---

and could not be used to impeach; court did not address whether it could lead to admissible evidence). *But cf.* Hoke v. Netherland, 92 F.3d 1350, 1356 at n.3 (4th Cir. 1996) (reading *Wood* to hold that inadmissible evidence is, "as a matter of law, 'immaterial' for *Brady* purposes").

6. *See also* Porter v. White, 483 F.3d 1294, 1305 (11th Cir. 2007) ("The *Brady* rule thus imposes a no-fault standard of care on the prosecutor. If favorable, material evidence exclusively in the hands of the prosecution team fails to reach the defense—for whatever reason—and the defendant is subsequently convicted, the prosecution is charged with a *Brady* violation, and the defendant is entitled to a new trial."); *Gantt v. Roe*, 389 F.3d 908, 912 (9th Cir. 2004) ("*Brady* has no good faith or inadvertence defense").

7. *See, e.g.,* Parker v. Allen, 565 F.3d 1258, 1277 (11th Cir. 2009) ("there is no suppression if the defendant knew of the information or had equal access to obtaining it"); United States v. Zichittello, 208 F.3d 72, 103 (2d Cir. 2000) ("Even if evidence is material and exculpatory, it 'is not "suppressed"' by the government within the meaning of *Brady* 'if the defendant either knew, or should have known, of the essential facts permitting him to take advantage of any exculpatory evidence.'") (citations omitted); Rector v. Johnson, 120 F.3d 551, 558–59 (5th Cir. 1997) (same); United States v. Clark, 928 F.2d 733, 738 (6th Cir. 1991) ("No *Brady* violation exists where a defendant 'knew or should have known the essential facts permitting him to take advantage of any exculpatory information,' ... or where the evidence is available to defendant from another source.") (citations omitted). *Cf.* United States v. Quintanilla, 193 F.3d 1139, 1149 (10th Cir. 1999) ("a defendant's independent awareness of the exculpatory evidence is critical in determining whether a *Brady* violation has occurred. If a defendant already has a particular piece of evidence, the prosecution's disclosure of that evidence is considered cumulative, rendering the suppressed evidence immaterial.").

8. United States v. Rodriguez, 162 F.3d 135, 147 (1st Cir. 1998) ("government has no *Brady* burden when the necessary facts for impeachment are readily available to a diligent defender"); United States v. Dimas, 3 F.3d 1015, 1019 (7th Cir. 1993) (when "the defendants might have obtained the evidence themselves with reasonable diligence . . . , then the evidence was not 'suppressed' under *Brady* and they would have no claim"); *Hoke*, 92 F.3d at

fendant did not investigate further because the prosecution represented that it had turned over all disclosable information or that there was no disclosable material. In *Strickler,* the prosecutor had an "open file" policy, but exculpatory information had been kept out of the files. The Supreme Court held that the "petitioner has established cause for failing to raise a *Brady* claim prior to federal habeas because (a) the prosecution withheld exculpatory evidence; (b) petitioner reasonably relied on the prosecution's open file policy as fulfilling the prosecution's duty to disclose such evidence; and (c) the Commonwealth confirmed petitioner's reliance on the open file policy by asserting during state habeas proceedings that petitioner had already received 'everything known to the government.'" 527 U.S. at 283–89.[9] The Court reached the same conclusion in a later case in which the prosecution withheld disclosable information after having "asserted, on the eve of trial, that it would disclose all *Brady* material."[10]

Suppression may also be found when disclosure is so late that the defense is unable to make effective use of the information at trial. See discussion in *infra* section C: Timing of disclosure.

3. Materiality

(a) Definition

The most problematic aspect of *Brady* for prosecutors and trial judges is the third element: the requirement that the favorable information suppressed by the government be "material." Under *Brady,* information is considered "material" "when there is a reasonable probability that, had the evidence

---

1355 ("The strictures of *Brady* are not violated, however, if the information allegedly withheld by the prosecution was reasonably available to the defendant.").

9. The Court cautioned, however, that "[w]e do not reach, because it is not raised in this case, the impact of a showing by the State that the defendant was aware of the existence of the documents in question and knew, or could reasonably discover, how to obtain them." *Id.* at 288 n.33. *See also* Carr v. Schofield, 364 F.3d 1246, 1255 (11th Cir. 2004) (citing and quoting *Strickler* for proposition that "if a prosecutor asserts that he complies with *Brady* through an open file policy, defense counsel may reasonably rely on that file to contain all materials the State is constitutionally obligated to disclose under *Brady*").

10. Banks v. Dretke, 540 U.S. 668, 693–96 (2004) ("Our decisions lend no support to the notion that defendants must scavenge for hints of undisclosed *Brady* material when the prosecution represents that all such material has been disclosed. As we observed in *Strickler,* defense counsel has no 'procedural obligation to assert constitutional error on the basis of mere suspicion that some prosecutorial misstep may have occurred.' 527 U.S. at 286–287"). *See also* Gantt v. Roe, 389 F.3d at 912–13 ("While the defense could have been more diligent, ... this does not absolve the prosecution of its *Brady* responsibilities. ... Though defense counsel could have conducted his own investigation, he was surely entitled to rely on the prosecution's representation that it was sharing the fruits of the police investigation."). *Cf.* Bell v. Bell, 512 F.3d 223, 236 (6th Cir. 2008) (distinguishing *Banks* from instant case, in which the facts known to defendant "strongly suggested that further inquiry was in order, whether or not the prosecutor said he had turned over all the discoverable evidence in his file, and the information was a matter of public record").

been disclosed, the result of the proceeding would have been different." *Smith v. Cain*, 132 S. Ct. 627, 630 (2012) (quotations omitted). "A reasonable probability does not mean that the defendant 'would more likely than not have received a different verdict with the evidence,' only that the likelihood of a different result is great enough to 'undermine[] confidence in the outcome of the trial.'" *Id.* (quoting *Kyles v. Whitley*, 514 U.S. at 434) (alteration in original).[11]

This definition of "materiality" necessarily is retrospective. It is used by an appellate court after trial to review whether a failure to disclose on the part of the government was so prejudicial that the defendant is entitled to a new trial. While *Brady* requires that materiality be considered even before or during trial, obviously it may not always be apparent in advance whether the suppression of a particular piece of information ultimately might "undermine [] confidence in the outcome of the trial."[12] For this reason, as noted earlier, the Supreme Court explicitly has recommended erring on the side of disclosure when there is uncertainty before or during trial about an item's materiality: "[T]here is a significant practical difference between the pretrial decision of the prosecutor and the post-trial decision of the judge. Because we are dealing with an inevitably imprecise standard, and because the significance of an item of evidence can seldom be predicted accurately until the entire record is complete, the prudent prosecutor will resolve doubtful questions in favor of disclosure."[13] At the same time, the Court reiterated the

---

11. *See also* Banks v. Dretke, 540 U.S. at 698–99 ("[o]ur touchstone on materiality is *Kyles v. Whitley*"); Kyles v. Whitley, 514 U.S. at 434 ("The question is not whether the defendant would more likely than not have received a different verdict with the evidence, but whether in its absence he received a fair trial, understood as a trial resulting in a verdict worthy of confidence."); United States v. Bagley, 473 U.S. 667, 682 (1985) ("A 'reasonable probability' is a probability sufficient to undermine confidence in the outcome.").

12. Smith v. Cain, 132 S. Ct. at 630. *See also* United States v. Jordan, 316 F.3d 1215, 1252 n.79 (11th Cir. 2003) ("In the case at hand, . . . the defendants' *Brady* claims involve material that was produced both before and during the defendants' trial. In such a scenario, because the trial has just begun, the determination of prejudice is inherently problematical.").

13. United States v. Agurs, 427 U.S. 97, 108 (1976). *See also* Cone v. Bell, 556 U.S. at 470 n.15 ("As we have often observed, the prudent prosecutor will err on the side of transparency, resolving doubtful questions in favor of disclosure."); United States v. Starusko, 729 F.2d 256, 261 (3d Cir. 1984) ("it is difficult to analyze, prior to trial, whether potential impeachment evidence falls within *Brady* without knowing what role a certain witness will play in the government's case"). *Cf. Jordan*, 316 F.3d at 1251 ("under *Brady*, the government need only disclose during pretrial discovery (or later, at the trial) evidence which, in the eyes of a neutral and objective observer, could alter the outcome of the proceedings. Not infrequently, what constitutes *Brady* material is fairly debatable. In such cases, the prosecutor should mark the material as a court exhibit and submit it to the court for in camera inspection."); United States v. Cadet, 727 F.2d 1453, 1469 (9th Cir. 1984) ("Any doubt concerning the applicability of *Brady* to any specific document . . . should have been submitted to the court for an in camera review.").

Some district courts have enacted local rules that eliminate the *Brady* materiality requirement for pretrial disclosure of exculpatory information. *See* discussion at pp. 16–17 in "critical point" that "the prosecutor will not have violated his constitutional duty of disclosure unless his omission is of sufficient significance to result in the denial of the defendant's right to a fair trial."[14]

(b) Cumulative effect of suppressed evidence

Although each instance of nondisclosure is examined separately, the "suppressed evidence [is] considered collectively, not item by item" in determining materiality. *Kyles v. Whitley,* 514 U.S. at 436–37 & n.10 ("showing that the prosecution knew of an item of favorable evidence unknown to the defense does not amount to a *Brady* violation, without more. But the prosecution, which alone can know what is undisclosed, must be assigned the consequent responsibility to gauge the likely net effect of all such evidence and make disclosure when the point of 'reasonable probability' is reached").[15] The undisclosed evidence "must be evaluated in the context of the entire

---

Laural Hooper et al., Fed. Judicial Ctr., A Summary of Responses to a National Survey of Rule 16 of the Federal Rules of Criminal Procedure and Disclosure Practices in Criminal Cases (2011). *See also* United States v. Price, 566 F.3d 900, 913 n.14 (9th Cir. 2009) ("[f]or the benefit of trial prosecutors who must regularly decide what material to turn over, we note favorably the thoughtful analysis" of two district courts that held that "the 'materiality' standard usually associated with *Brady* . . . should not be applied to pretrial discovery of exculpatory materials").

14. *Agurs,* 427 U.S. at 109–10 (also cautioning that "[t]he mere possibility that an item of undisclosed information might have helped the defense, or might have affected the outcome of the trial, does not establish 'materiality' in the constitutional sense"). *See also* United States v. Lemmerer, 277 F.3d 579, 588 (1st Cir. 2002) ("The same standard applies when the claim is one of delayed disclosure rather than complete suppression. However, in delayed disclosure cases, we need not reach the question whether the evidence at issue was 'material' under *Brady* unless the defendant first can show that defense counsel was 'prevented by the delay from using the disclosed material effectively in preparing and presenting the defendant's case.'"); United States v. Coppa, 267 F.3d 132, 140 (2d Cir. 2001) ("Although the government's obligations under *Brady* may be thought of as a constitutional duty arising before or during the trial of a defendant, the scope of the government's constitutional duty—and, concomitantly, the scope of a defendant's constitutional right—is ultimately defined retrospectively, by reference to the likely effect that the suppression of particular evidence had on the outcome of the trial. . . . The government therefore has a so-called '*Brady* obligation' only where non-disclosure of a particular piece of evidence would deprive a defendant of a fair trial."); *Starusko,* 729 F.2d at 261 (there is "no violation of *Brady* unless the government's nondisclosure infringes the defendant's fair trial right").

15. *See also* Jackson v. Brown, 513 F.3d 1057, 1071–72 (9th Cir. 2008) ("The materiality of suppressed evidence is 'considered collectively, not item by item.' . . . [E]ach additional . . . *Brady* violation further undermines our confidence in the decision-making process") (quoting *Kyles*); Maharaj v. Sec'y for Dept. of Corrections, 432 F.3d 1292, 1310 (11th Cir. 2005) ("the district court followed the appropriate methodology, considering each *Brady* item individually, and only then making a determination about the cumulative impact"); United States v. Sipe, 388 F.3d 471, 477 (5th Cir. 2004) ("Even if none of the nondisclosures standing alone could have affected the outcome, when viewed cumulatively in the context of the full array of facts, we cannot disagree with the conclusion of the district judge that the government's nondisclosures undermined confidence in the jury's verdict.").

record. If there is no reasonable doubt about guilt whether or not the additional evidence is considered, there is no justification for a new trial. On the other hand, if the verdict is already of questionable validity, additional evidence of relatively minor importance might be sufficient to create a reasonable doubt." *Agurs*, 427 U.S. at 112.[16]

C. Timing of disclosure

1. In time for effective use at trial

As noted earlier, information may be considered "suppressed" for *Brady* purposes if disclosure is delayed to the extent that the defense is not able to make effective use of the information in the preparation and presentation of its case at trial. How much preparation a defendant needs in order to use *Brady* material effectively—which determines how early disclosure must be made by the prosecution—depends upon the circumstances of each case. Disclosure before trial (and often well before trial) is always preferable and may be required if the material is significant, complex, or voluminous, or may lead to other exculpatory material after further investigation.[17] In some circumstances, however, disclosure right before, or even during, trial has been found to be sufficient.[18] "It is not feasible or desirable to specify the

---

16. *See also* United States v. Bowie, 198 F.3d 905, 912 (D.C. Cir. 1999) (court must "evaluate the impact of the undisclosed evidence not in isolation, but in light of the rest of the trial record"); Porretto v. Stalder, 834 F.2d 461, 464 (5th Cir. 1987) ("Omitted evidence is deemed material when, viewed in the context of the entire record, it creates a reasonable doubt as to the defendant's guilt that did not otherwise exist.").

17. *See* DiSimone v. Phillips, 461 F.3d 181, 197 (2d Cir. 2006) ("The more a piece of evidence is valuable and rich with potential leads, the less likely it will be that late disclosure provides the defense an 'opportunity for use.'"); Leka v. Portuondo, 257 F.3d 89, 101 (2d Cir. 2001) ("When such a disclosure is first made on the eve of trial, or when trial is under way, the opportunity to use it may be impaired. The defense may be unable to divert resources from other initiatives and obligations that are or may seem more pressing. And the defense may be unable to assimilate the information into its case. ... Moreover, new witnesses or developments tend to throw existing strategies and preparation into disarray."). *See also* United States v. Garner, 507 F.3d 399, 405–07 (6th Cir. 2007) (defendant "did not receive a fair trial" where cell phone records that would have allowed impeachment of critical prosecution witness were not disclosed until the morning of trial and the defense was not given sufficient time to investigate records: "The importance of the denial of an opportunity to impeach this witness cannot be overstated."); United States v. Fisher, 106 F.3d 622, 634–35 (5th Cir. 1997) (new trial warranted where government did not disclose until last day of trial an FBI report containing impeachment evidence that directly contradicted testimony of key witness and defense was not able to make meaningful use of evidence), *abrogated on other grounds by* Ohler v. United States, 529 U.S. 753, 758–59 (2000).

18. A majority of the circuits that have addressed this point have held that disclosure may be deemed timely, at least in some circumstances, when the defendant is able to effectively use the information at trial, even if disclosure occurs after the trial has begun. *See, e.g.,* United States v. Houston, 648 F.3d 806, 813 (9th Cir. 2011) ("there is no *Brady* violation so long as the exculpatory or impeaching evidence is disclosed at a time when it still has value"); United States v. Celis, 608 F.3d 818, 836 (D.C. Cir. (2010) ("the critical point is that

extent or timing of disclosure *Brady* and its progeny require, except in terms of the sufficiency, under the circumstances, of the defense's opportunity to use the evidence when disclosure is made. Thus, disclosure prior to trial is not [always] mandated. . . . At the same time, however, the longer the prosecution withholds information, or (more particularly) the closer to trial the disclosure is made, the less opportunity there is for use." *Leka v. Portuondo*, 257 F.3d 89, 100 (2d Cir. 2001).[19]

In light of these considerations, and because the effect of suppression usually cannot be evaluated fully until after trial, potential *Brady* material ordinarily should be disclosed as soon as reasonably possible after its existence is known by the government, and disclosures on the eve of or during trial should be avoided unless there is no other reasonable alternative.

2. Prior to a guilty plea?

The Supreme Court has held that disclosure of impeachment information is not required before a guilty plea is negotiated or accepted. *See United States*

---

disclosure must occur in sufficient time for defense counsel to be able to make effective use of the disclosed evidence"); Powell v. Quarterman, 536 F.3d 325, 335 (5th Cir. 2008) ("a defendant is not prejudiced [by untimely disclosure] if the evidence is received in time for its effective use at trial"); United States v. Rodriguez, 496 F.3d 221, 226 (2d Cir. 2007) ("the Government must make disclosures in sufficient time that the defendant will have a reasonable opportunity to act upon the information efficaciously," that is, "in a manner that gives the defendant a reasonable opportunity either to use the evidence in the trial or to use the information to obtain evidence for use in the trial"); Blake v. Kemp, 758 F.2d 523, 532 n.10 (11th Cir. 1985) ("In some instances [disclosure of potential *Brady* material the day before trial] may be sufficient. . . . However, . . . some material must be disclosed earlier. . . . This is because of the importance of some information to adequate trial preparation.") (citations omitted).

19. *See also* Gantt v. Roe, 389 F.3d at 912 ("That [relevant] pieces of information were found (or their relevance discovered) only in time for the last day of testimony underscores that disclosure should have been *immediate:* Disclosure must be made 'at a time when [it] would be of value to the accused.'") (citation omitted); United States v. McKinney, 758 F.2d 1036, 1049–50 (5th Cir. 1985) ("If the defendant received the material in time to put it to effective use at trial, his conviction should not be reversed simply because it was not disclosed as early as it might have and, indeed, should have been."); United States v. Pollack, 534 F.2d 964, 973–74 (D.C. Cir. 1976) ("Disclosure by the government must be made at such a time as to allow the defense to use the favorable material effectively in the preparation and presentation of its case, even if satisfaction of this criterion requires pre-trial disclosure. . . . The trial judge must be given a wide measure of discretion to ensure satisfaction of this standard. . . . Courts can do little more in determining the proper timing for disclosure than balance in each case the potential dangers of early discovery against the need that *Brady* purports to serve of avoiding wrongful convictions."); Grant v. Alldredge, 498 F.2d 376, 382 (2d Cir. 1976) ("Although it well may be that marginal *Brady* material need not always be disclosed upon request prior to trial," evidence indicating that another suspect may have committed the crime "was without question 'specific, concrete evidence' of a nature requiring pretrial disclosure to allow for full exploration and exploitation by the defense" that "would have had a 'material bearing on defense preparation' . . . and therefore should have been revealed well before the commencement of the trial.") (citations omitted).

v. Ruiz, 536 U.S. 622, 629–30 (2002) ("impeachment information is special in relation to the *fairness of a trial*, not in respect to whether a plea is *voluntary*," and due process does not require disclosure of such impeachment information before a plea) (emphasis in original). The holding in *Ruiz* was limited to impeachment material because "the proposed plea agreement at issue ... specifie[d that] the Government [would] provide 'any information establishing the factual innocence of the defendant,'" *Id.* at 631. The Court "has not addressed the question of whether the *Brady* right to *exculpatory* information, in contrast to *impeachment* information, might be extended to the guilty plea context." *United States v. Moussaoui*, 591 F.3d 263, 286 (4th Cir. 2010) (emphasis in original).[20]

3. Remedies for untimely disclosure

Untimely disclosure that effectively suppresses *Brady* information may result in sanctions. The decision whether to impose sanctions is within the sound discretion of the trial judge: "Where the district court concludes that the government was dilatory in its compliance with *Brady*, to the prejudice of the defendant, the district court has discretion to determine an appropriate remedy, whether it be exclusion of the witness, limitations on the scope of permitted testimony, instructions to the jury, or even mistrial. The choice of remedy also is within the sound discretion of the district court. Fed. R. Crim. P. 16(d)(2) authorizes the district court in cases of non-compliance with discovery obligations to 'permit the discovery or inspection,' 'grant a continu-

---

20. *Compare* United States v. Conroy, 567 F.3d 174, 179 (5th Cir. 2009) (rejecting defendant's argument that the limitation on the Supreme Court's discussion in *Ruiz* "to impeachment evidence implies that exculpatory evidence is different and must be turned over before entry of a plea"), *with* McCann v. Mangialardi, 337 F.3d 782, 787–88 (7th Cir. 2003) ("*Ruiz* indicates a significant distinction between impeachment information and exculpatory evidence of actual innocence. Given this distinction, it is highly likely that the Supreme Court would find a violation of the Due Process Clause if prosecutors or other relevant government actors have knowledge of a criminal defendant's factual innocence but fail to disclose such information to a defendant before he enters into a guilty plea"). *See also* United States v. Mathur, 624 F.3d 498, 504–07 (1st Cir. 2010) (rejecting defendant's claim that "potentially exculpatory" information and impeachment information should have been disclosed before his plea, court held that the information was not material and added, "Although we recognize that plea negotiations are important, that fact provides no support for an unprecedented expansion of *Brady*."); Jones v. Cooper, 311 F.3d 306, 315 n.5 (4th Cir. 2002) (in a death penalty case, "[t]o the extent that appellant contends that he would not have pled guilty had he been provided the [potentially mitigating] information held by the jailor, this claim is foreclosed by" *Ruiz*). *Cf.* Ferrara v. United States, 456 F.3d 278, 293 (1st Cir. 2006) (prosecution's "blatant misconduct" and "affirmative misrepresentations" in withholding material exculpatory information—which it was obligated to disclose not only under *Brady v. Maryland* but also under local court rules and a court order—rendered defendant's guilty plea involuntary under *Brady v. United States,* 397 U.S. 742 (1970)); United States v. Wright, 43 F.3d 491, 496 (10th Cir. 1994) ("under certain limited circumstances, the prosecution's violation of *Brady* can render a defendant's plea involuntary").

ance,' 'prohibit the party from introducing the evidence not disclosed,' or 'enter any other order that is just under the circumstances.'"[21]

In most cases, "[t]he customary remedy for a *Brady* violation that surfaces mid-trial is a continuance and a concomitant opportunity to analyze the new information and, if necessary, recall witnesses."[22] In fact, failure to request a continuance, or an "outright rejection of a proffered continuance," is taken as an indication that the defendant is able to use the information effectively despite the delay.[23]

In an extreme case, dismissal may be warranted: "*Brady* violations are just like other constitutional violations. Although the appropriate remedy will usually be a new trial, ... a district court may dismiss the indictment when the prosecution's actions rise ... to the level of flagrant prosecutorial misconduct."[24]

4. Jencks Act

There is no consensus among the circuits as to whether the government's constitutional obligation to produce *Brady* information in a timely manner

---

21. United States v. Burke, 571 F.3d 1048, 1054 (10th Cir. 2009). *See also* United States v. Johnston, 127 F.3d 380, 391 (5th Cir. 1997) (district court has "real latitude" to fashion appropriate remedy for alleged *Brady* errors, including delayed disclosure); United States v. Josleyn, 99 F.3d 1182, 1196 (1st Cir. 1996) ("The district court has broad discretion to redress discovery violations in light of their seriousness and any prejudice occasioned the defendant," and court properly refused to dismiss indictment for delay in disclosing *Brady* material).

22. *Mathur,* 624 F.3d at 506. *See also* United States v. Collins, 415 F.3d 304, 311 (4th Cir. 2005) (continuance is preferable to motion to dismiss as remedy for late disclosure); United States v. Kelly, 14 F.3d 1169, 1176 (7th Cir. 1994) (when "a *Brady* disclosure is made during trial, the defendant can seek a continuance of the trial to allow the defense to examine or investigate, if the nature or quantity of the disclosed *Brady* material makes an investigation necessary").

23. *Mathur,* 624 F.3d at 506. *See also* Lawrence v. Lensing, 42 F.3d 255, 258 (5th Cir. 1994) (petitioner "cannot convert his tactical decision not to seek a recess or continuance into a *Brady* claim in this habeas petition"); United States v. Adams, 834 F.2d 632, 635 (7th Cir. 1987) (holding that delayed disclosure did not prejudice defendant partly based on fact that defendant did not request continuance or recess); United States v. Holloway, 740 F.2d 1373, 1381 (6th Cir. 1984) (where defense counsel made no request for a continuance after delayed disclosure, "we conclude that the timing of the disclosure did not prejudice" the defendant).

24. United States v. Chapman, 524 F.3d 1073, 1086 (9th Cir. 2008) ("Because the district court did not clearly err in finding that the government recklessly violated its discovery obligations and made flagrant misrepresentations to the court, we hold that the dismissal was not an abuse of discretion."). *Accord* Government of Virgin Islands v. Fahie, 419 F.3d 249, 255 (3d Cir. 2005) ("While retrial is normally the most severe sanction available for a *Brady* violation, where a defendant can show both willful misconduct by the government, and prejudice, dismissal may be proper.").

supersedes the timing requirements of the Jencks Act, 18 U.S.C. § 3500.[25] Some courts have attempted to harmonize the two rules, usually by finding that the timing of disclosure was sufficient under either standard to allow the defendant to make effective use of the information.[26]

There may be instances in which the nature of impeaching information warrants a delay in disclosure by the government. Even if the information might be helpful to a defendant in impeaching a witness's testimony, the government might not determine whether it actually will call the witness until shortly before, or even during, the trial. There is also the chance that a witness will choose not to cooperate or could be put in jeopardy by early disclosure.[27]

Brady and the Jencks Act serve different purposes, and although their disclosure obligations often overlap, they are not always coextensive, and

---

25. *Compare, e.g.,* United States v. Rittweger, 524 F.3d 171, 181 n.4 (2d Cir. 2008) ("Complying with the Jencks Act, of course, does not shield the government from its independent obligation to timely produce exculpatory material under *Brady*—a constitutional requirement that trumps the statutory power of 18 U.S.C. § 3500."), *with* United States v. Presser, 844 F.2d 1275, 1283–84 (6th Cir. 1988) ("If impeachment evidence is within the ambit of the Jencks Act, then the express provisions of the Jencks Act control discovery of that kind of evidence. The clear and consistent rule of this circuit is that the intent of Congress expressed in the Act must be adhered to and, thus, the government may not be compelled to disclose Jencks Act material before trial. . . . Accordingly, neither *Giglio* nor *Bagley* alter the statutory mandate").

26. *See, e.g., Presser,* 844 F.2d at 1283–84 ("so long as the defendant is given impeachment material, even exculpatory impeachment material, in time for use at trial, we fail to see how the Constitution is violated. Any prejudice the defendant may suffer as a result of disclosure of the impeachment evidence during trial can be eliminated by the trial court ordering a recess in the proceedings in order to allow the defendant time to examine the material and decide how to use it."); United States v. Kopituk, 690 F.2d 1289, 1339 n.47 (11th Cir. 1982) ("It has been held that 'when alleged *Brady* material is contained in Jencks Act material, disclosure is generally timely if the government complies with the Jencks Act.'") (citations omitted).

27. *See, e.g.,* United States v. Rodriguez, 496 F.3d 221, 228 n.6 (2d Cir. 2007) ("We recognize that in many instances the Government will have good reason to defer disclosure until the time of the witness's testimony, particularly of material whose only value to the defense is as impeachment of the witness by reference to prior false statements. In some instances, earlier disclosure could put the witness's life in jeopardy, or risk the destruction of evidence. Also at times, the Government does not know until the time of trial whether a potential cooperator will plead guilty and testify for the Government or go to trial as a defendant."); United States v. Pollack, 534 F.2d 964, 973–74 (D.C. Cir. 1976) (noting that there can be "situations in which premature disclosure would unnecessarily encourage those dangers that militate against extensive discovery in criminal cases, *e.g.,* potential for manufacture of defense evidence or bribing of witnesses. Courts can do little more in determining the proper timing for disclosure than balance in each case the potential dangers of early discovery against the need that *Brady* purports to serve of avoiding wrongful convictions."). *Cf.* United States v. Starusko, 729 F.2d 256, 261 (3d Cir. 1984) ("We recognize that, generally, it is difficult to analyze, prior to trial, whether potential impeachment evidence falls within *Brady* without knowing what role a certain witness will play in the government's case.").

there may or may not be a conflict between their respective timing requirements. "All Jencks Act statements are not necessarily *Brady* material. The Jencks Act requires that any statement in the possession of the government—exculpatory or not—that is made by a government witness must be produced by the government during trial at the time specified by the statute. *Brady* material is not limited to *statements* of witnesses but is defined as exculpatory *material*; the precise time within which the government must produce such material is not limited by specific statutory language but is governed by existing case law. Definitions of the two types of investigatory reports differ, the timing of production differs, and compliance with the statutory requirements of the Jencks Act does not necessarily satisfy the due process concerns of *Brady*." *Starusko*, 729 F.2d at 263 (emphasis in original).[28]

5. Supervisory authority of district court

"[I]t must be remembered that *Brady* is a constitutional mandate. It exacts the *minimum* that the prosecutor, state or federal, must do" to avoid violating a defendant's due process rights. *United States v. Beasley*, 576 F.2d 626, 630 (5th Cir. 1978) (emphasis added). As it is not otherwise specified by rule or case law, district courts have the discretionary authority "to dictate by court order when *Brady* material must be disclosed." *Starusko*, 729 F.2d at 261 ("the district court has general discretionary authority to order the pretrial disclosure of *Brady* material 'to ensure the effective administration of the criminal justice system.'") (citation omitted).[29] Some districts have done

---

28. *See also Rodriguez*, 496 F.3d at 224–26 (oral statements by witness that were never written down or recorded did not fall under Jencks Act but could be disclosable under *Brady/Giglio*: "The Jencks Act requires the Government to produce to the defendant any 'statement' by the witness that 'relates to the subject matter as to which the witness has testified.' 18 U.S.C. § 3500(b); *see id.* § 3500(e) (defining 'statement'). The term 'statement,' however, is defined to include only statements that have been memorialized in some concrete form, whether in a written document or electrical recording. . . . The obligation to disclose information covered by the *Brady* and *Giglio* rules exists without regard to whether that information has been recorded in tangible form."); United States v. Phibbs, 999 F.2d 1053, 1088 (6th Cir. 1993) ("Unlike the Jencks Act, the force of *Brady* and its progeny is not limited to the statements and reports of witnesses."). *Cf.* United States v. Coppa, 267 F.3d 132, 146 (2d Cir. 2001) ("a District Court's power to order pretrial disclosure is constrained by the Jencks Act," and the district court exceeded its authority in ordering disclosure "of not only those witness statements that fall within the ambit of *Brady/Giglio*, and thus may be required to be produced in advance of trial despite the Jencks Act, but also those witness statements that, although they might indeed contain impeachment evidence, do not rise to the level of materiality prescribed by *Agurs* and *Bagley* for mandated production").

29. *See generally* United States v. Hasting, 461 U.S. 499, 505 (1983) ("[I]n the exercise of supervisory powers, federal courts may, within limits, formulate procedural rules not specifically required by the Constitution or the Congress. The purposes underlying use of the supervisory powers are threefold: to implement a remedy for violation of recognized rights . . . ; to preserve judicial integrity by ensuring that a conviction rests on appropriate considerations validly before the jury . . . ; and finally, as a remedy designed to deter illegal con-

this through local rules, setting pretrial deadlines for disclosure of *Brady* and *Giglio* material.[30] Otherwise, "[h]ow the trial court proceeds to enforce disclosure requirements is largely a matter of discretion to be exercised in light of the facts of each case." *United States v. Valera*, 845 F.2d 923, 927 (11th Cir. 1988).[31]

D. Disputed disclosure

If a defendant requests disclosure of materials that the government contends are not discoverable under *Brady*, the trial court may conduct an in camera review of the disputed materials.[32] "To justify such a review, the defendant must make some showing that the materials in question could contain favorable, material evidence. ... This showing cannot consist of mere speculation. ... Rather, the defendant should be able to articulate with some specificity what evidence he hopes to find in the requested materials, why he thinks the materials contain this evidence, and finally, why this evidence would be both favorable to him and material."[33]

---

duct.") (citations omitted); United States v. W.R. Grace, 526 F.3d 499, 508–09 (9th Cir. 2008) (en banc) ("We begin with the principle that the district court is charged with effectuating the speedy and orderly administration of justice. There is universal acceptance in the federal courts that, in carrying out this mandate, a district court has the authority to enter pretrial case management and discovery orders designed to ensure that the relevant issues to be tried are identified, that the parties have an opportunity to engage in appropriate discovery and that the parties are adequately and timely prepared so that the trial can proceed efficiently and intelligibly"). *See also* Fed. R. Crim. P. 57(b) ("Procedure when there is no controlling law: A judge may regulate practice in any manner consistent with federal law, these rules, and the local rules of the district.").

30. *See* discussion of local rules in Laural Hooper et al., Fed. Judicial Ctr., A Summary of Responses to a National Survey of Rule 16 of the Federal Rules of Criminal Procedure and Disclosure Practices in Criminal Cases 11–18 (2011).

31. *See also* United States v. Caro-Muniz, 406 F.3d 22, 29 (1st Cir. 2005) ("methods of enforcing disclosure requirements in criminal trials are generally left to the discretion of the trial court"); United States v. Runyan, 290 F.3d 223, 245 (5th Cir. 2002) (same); United States v. Campagnuolo, 592 F.2d 852, 857 n.2 (5th Cir. 1979) ("The government argues that it was not required to follow certain provisions of . . . the standing discovery order because those provisions were broader in scope than the requirements adopted by the Supreme Court in *Brady*. This argument is without merit. It is within the sound discretion of the district judge to make any discovery order that is not barred by higher authority.").

32. *See, e.g.,* United States v. Prochilo, 629 F.3d 264, 268 (1st Cir. 2011).

33. *Id.* at 268–69 (citing Pennsylvania v. Ritchie, 480 U.S. 39, 58 n.15 (1987)). *See also* Riley v. Taylor, 277 F.3d 261, 301 (3d Cir. 2001) ("A defendant seeking an in camera inspection to determine whether files contain *Brady* material must at least make a 'plausible showing' that the inspection will reveal material evidence. ... Mere speculation is not enough."); United States v. Lowder, 148 F.3d 548, 551 (5th Cir. 1998) (same); Love v. Johnson, 57 F.3d 1305, 1313 (4th Cir. 1995) (same); United States v. Navarro, 737 F.2d 625, 631 (7th Cir. 1984) ("Mere speculation that a government file may contain *Brady* material is not sufficient to require a remand for *in camera* inspection, much less reversal for a new trial. A due

E. Protective orders

For good cause, such as considerations of witness safety or national security, a trial judge may fashion an appropriate protective order to the extent necessary in a particular case, consistent with the defendant's constitutional rights. *See, e.g., United States v. Williams Companies, Inc.*, 562 F.3d 387, 396 (D.C. Cir. 2009) (discussing balancing of "the prosecution's affirmative duty to disclose material evidence 'favorable to an accused,'" Rule 16(d)(1)'s provision that, "'for good cause,' the district court may 'deny, restrict, or defer discovery or inspection or grant other appropriate relief,'" and defendant's right to fair trial). *See also* the Classified Information Procedures Act, 18 U.S.C. App. 3, for procedures regarding protective orders for classified information.

F. Summary

This section of the *Benchbook* is meant to provide a general guide to the *Brady* line of case law. Every case is different, however, and presents its own particular facts and circumstances that will affect the types of *Brady/Giglio* disclosure issues (if any) that may arise and how such issues may be handled most appropriately. Ideally, both prosecutors and defense attorneys will know and fulfill their respective responsibilities without significant judicial intervention. However, even if things appear to be going smoothly, a judge may want to monitor the situation, perhaps using status conferences to ask if information is being fully and timely exchanged. A district's particular legal culture is important. In districts where there is a history of poor cooperation between prosecutors and the defense bar, judges may need to take a more active role in ensuring *Brady* compliance than they might in districts where there is an "open file" discovery policy and a history of trust. A district's local rules or standing orders also may provide specific rules for handling disclosure.

---

process standard which is satisfied by mere speculation would convert *Brady* into a discovery device and impose an undue burden upon the district court.").

Appendix A. FJC survey

The Federal Judicial Center recently conducted a comprehensive review of *Brady* practices in federal courts, surveying "all federal district and magistrate judges, U.S. Attorneys' Offices, and federal defenders, and a sample of defense attorneys in criminal cases that terminated during calendar year 2009. The surveys collected empirical data on whether to amend Rule 16 and collected views regarding issues, concerns, or problems surrounding pretrial discovery and disclosure in the federal district courts." Laural Hooper et al., Federal Judicial Center, A Summary of Responses to a National Survey of Rule 16 of the Federal Rules of Criminal Procedure and Disclosure Practices in Criminal Cases 7 (2011).

In addition to the survey results, the FJC report contains an analysis of district court rules and standing orders that cover disclosure requirements under *Brady* and *Giglio*. A separate appendix reprints the rules and orders from thirty-eight districts. The rules range from basic reiterations of *Brady* and *Giglio* to very detailed instructions and deadlines. The report and the appendices can be accessed at http://cwn.fjc.dcn/fjconline/home.nsf/pages/1356.

Appendix B. Justice Department policies and guidance

Two documents set forth the current criminal discovery policies of the Department of Justice. The first is Section 9-5.001 of the *United States Attorney's Manual*, titled "Policy Regarding Disclosure of Exculpatory and Impeachment Information" (as updated June 10, 2010), which largely follows established case law in outlining a prosecutor's responsibilities to disclose exculpatory information, though in some instances it goes beyond what is required. It can be accessed at http://www.justice.gov/usao/eousa/foia_reading_room/usam/title9/5mcrm.htm#9-5.001.

The second document is a memorandum issued by Deputy Attorney General David Ogden on January 4, 2010, which provides "Guidance for Prosecutors Regarding Criminal Discovery." It goes beyond *Brady* and *Giglio* and also outlines a prosecutor's obligations under Rules 16 and 26.2, as well as the Jencks Act, 18 U.S.C. § 3500. Usually called "The Ogden Memorandum," it is "intended to assist Department prosecutors to understand their obligations and to manage the discovery process" and can be found at http://www.justice.gov/usao/eousa/foia_reading_room/usam/title9/crm00165.htm.

Note that these documents are internal policy guidelines. They do not, as the "Policy" states, "provide defendants with any additional rights or remedies," and they are "not intended to have the force of law or to create or confer any rights, privileges, or benefits." While it may be useful to know what information prosecutors are gathering and should be disclosing, these guidelines are not legal obligations to be enforced by a court. Unlike a violation of *Brady* or *Giglio*, a failure to follow Justice Department policies is not by itself a basis for a trial judge to impose sanctions, exclude evidence, or declare a mistrial, or for an appellate court to reverse a conviction.

Appendix C. Potential *Brady* or *Giglio* information

The following is a list of the types of material that may be discoverable under *Brady* or *Giglio*. The examples are culled from case law, district court local rules, and Department of Justice guidelines for prosecutors. Citations from Supreme Court and appellate cases are provided to assist judges who may be faced with similar situations. The list is not exhaustive, and whether the disclosure of any item is or is not required must be determined in light of the specific facts and circumstances of each case.

1. Exculpatory information under Brady

(a) information that is inconsistent with any element of any crime charged in the indictment or that tends to negate the defendant's guilt of any of the crimes charged

Brady v. Maryland, 373 U.S. 83, 84 (1963) (confession by codefendant); *Finley v. Johnson,* 243 F.3d 215, 221–22 (5th Cir. 2001) (affirmative defense: necessity); *United States v. Udechukwu,* 11 F.3d 1101, 1106 (1st Cir. 1993) (prosecution had independently corroborated information that would have strengthened defendant's credibility in claiming duress); *United States v. Spagnoulo,* 960 F.2d 990, 993–95 (11th Cir. 1992) (psychiatric evaluation done during pretrial detention could have strengthened insanity defense).

(b) failure of any person who participated in an identification procedure to make a positive identification of the defendant, whether or not the government anticipates calling the person as a witness at trial

Smith v. Cain, 132 S. Ct. 627, 629–30 (2012) (the only eyewitness told police on night of murder and a few days later that he could not make an identification); *Kyles v. Whitley,* 514 U.S. 419, 423–25 (1995) (six eyewitness statements contained physical details that were inconsistent with defendant and more closely resembled state's key witness).

(c) any information that links someone other than the defendant to the crime (e.g., a positive identification of someone other than the defendant)

DiSimone v. Phillips, 461 F.3d 181, 195 (2d Cir. 2006) (evidence that another person confessed to stabbing the victim); *Monroe v. Angelone,* 323 F.3d 286, 313, 316 n.20 (4th Cir. 2003) (undisclosed evidence that car driven by someone other than defendant was seen speeding away from murder scene); *United States v. Robinson,* 39 F.3d 1115, 1116–19 (10th Cir. 1994) (description by eyewitness of person who picked up cocaine closely matched another witness rather than defendant).

(d) information that casts doubt on the accuracy of any evidence—including witness testimony—that the prosecutor intends to rely on to prove an element of any of the crimes charged in the indictment, or that might have a significant bearing on the admissibility of that evidence in the case-in-chief

United States v. Triumph Capital Group, Inc., 544 F.3d 149, 162–65 (2d Cir. 2008) (suppressed notes of FBI agent cast doubt on whether defendant had intent to commit offense); *Benn v. Lambert*, 283 F.3d 1040, 1060–62 (9th Cir. 2002) (investigative report concluding that fire was accidental and not arson, which prosecution had used as aggravating factor in murder case); *Ballinger v. Kerby*, 3 F.3d 1371, 1376 (10th Cir. 1993) (undisclosed photograph most likely would have "destroyed" credibility of key prosecution witness); *United States ex rel. Smith v. Fairman*, 769 F.2d 386, 391 (7th Cir. 1985) (evidence that the gun defendant allegedly fired at police was inoperable).

(e) any classified or otherwise sensitive national security material disclosed to defense counsel or made available to the court in camera that tends directly to negate the defendant's guilt

United States v. Amawi, 695 F.3d 457, 471 (6th Cir. 2012) (standard for discovery under Classified Information Procedures Act is whether evidence is "relevant and helpful" to defense, not *Brady*'s stricter materiality standard); *United States v. Mejia*, 448 F.3d 436, 456–57 (D.C. Cir. 2006) (same). *See also United States v. Aref*, 533 F.3d 72, 79–80 (2d Cir. 2008) (classified information must be "relevant and helpful," interpreted by the court as "material to the defense," but to be "helpful or material to the defense, evidence need not rise to the level that would trigger the Government's obligation under *Brady*"; information can be "helpful" without being "'favorable' in the *Brady* sense").

(f) any information favorable and material to the defendant in the sentencing phase

Brady v. Maryland, 373 U.S. 83, 85–86 (1963) (defendant's sentence of death could have been affected by codefendant's admission that he, rather than defendant, committed actual killing during robbery); *Cone v. Bell*, 556 U.S. 449, 474–75 (2009) (death sentence could have been affected by evidence that defendant may have been drunk or high when committing murders); *United States v. Weintraub*, 871 F.2d 1257, 1261–65 (5th Cir. 1989) (prior inconsistent statement by key witness describing lower amount of drugs sold by defendant that could affect his sentence).

2. *Impeachment information under* Giglio

(a) all statements made orally or in writing by any witness the prosecution intends to call in its case-in-chief that are inconsistent with other statements made by that same witness

Strickler v. Greene, 527 U.S. 263, 282 (1999) (undisclosed witness statements inconsistent with trial testimony); *Kyles v. Whitley,* 514 U.S. 419, 441–46 (1995) (same); *Youngblood v. West Virginia,* 547 U.S. 867, 868–70 (2006) (per curiam) (note written by two victim witnesses that contradicted testimony).

(b) all plea agreements entered into by the government in this case or related cases with any witness the government intends to call

Douglas v. Workman, 560 F.3d 1156, 1174–75 (10th Cir. 2009) (undisclosed deal between prosecutor and key witness); *Silva v. Brown,* 416 F.3d 980, 986–87 (9th Cir. 2005) (as part of his plea deal reducing charges against him and limiting his sentence in return for testifying, one of three murder suspects agreed to refrain from undergoing psychiatric evaluation so as to avoid questions about his mental capacity).

(c) any favorable dispositions of criminal charges pending against witnesses the prosecutor intends to call

Akrawi v. Booker, 572 F.3d 252, 263 (6th Cir. 2009) (informal agreement to reduce charges against witness in different case in return for his testimony against defendant); *Douglas v. Workman,* 560 F.3d 1156, 1166–67 (10th Cir. 2009) (several instances of prosecutor dropping charges in other cases against witness in exchange for testimony against defendant); *Singh v. Prunty,* 142 F.3d 1157, 1162 (9th Cir. 1998) (key witness had several pending charges against him dropped during prosecution of defendant).

(d) offers or promises made or other benefits provided, directly or indirectly, to any witness in exchange for cooperation or testimony, including:

   (1) dismissed or reduced charges

   Wolfe v. Clarke, 691 F.3d 410, 417–18 (4th Cir. 2012) (witness who actually killed drug supplier was told he might have capital murder charges reduced if he testified that defendant drug dealer hired him to do the shooting); *United States v. Smith,* 77 F.3d 511, 513–16 (D.C. Cir. 1996) (key prosecution witness, who was originally charged as codefendant, had other felony charges dismissed); *Blankenship v. Estelle,* 545 F.2d 510, 513–14 (5th Cir. 1977) (promise to drop all charges against two witnesses in exchange for testimony against defendant);

(2) immunity or offers of immunity

Horton v. Mayle, 408 F.3d 570, 578–81 (9th Cir. 2005) (alleged promise of immunity to key witness); *Haber v. Wainwright*, 756 F.2d 1520, 1523 (11th Cir. 1985) (alleged promise by state attorney to grant immunity from prosecution on numerous prior offenses in exchange for testimony);

(3) expectations of downward departures or reduction of sentence

Douglas v. Workman, 560 F.3d 1156, 1174–75 (10th Cir. 2009) (assistance to key witness with pre-parole release and reinstatement of lost good-time credits); *Tassin v. Cain*, 517 F.3d 770, 778–79 (5th Cir. 2008) (key witness led to believe she would receive reduced sentence in her case if she testified against husband in his case); *Reutter v. Solem*, 888 F.2d 578, 581–82 (8th Cir. 1989) (state's key witness was scheduled to go before parole board—of which prosecutor was a member—seeking a sentence commutation just a few days after he was to testify against defendant); *United States v. Gerard*, 491 F.2d 1300, 1303–04 (9th Cir. 1974) (promise to testifying codefendant, who earlier pled guilty, to recommend probation);

(4) assistance in other criminal proceedings—federal, state, or local

Bell v. Bell, 512 F.3d 223, 233 (6th Cir. 2008) (district attorney's office dropped four pending charges after witness met with prosecutor with offer to testify); *United States v. Risha*, 445 F.3d 298, 299–302 (3d Cir. 2006) (key witness expected, and later received, "an extremely favorable plea agreement" on unrelated state charges); *Benn v. Lambert*, 283 F.3d 1040, 1057 (9th Cir. 2002) (prosecutor arranged for informant to be released without being charged after stop for traffic offense led to arrest on outstanding warrants);

(5) considerations regarding forfeiture of assets, forbearance in seeking revocation of professional licenses or public benefits, waiver of tax liability, or promises not to suspend or debar a government contractor

United States v. Shaffer, 789 F.2d 682, 688–89 (9th Cir. 1986) (government's failure to initiate asset forfeiture proceedings or enforce civil liability for unpaid taxes related to key witness's former drug dealing indicated leniency in return for cooperation);

(6) stays of deportation or other immigration benefits

United States v. Blanco, 392 F.3d 382 (9th Cir. 2004) (undocumented alien working as paid confidential informant was given "special parole visa through INS" in return for cooperation with DEA); *United States v. Sipe*, 388 F.3d 471, 488–89 (5th Cir. 2004) (while waiting to testify against defendant, illegal aliens who were caught trying to enter the United States received "significant benefits, including Social

Security cards, witness fees, permits allowing travel to and from Mexico, travel expenses, living expenses, some phone expenses, and other benefits");

(7) monetary or other benefits, paid or promised

United States v. Bagley, 473 U.S. 667, 683–84 (1985) (payments to witnesses for assistance in undercover drug operation and testimony in court); *Robinson v. Mills,* 592 F.3d 730, 737–38 (6th Cir. 2010) (witness who provided the only evidence contradicting defendant's self-defense claim worked as paid confidential informant for local authorities before and after defendant's trial); *United States v. Boyd,* 55 F.3d 239, 244–45 (7th Cir. 1995) (witness gang members "received a continuous stream of unlawful, indeed scandalous, favors from staff at the U.S. Attorney's office while jailed [and] awaiting the trial of the defendants," including lax supervision that allowed drug use and drug dealing, long distance telephone calls, and sexual contact with visitors); *United States v. Librach,* 520 F.2d 550, 553 (8th Cir. 1975) ("Government's failure to disclose protective custody and its substantial payment of almost $10,000 to" primary witness). *Cf. Wilson v. Beard,* 589 F.3d 651, 662 (3d Cir. 2009) (officer "loaned money, interest free, to [witness] during the time period when [witness] acted as a police informant");

(8) non-prosecution agreements

Giglio v. United States, 405 U.S. 150, 152–55 (1972) (promise to key witness—and alleged coconspirator—that he would not be prosecuted if he testified against defendant); *Monroe v. Angelone,* 323 F.3d 286, 312–14 (4th Cir. 2003) (prosecution promised not to prosecute key witness—a convicted felon—for possession of a firearm); *United States v. Sanfilippo,* 564 F.2d 176, 177–79 (5th Cir. 1977) (witness was promised he would not be prosecuted in a separate case if he testified);

(9) letters to other law enforcement officials setting forth the extent of a witness's assistance or making recommendations on the witness's behalf

Jackson v. Brown, 513 F.3d 1057, 1070–72 (9th Cir. 2008) (law enforcement personnel promised prisoner-witness to bring his cooperation to attention of judges and prosecutors in other cases to help him get reduced sentences); *United States v. Bigeleisen,* 625 F.2d 203, 208 (8th Cir. 1980) (in exchange for testimony, government agreed to write letter to Parole Commission outlining cooperation of witness who was imprisoned for other offense);

(10) relocation assistance or more favorable conditions of confinement

Quezada v. Scribner, 611 F.3d 1165, 1168–69 (9th Cir. 2010) (question whether relocation payments witness received were sufficient to warrant evidentiary hearing for *Brady* violation); *Jackson v. Brown,* 513 F.3d 1057, 1070–71 (9th Cir. 2008) (promise to recommend that witness be allowed to serve California sentence in Arizona to be closer to his family); *Bell v. Bell,* 512 F.3d 223, 232–33 (6th Cir. 2008) (in exchange for testifying, witness who was in jail for other offenses sought placement in different building and participation in work-release program). *Cf. United States v. Talley,* 164 F.3d 989, 1003 (6th Cir. 1999) (where witness "was the government's key witness and his credibility was at issue throughout the trial, failure to disclose a relocation benefit to the jury would have violated the rule set forth in *Giglio*");

(11) consideration or benefits to culpable or at-risk third parties

LaCaze v. Warden Louisiana Correctional Institute for Women, 645 F.3d 728, 735–36 (5th Cir.) (before admitting to shooting victim and implicating defendant, witness received assurances from prosecutor that his 14-year-old son would not be prosecuted), *opinion amended on denial of reh'g en banc,* 647 F.3d 1175 (2011); *Harris v. Lafler,* 553 F.3d 1028, 1033–35 (6th Cir. 2009) (key witness was promised his girlfriend would be released from custody if he incriminated defendant). *Cf. Graves v. Dretke,* 442 F.3d 334, 342–44 (5th Cir. 2006) (prosecution did not reveal that the key witness—himself a possible suspect in murder case—tried to protect his wife from prosecution but had earlier made statement that she was present during crime).

(e) prior convictions of witnesses the prosecutor intends to call

United States v. Bernal-Obeso, 989 F.2d 331, 332–33 (9th Cir. 1993) (misinformation about criminal record of key government witness who was confidential informant); *Ouimette v. Moran,* 942 F.2d 1, 10–11 (1st Cir. 1991) (prosecution failed to disclose main witness's numerous convictions and deals he made with prosecution to testify); *United States v. Auten,* 632 F.2d 478 (5th Cir. 1980) (codefendant granted immunity for testimony had prior criminal record).

(f) pending criminal charges against any witness known to the government

Sivak v. Hardison, 658 F.3d 898, 909–11 (9th Cir. 2011) (letters to other county prosecutor urging dismissal of pending charge against witness); *United States v. Kohring,* 637 F.3d 895, 903–04 (9th Cir. 2010) (key witness faced charges of sexual misconduct with minor); *Cargall v. Mullin,* 317 F.3d 1196, 1215–16 (10th Cir. 2003) ("forbearance on potential charges . . . to secure the cooperation of a witness" must be disclosed to defense).

(g) prior specific instances of conduct by any witness known to the government that could be used to impeach the witness under Rule 608 of the
Federal Rules of Evidence, including any finding of misconduct that reflects upon truthfulness

United States v. Kohring, 637 F.3d 895, 906 (9th Cir. 2010) (alleged attempts by key witness to suborn perjurious testimony in different case);
United States v. Torres, 569 F.3d 1277, 1282–83 (10th Cir. 2009) (evidence
that confidential informant breached prior agreement with DEA and
continued to use illegal drugs despite testifying that she had stopped);
United States v. Velarde, 485 F.3d 553, 561–63 (10th Cir. 2007) (information that victim had made false accusations of similar nature); *Benn v.
Lambert,* 283 F.3d 1040, 1054–56 (9th Cir. 2002) (informant's history of
committing crimes and "regularly" lying while acting as informant);
United States v. O'Conner, 64 F.3d 355, 357–59 (8th Cir. 1995) (per curiam)
(two witnesses attempted to influence testimony of another witness by
threatening him and his family).

(h) substance abuse, mental health issues, or physical or other impairments
known to the government that could affect any witness's ability to per-
ceive and recall events

Gonzalez v. Wong, 667 F.3d 965, 983–84 (9th Cir. 2011) (medical reports
indicating "jailhouse informant" witness was schizophrenic and had history of lying); *Wilson v. Beard,* 589 F.3d 651, 660–62 (3d Cir. 2009) (government witness's history of severe mental problems which showed witness was prescribed psychotropic drugs during relevant time period;
another witness also had undisclosed mental issues); *Benn v. Lambert,*
283 F.3d 1040, 1056 (9th Cir. 2002) (evidence that key witness was using
drugs during trial).

(i) information known to the government that could affect any witness's
bias, such as:

(1) animosity toward the defendant

United States v. Aviles-Colon, 536 F.3d 1, 19–21 (1st Cir. 2008) (evidence that defendant and codefendant were "at war" would have
advanced defendant's claim that he was not part of charged drug
conspiracy); *United States v. Sipe,* 388 F.3d 471, 477 (9th Cir. 2004)
(evidence not revealed until presentence report that key witness
"personally disliked" defendant). *Cf. Schledwitz v. United States,* 169
F.3d 1003, 1014–15 (6th Cir. 1999) (key witness, portrayed as "neutral
and disinterested expert" during petitioner's fraud prosecution, actually had for years been actively involved in investigating petitioner
and interviewing witnesses against him); *United States v. Steinberg,*
99 F.3d 1486, 1491 (9th Cir. 1996) (informant, who was key witness,

owed defendant money, thus giving him incentive to send defendant to prison).

(2) previous relationship with law enforcement authorities

Robinson v. Mills, 592 F.3d 730, 737 (6th Cir. 2010) (key government witness worked as paid informant in other criminal cases before and after defendant's trial); *United States v. Torres*, 569 F.3d 1277, 1282–83 (10th Cir. 2009) (two prior undisclosed contracts between confidential informant witness and DEA); *United States v. Shaffer*, 789 F.2d 682, 688–89 (9th Cir. 1986) (key witness was informant for government in earlier, different drug investigation).

(j) Prosecutorial misconduct

United States v. Scheer, 168 F.3d 445, 449–53 (11th Cir. 1999) (threatening remark by prosecutor to "critical" prosecution witness who was on probation that if he did not "come through for us" he would be sent back to jail); *United States v. Alzate*, 47 F.3d 1103, 1110 (11th Cir. 1995) (prosecutor failed to correct representations he made to jury which were damaging to defendant's duress defense, despite learning before trial ended that they were actually false); *United States v. Kojayan*, 8 F.3d 1315, 1318–19 (9th Cir. 1993) (prosecution refused to reveal that a witness it chose not to call had signed a cooperation agreement to testify truthfully if requested and instead falsely claimed at trial that witness had invoked Fifth Amendment right to refuse to testify). *Cf. Douglas v. Workman*, 560 F.3d 1156, 1192–94 (10th Cir. 2009) (prosecutor's "active concealment" of *Brady* violation that prevented defendant from presenting claim in timely fashion warranted allowing claim as a second or successive request for habeas relief).

6.01   Civil case management

Fed. R. Civ. P. 16 and 26

Introduction

This section is designed to provide guidance for managing both simple and complex civil cases. It includes actions that are required by rule along with factors to consider, alternative methods, and recommendations that experienced judges have found to be helpful. Not all of the recommendations given will be appropriate for every case, and judges should tailor the advice to the case at hand. Also, a district's local rules may recommend or require a different practice or procedure, or even use different terminology.

Magistrate judges routinely handle many of the pretrial functions referred to below (see *infra* section II), and the term "judge" is meant to include both district and magistrate judges.

I.   The judge's role

The Civil Rules contemplate that the judge will be an active case manager. The rules apply across case types and sizes, but different cases have different pretrial needs. Some cases may require extensive discovery and motions practice, while others may involve little or no discovery or pretrial motions. The Civil Rules provide a flexible template to be tailored to the needs of each case.

The judge and the parties share case-management responsibility. The parties exercise first-level control and are the principal managers of their cases, but they do so under a schedule and other limits established by the judge. Many parties will not manage, or will manage in ways that are disproportionate to the needs of the case, or will otherwise frustrate the just, speedy, and inexpensive determination of the action. Judges may meet their own responsibility for the efficient resolution of cases both by guiding the parties to sound self-management and by intervening to impose effective management when necessary.

Active judicial case management is an essential part of the civil pretrial process. No party has the right to impose disproportionate or unnecessary costs on the court or the other side. Many parties and lawyers want and welcome active judicial case management, viewing it as key to controlling unnecessary cost and delay.

Active case management does involve additional judge time at the start of the case, but it pays valuable dividends. It ensures that the case will proceed under an efficient but reasonable schedule, that time and expense will not be wasted on unnecessary discovery or motions practice, and that court and lawyer time will be devoted to the issues most important to the resolution of the case. When lawyers know the judge will be managing them, they are more likely to engage in sound self-management. Early attention to case management may also identify potential problems before they arise or address them before they worsen. Active case management promotes justice by focusing the parties and the court on what is truly in dispute and by reducing undue cost and delay.

There are three stages of pretrial case management:

1. activities before the Rule 16 conference and/or order;

2. holding a Rule 16 case-management conference and issuing a case-management order; and

3. ongoing case management.

II. Initial case management (pre-Rule 16 conference)

The Rule 16 case-management conference between the lawyers and the judge is the primary opportunity for the judge to assess the pretrial needs of the case in time to craft an appropriately tailored case-management order. The effectiveness of the Rule 16 conference depends in large part on the information the parties provide. Rule 26(f) requires the parties to confer and prepare a discovery planning report to use in the Rule 16 conference with the court. The judge can take steps to promote the parties' effective use of Rule 26(f).

A. Rule 26(f) discovery planning conference and report

1. Fed. R. Civ. P. 26(f) requires the parties to confer at least 21 days before the scheduling conference is to be held or a scheduling order is due under Rule 16(b), except in proceedings exempted from the Rule 26(a)(1)(B) initial disclosures or when the court orders otherwise.

2. The parties must, among other things, consider the nature and basis of their claims, discuss their expected discovery needs, and make a good-faith effort to agree on a proposed discovery plan, which they must submit to the court within 14 days.

3. The Rule 26(f) conference and report serve two purposes. One is to have the parties discuss discovery before engaging in it, to prevent a "shoot first, ask questions later" approach. The second is to generate information for the court to consider at the Rule 16 conference in determining the reasonable pretrial needs of the case.

B. Initial case-management orders (pre-Rule 16 conference)

1. Too often, the lawyers' Rule 26(f) conferences are perfunctory. As a result, the reports supply little useful information to the court. To improve the quality of the Rule 26(f) process, some judges issue initial case-management orders that spell out the topics the judge expects the parties to discuss at their Rule 26(f) conferences and address in their Rule 26(f) report. The order can also make clear that the judge will be asking about these topics at the Rule 16 case-management conference, creating an incentive for the lawyers to carry out their Rule 26(f) obligations responsibly.

2. Consider issuing an order (or developing case-management guidelines) that structures the parties' initial planning activities in order to facilitate an effective and efficient case-management conference with you later. The order or guidelines can be a standardized form issued by your staff when the Rule 16 case-management conference is scheduled.

3. Consider reminding the parties that Rule 26(f) requires them to discuss issues relating to discovery of electronically stored information and advising them that you will ask about such issues at the Rule 16(b) case-management conference.

4. Consider reminding the parties that Rule 26(b) and (g) require their discovery activities to be proportional to the needs of the case and that you will ask about proportionality at the Rule 16(b) case-management conference.

C. Supplementing the Rule 26(f) agenda for the parties

1. Your order or guidelines can also direct the parties to discuss at their Rule 26(f) conference matters that go beyond those listed in Rule 26(f), and to address those matters in their Rule 26(f) report or in a separate pre-Rule 16 conference submission. A district's local rules may have specific requirements for the conference.

2. Possible topics—for discussion or report or both—could be anything that will aid in your assessing and managing the case, including

   (a) the basis for federal-court subject-matter jurisdiction;

   (b) a brief description of the facts and issues in the case;

   (c) the status of any initial settlement discussions or a statement of whether the parties will engage in initial settlement discussions; and

   (d) any other case-management topics listed in Rule 16(c)(2).

3. One factor to consider is that supplemental discussions or supplemental pre-Rule 16 conference reports will increase the parties' upfront costs and burdens of litigation. While some judges effectively

use supplemental submissions, other judges prefer to raise these topics at the Rule 16(b) conference if appropriate for the case. Each judge must determine how best to balance the costs and benefits of additional pre-Rule 16 conference requirements in different types of cases.

III. Rule 16 case-management conferences and orders

Before issuing a scheduling order, most judges find it advisable to hold a case-management conference with the lawyers—and sometimes the parties—to learn more about the case. The exchange with the lawyers, preferably face-to-face but by telephonic conference if circumstances require, is usually much more valuable for the court and the lawyers than just reviewing the parties' report. The exchange provides the court with the information it needs to develop a scheduling order or case-management order that is tailored to the needs of the case. The Rule 26(f) report, even when well done, is typically no substitute for a live dialogue in which a judge asks questions, probes behind the parties' representations, and fills in gaps.

A tailored case-management order can address several critical areas:

1. the issues to be resolved and the best methods for resolving them in a timely and efficient manner;
2. the scope of discovery, the best methods for the timely and cost-effective exchange of information, and limits on the amount and type of discovery allowed in the case;
3. procedures the parties must follow in the case, such as procedures for obtaining the court's assistance in resolving discovery disputes;
4. whether and when the parties might participate in processes designed to facilitate settlement; and
5. a schedule for the topics addressed below.

A. Rule 16(b) minimum requirements

1. The district judge—or a magistrate judge when authorized by local rule—must issue a basic scheduling order in every civil case unless it is in a category of cases exempted by local rule.
2. The basic scheduling order must set four deadlines:
    (a) to join new parties;
    (b) to amend the pleadings;
    (c) to complete discovery; and
    (d) to file motions.
3. The judge must issue the scheduling order as soon as practicable, but in any event within 120 days after any defendant has been served or 90 days after any defendant has appeared, whichever occurs earlier.

B. Rule 16(b) case-management orders; case-management conferences

1. *Scope.* Most judges issue orders that go well beyond the minimum basic deadlines required by Rule 16(b). A Rule 16(b) order that provides extensive case management may be styled as a scheduling order; the label used is not controlling.

2. *Format.* As noted earlier, most judges hold a Rule 16 conference with the lawyers, either face-to-face or by conference call, to learn about the case in order to issue a scheduling order/case-management order tailored to the case. In some cases, it will be clear in advance that such a conference is not necessary. In some categories of suits, the pretrial needs do not vary by case. In that event, the court can issue a scheduling order based on established practice as informed by the parties' Rule 26(f) submissions. In general, however, it is better to hold a case-management conference, either in person or by telephone, even if the parties agree on deadlines and no motions are pending. The conference often reveals information and issues not apparent to the parties or the judge in the submissions. That information and those issues are often important in preparing a tailored case-management order.

3. *Length.* The length of the conference will depend on the complexity of the case and the scope of the matters to be addressed. In many cases, 20 to 30 minutes should be adequate to explore the matters discussed below. More complicated cases will probably require more time. Cases that might seem simple and organized often turn out to have unforeseen complications and call for a longer conference to get them on a productive and efficient path. Allotting enough time for every conference maximizes the benefits of early case management.

4. *Judge participation.* The judge who is conducting the pretrial activities should lead the conference.

5. *Party participation.* Consider whether represented parties should be present at the case-management conference. Having the parties present can make it easier to identify the issues and can greatly add to a meaningful discussion of the litigation costs and the importance of limiting pretrial work to what is reasonable and proportional to the case. Note that some districts have a local rule that requires the parties to meet and discuss settlement or ADR before the pretrial conference.

C. Addressing merits issues

1. *Narrowing the issues.* The pleadings often fail to clearly identify what claims or defenses—or elements of claims or defenses—are genuinely in dispute. The case-management conference is an ideal time

to probe the parties' contentions to determine what issues actually need to be resolved.

2. *Initial disclosures.* Because initial disclosures are required in most cases, it is useful to ask counsel whether initial disclosures have been exchanged and, if not, include that in the scheduling order.

3. *Motions to dismiss.* The case-management conference is an important opportunity to address any pending motions to dismiss and determine whether the plaintiff intends to file an amended complaint that might moot the need to resolve a pending motion. Consider discussing with counsel other ways of limiting dismissal motions and whether it may be better to address the issues by summary judgment than by pleading challenges. For example, if a party wishes to raise a statute of limitations issue, it may be better to address that in a summary judgment motion after some discovery rather than by a motion to dismiss.[1]

4. *Staging motions.* Explore whether there are any threshold issues that should be resolved first. Where appropriate, phase the pretrial process (including discovery) so that critical or case-dispositive threshold issues are resolved before the parties begin work on other issues.

5. *Stipulations.* Consider asking counsel whether they will stipulate to facts that do not appear to be genuinely contested. Such stipulations can streamline the issues to be resolved and can eliminate the need for costly discovery on uncontested issues.

6. *Experts.* Explore the need for experts. Counsel often say they need experts in cases or on issues but, on examination, it is apparent that experts are neither needed nor appropriate. If experts are needed, deadlines should be included in the case-management order for expert disclosures, reports, and discovery, and for the filing of motions raising *Daubert* challenges under Rule 702 of the Federal Rules of Evidence if those are expected. Such motions should not be deferred until the final pretrial conference.

7. *Class actions.* If the case is styled as a class action, the conference is often the best time to set dates for class certification motions and to establish a process for any certification discovery that may be needed. The conference provides an effective opportunity to explore with counsel the relationship between, and possible overlap of, dis-

---

1. Consider establishing a process for the submission of premotion letters or for premotion conferences before a party can file a motion to dismiss or for summary judgment. Such motions can be expensive and time-consuming for both the parties and the court. Some judges have found that a premotion letter or conference requirement avoids or limits motions to dismiss or for summary judgment without the need for full briefing, or clarifies and focuses the issues for those motions that do proceed to full briefing.

covery on class certification and on the merits, the limits that should be imposed on class-certification discovery, and staging discovery to decide the certification motion before proceeding to other merits discovery.

D. Addressing discovery issues

1. *Managing discovery.* Excessive discovery is one of the chief causes of undue cost and delay in the pretrial process. The case-management conference can help ensure that discovery proceeds fairly and efficiently in light of the needs of the case. Although you should ask the parties what discovery they need and how much time they will need to do it, do not rely solely on what the parties say in the Rule 26(f) discovery plan. Even if the parties agree, that does not guarantee that discovery will be proportional or proceed on a timely basis.

   Remember that parties are not entitled to all discovery that is relevant to the claims and defenses. The judge has a duty to ensure that discovery is proportional to the needs of the case. Under Rule 26(b)(2)(C), the court must limit discovery that would be "unreasonably cumulative or duplicative" or when "the burden or expense of the proposed discovery outweighs its likely benefit, considering the needs of the case, the amount in controversy, the parties' resources, the importance of the issues at stake in the action, and the importance of the discovery in resolving the issues."

2. *Proportionality.* When needed, consider these techniques for imposing proportionality limits on discovery:

   (a) limiting the number of depositions (or their length), interrogatories, document requests, and/or requests for admission;

   (b) identifying whether discovery should initially focus on particular issues that are most important to resolving the case;

   (c) phasing discovery so that the parties initially focus on the sources of information that are most readily available and/or most likely to yield key information. Guide the parties to go after the "low hanging fruit" first;

   (d) limiting the number of custodians and sources of information to be searched;

   (e) delaying contention interrogatories until the end of the case, after discovery is substantially completed; and

   (f) otherwise modifying the type, amount, or timing of discovery to achieve proportionality.

3. *Evidence Rule 502 non-waiver order.* Consider whether to enter a "non-waiver order" under Federal Rule of Evidence 502(d). This order, which does not require party agreement, precludes the assertion of a waiver claim based on production in the litigation. It avoids the

need to litigate whether an inadvertent production was reasonable. By reducing the risk of waiver, the order removes one reason parties conduct exhaustive and expensive preproduction review. Many parties still are not aware of this opportunity for reducing the cost of discovery by reducing privilege review.

4. *Electronic discovery.* Because electronic discovery is often a source of dispute, excessive costs, and delays, it can be important to ask whether the parties have considered any issues on discovery of electronically stored information (ESI). While the parties have a duty to discuss the discovery of ESI at their Rule 26(f) conference and include it in their Rule 26(f) report, experience shows that many lawyers do not.

   If they have not already done so, see if the parties can reach agreement on basic electronic discovery issues, including the following:

   (a) the form in which ESI will be produced (i.e., native format, PDF, paper, etc.). The form of production can affect whether the material produced will include metadata and whether it will be computer searchable;

   (b) whether to limit discovery of ESI to particular sources or custodians, at least as an initial matter (see the "low hanging fruit" principle above); and

   (c) whether to seek agreement on search terms or methods before conducting computer searches to identify responsive materials.

5. *Preservation.* Explore whether the parties have discussed the preservation of discoverable information, especially ESI. See if the parties can reach agreement on what will be preserved. If there are disputes, it is important to resolve them quickly to keep the case on track and avoid spoliation issues later. The principles of reasonableness and proportionality that guide discovery generally apply.

6. *Resolving discovery disputes.* Consider requiring the parties to present discovery disputes informally (e.g., via a telephone conference or a short letter) before allowing the parties to file formal discovery motions and briefs. Many courts have found that they are able to resolve most discovery disputes using these less formal—and considerably less expensive and less time-consuming—methods. These courts do not allow counsel to file motions to compel or for sanctions before getting the judge on the phone (with a court reporter or a tape machine) to discuss the issue. Many courts find that they are able to resolve most discovery disputes over the telephone and that simply being available encourages the parties to resolve many disputes on their own.

7. *Cooperation.* The discovery process is adversarial in the sense that the adversaries make choices about what information to seek and how to seek it. But that does not mean that lawyers cannot cooperate or that they must act in a hostile and contentious manner while conducting discovery. It is helpful to let the parties know that you expect them to be civil, to find ways to streamline the discovery process where possible, and to avoid needless cost and delay.

E. Addressing settlement or other means of alternative dispute resolution

   1. Most courts will ask about the prospects of settlement and whether it would be useful for the parties to have an early settlement conference before the magistrate judge or another adjunct of the court.

   2. Some judges set a deadline in the scheduling order by which parties must engage in face-to-face settlement talks (whether assisted by a neutral or not), and require the parties to file a short status report on settlement talks after the deadline. This may prompt the parties to address settlement sooner than would otherwise occur. However, judges should be attuned to the parties' views on settlement discussions. Sometimes counsel are prepared for early settlement discussion. But at other times, counsel will want to hold off discussing settlement until they have learned more about the case.

   3. Consider discussing whether the parties would be interested in pursuing other forms of alternative dispute resolution, such as early neutral evaluation, private mediation, nonbinding arbitration, or a summary jury trial.

F. Trial date and joint pretrial order

   1. Most courts set a trial date in the scheduling order and try to adhere to it. Empirical data show that setting a firm trial date and sticking to it when possible is one of the best ways to ensure that the case moves forward without undue cost or delay.

   2. Consider whether a simpler and less costly joint pretrial order would suffice for the case. For example, for some cases, it is sufficient to have the parties submit exhibit and witness lists, proposed voir dire questions, and proposed jury instructions.

IV. Ongoing case management

Case management does not end when the case-management order is entered. Not all cases will require active ongoing case management, but many will. It is helpful to make clear up front that you stand prepared to re-engage when needed.

A. Scheduling future conferences

   1. At the initial case-management conference, consider whether to schedule one or more follow-up conferences. These may include in-

terim pretrial conferences to manage discovery and resolve any disputes, schedule deadlines for potential summary judgment motions, or narrow the issues. These may also include a conference at the end of discovery to identify remaining issues, hear oral argument on motions if that would be helpful, and address any problems that presenting proof at trial may raise.

2. In cases with heavy or contentious discovery, some judges schedule a standing discovery conference at set periods (e.g., once a month). This ensures that time is available to address any issues. Experience shows that the lawyers often call shortly before the regularly scheduled conference date to cancel it, as the impending conference date motivates them to resolve the issues on their own.

3. In cases with extensive electronic discovery, the judge and the parties often adopt an iterative approach, in which the parties initially limit discovery to specific sources or custodians, deferring until later the decision whether to pursue further discovery. In cases that follow that approach, it is advisable to schedule a follow-up discovery management conference in advance, subject to cancellation if it is not needed.

4. If you have deferred exploring settlement or other alternative dispute resolution activities until the parties have conducted discovery, it may be advisable to schedule a conference after the initial discovery to reassess the prospects of settlement or other resolution activity.

B. Modifying the litigation schedule

1. In some cases, it may be necessary to modify the schedule set in the initial case-management order. Under Rule 16(b)(4), any modification requires an order and a finding of good cause.

2. Only the judge can modify the case-management order. The parties cannot extend the schedule on their own, even by agreement. It is common for the parties to seek a modification by stipulation, but the stipulation has no force of its own and should not be adopted automatically because of the need to determine whether there is good cause for the proposed modification.

3. Modifying the case-management order requires a good-cause showing. The dominant factor is whether the existing schedule cannot reasonably be met despite the diligence of the party seeking extension. If that party has not been diligent in meeting the schedule, good cause to extend it may be lacking.

4. Effective case management requires holding the parties and their lawyers to reasonable schedules. Parties and lawyers who disregard reasonable deadlines interfere with the "just, speedy, and inexpen-

sive determination of every action and proceeding." Fed. R. Civ. P. 1. When judges adhere to the schedules they have imposed and enforce the good-cause requirement for modification, cases tend to be resolved more efficiently.

C. Addressing issues promptly

1. Addressing disputed issues promptly is the key to capitalizing on early case-management work and keeping the case moving. If the parties contact chambers with an issue, prompt attention—whether by conference call, a quickly scheduled case-management conference, or other means—can help keep the parties and the schedule on track.

2. The way a dispute or motion is decided will often define or limit the pretrial activities to follow. For example, the way a motion for summary judgment is decided might dramatically narrow the issues in the case and therefore affect the scope of discovery. The way a discovery dispute is resolved also affects the cost, burden, and time of discovery. The prompt resolution of motions and disputes that intersect with the management of the case can be critical to reducing costs and delays.

3. Rule 16(f) provides tools for promoting the purposes of Rule 16 and for enforcing the court's case-management order.

V. Final pretrial conference

A. A valuable case-management tool

Rule 16(e) states that a court may hold a final pretrial conference to "formulate a trial plan." While not mandatory, a final pretrial conference is strongly encouraged. It is the judge's primary way to ensure that the lawyers and the parties are prepared to try the case and that the trial starts and ends on time, and to avoid surprises. The final pretrial conference allows the judge, with the parties and counsel, to identify the legal issues that still need to be resolved. It also provides an opportunity to identify and address problems that otherwise might disrupt, delay, or unnecessarily complicate the trial.

B. Scheduling the conference and setting the agenda

1. *Timing and participation.* The purpose of the final pretrial conference is to plan the trial. Rule 16(e) provides that it must be held "as close to the start of trial as is reasonable." Rule 16(e) also addresses who should be in attendance, stating that each party must be represented at the conference by at least one attorney who will conduct the trial, or by the party if unrepresented. Many judges require the attorneys who will take the lead at the trial to be present.

2. *Final pretrial conference orders.* For a final pretrial conference to be effective, the lawyers and parties must prepare in advance. To facili-

tate that, many judges issue final pretrial conference orders that identify the specific steps the lawyers and parties must complete and the documents they must file before the conference. These steps and documents are designed to make the lawyers focus on what is actually needed to try the case. The final pretrial conference order does not have to be one-size-fits-all. The court can tailor or adapt the order to be sure that the steps the lawyers and parties are required to take are appropriate for the case, address the information needed for the trial, and do not unnecessarily increase the expense and burden of trial preparation.

C. Requiring the parties to submit materials before the conference

Most judges require the parties to prepare and submit materials in advance of the final pretrial conference, although specific practices vary both by district and by judge. Some districts have local rules, while others leave the matter to each judge. When local rules exist, they typically still allow for tailoring by the judge who will try the case. The two most important things to decide are what matters the judge wants the parties to address and the form the submissions should take.

1. *Matters to be addressed in the preconference submissions.* The judge may ask the parties to address any matters that will help in planning the trial. The following items illustrate the types of matters judges often ask the parties to address in preconference submissions:

   (a) *Factual issues.* Require the parties to identify the factual issues to be resolved at trial and to provide a brief summary of the party's position on each issue. This requires the parties to think through the trial ahead of time and enables the judge to discuss the nature and length of the trial and resolve issues that may simplify the trial.

   (b) *Legal issues.* Require the parties to identify disputed legal issues that must be resolved in connection with the trial. This prepares the judge to address those issues and, if possible, to decide them before trial.

   (c) *Rule 26(a)(3)(A) disclosures.* Rule 26(a)(3)(A) requires the parties to make pretrial disclosures on three topics. The parties must

      (i) identify their trial witnesses, separately identifying those they expect to present and those they may call if the need arises;

      (ii) designate any witness that will be presented by deposition transcript or videotape; and

      (iii) identify their documents and trial exhibits, separately identifying those they expect to offer and those they may offer if the need arises.

Rule 26(a)(3)(B) provides that these disclosures are due 30 days before trial unless the court sets a different due date. Many judges alter the deadline by ordering the parties to make their disclosures as part of the preconference submissions.

(d) *Marking exhibits.* To ensure that the evidence is ready for trial and to minimize surprises, consider requiring the parties to exchange not only lists of exhibits, but actual copies of exhibits marked for introduction into evidence.

(e) *Objections.* Rule 26(a)(3)(B) requires opposing parties to list objections to the use of a deposition under Rule 32(a), as well as any objection—together with the grounds for it—to the admissibility of trial exhibits. With the exception of objections under Federal Rules of Evidence 402 and 403, objections not so made are waived unless excused by the court for good cause.

These objections are due 14 days after the pretrial disclosures are made, unless the court sets a different deadline. Consider including in the final pretrial conference order instructions on how the parties should make any such objections.

(f) *Motions in limine.* Many judges require parties to file and brief motions in limine before the final pretrial conference. The judge has discretion to place page or number limits on the motions in limine that are filed. Resolving motions in limine at the final pretrial conference defines the issues and evidence to be presented at trial.

(g) *Voir dire.* Consider requiring the parties to submit proposed voir dire questions and a joint statement of the case to be read to the jury panel during voir dire.

(h) *Jury instructions.* Consider requiring the parties to submit proposed preliminary and final jury instructions.

(i) *Verdict.* Consider requiring the parties to submit proposed verdict forms or jury interrogatories.

(j) *Findings of fact and conclusions of law.* In a bench trial, consider requiring the parties to submit proposed findings of fact and conclusions of law.

As noted earlier, there is no one-size-fits-all requirement. In cases that are simple or straightforward or in which the stakes are small, an elaborate joint proposed pretrial order may not be needed. In such cases, consider conferring with the lawyers about tailoring the preconference submissions, including any joint proposed pretrial order, so that they are limited to what the court and parties reasonably need for a fair and efficient trial.

2. *Form of the preconference submissions.* Many judges require the parties to prepare and submit a joint proposed pretrial order that incorporates all of the matters they are required to address. Some judges prefer a shorter joint proposed pretrial order and additional matters, such as motions in limine, proposed voir dire questions, or proposed jury instructions, to be addressed separately, either in attachments or as freestanding submissions.

   The deadlines for submission should allow time for the parties to prepare and submit any materials that respond to other submitted materials. For example, time is needed to see and review the other side's exhibits and deposition designations before submitting objections to those exhibits and designations.

D. Conducting the final pretrial conference

1. *Narrowing and refining issues; ruling on motions in limine.* With the parties' preconference submissions, the judge works with the parties to narrow and refine the issues for trial. Ruling on motions in limine may be an important part of this work. Narrowing and refining the issues and ruling in advance on as many issues as the record permits allow the court and parties to conduct the trial more efficiently and within the time allotted on the court's calendar.

2. *Resolving other evidentiary issues*

   (a) The final pretrial conference provides an opportunity to preadmit exhibits if there will be no objections or if the court is able to resolve the objections and rule on admissibility under Federal Rule of Evidence 104.

   (b) The final pretrial conference can also be used to address evidence-related matters, such as which witnesses may be in the courtroom during the trial under Federal Rule of Evidence 615, the mode of questioning under Rule 611, and identifying exhibits suitable for summaries under Rule 1006.

3. *Other issues related to conducting the trial.* The final pretrial conference can address any other issues regarding the conduct of the trial, including

   (a) the order of presenting evidence, particularly if multiple parties are involved;

   (b) possible bifurcation of the trial;

   (c) witness-scheduling issues, such as calling witnesses out of order;

   (d) how to present depositions or electronic evidence;

   (e) the need for interpreters;

   (f) special equipment needs; and

   (g) jury questions.

4. *Firm trial dates and fixed trial times.* If the court has not previously set a firm trial date, that date should be set at the final pretrial conference. The order scheduling the conference can advise attorneys to come with their calendars and with information on the availability of their witnesses and clients. Once the issues and evidence have been identified, the judge, in consultation with the parties, can determine the length of the trial. Consider entering an order limiting the time for the trial, such as by allotting a specific number of trial hours to each party. The adage that work expands to fill the time available applies fully to trials. Trials with established time limits tend to be more focused and more efficient.

5. *Educating parties on the court's trial practices.* Many judges use the final pretrial conference to educate lawyers and parties on the court's trial practices, such as the extent of lawyer participation in jury voir dire; whether re-cross-examination generally is allowed; or whether jurors are permitted to take notes, to have copies of exhibits, or to submit questions to witnesses. It may also be helpful to educate the lawyers about the court's expectations for the conduct of trial counsel. For example, the judge can educate the parties about proper practice for marking and presenting exhibits, for approaching witnesses, or for the use of courtroom equipment. Such an education can be particularly valuable for trials involving pro se litigants.

6. *Promoting settlement.* If a final pretrial conference covers the kinds of issues identified above, parties leaving such a conference will never know more about their dispute, short of trial, than they do at that moment. The final pretrial conference may provide a valuable opportunity for settlement. Some judges encourage the parties to engage in settlement talks after the final pretrial conference and before trial.

E. The final pretrial order

1. *Issuing the final pretrial order.* After the final pretrial conference, the judge should issue a final pretrial order that reflects the decisions made during the conference. The final pretrial order should clearly identify the issues to be decided at trial, the witnesses to be called, the exhibits to be offered in evidence, and objections preserved for trial. The order should also reflect evidentiary or other rulings made by the judge for trial. A firm trial date should be fixed, as should the length of the trial, where appropriate. Judges may use a proposed final pretrial order submitted jointly by the parties, as modified by the judge, or an order written or dictated specifically for a particular case.

2. *Modifying the final pretrial order*
   (a) By adhering to the final pretrial order—that is, by holding the parties to the issues, evidence, objections, and schedule identified at the final pretrial conference—the judge can help avoid

surprises and ensure that the trial will be completed in the time allotted.

(b) Rule 16(e) provides that "[t]he court may modify the order issued after a final pretrial conference only to prevent manifest injustice." This is a higher standard than the "good cause" test found elsewhere in Rule 16 and is intended to reflect the relative finality of the final pretrial order. It may be useful to restate this standard in the final pretrial order itself.

VI. Conclusion

Case management, beginning early, is essential to controlling costs and burdens of discovery and motions practice, particularly given the challenges of electronic discovery issues. Ongoing judicial management as the case develops, which ends in a careful and thorough final pretrial conference, will reduce delays and unnecessary costs and increase the likelihood that the case will be resolved on terms that reflect the strength and weaknesses of the merits, rather than the desire to avoid disproportionate discovery or the costs of an unnecessarily protracted trial. Effective case management is a critical part of achieving "just, speedy, and inexpensive" case resolutions.

References

Civil Litigation Management Manual (Judicial Conference of the United States, 2d ed. 2010)

Federal Judicial Center's Case Management Seminar Materials

Steven S. Gensler, Federal Rules of Civil Procedure, Rules and Commentary (2011)

Manual for Complex Litigation, Fourth (2004)

Moore's Federal Practice, vols. 3 and 6

Wright, Miller & Kane, Federal Practice & Procedure, vol. 6A (2010)

Wright, Miller & Marcus, Federal Practice & Procedure, vol. 8 (2010)

Other FJC sources

The Elements of Case Management: A Pocket Guide for Judges (2d ed. 2006)

Managing Class Action Litigation: A Pocket Guide for Judges (3d ed. 2010)

Managing Discovery of Electronic Information: A Pocket Guide for Judges (2d ed. 2012)

6.02   Trial outline—civil

1. Have the case called for trial.
2. Jury is selected (see *infra* section 6.04: Jury selection—civil).
3. Give preliminary instructions to the jury (see *infra* section 6.06: Preliminary jury instructions—civil case).
4. Ascertain whether any party wishes to invoke the rule to exclude from the courtroom witnesses scheduled to testify in the case.
5. Plaintiff's counsel makes an opening statement.
6. Defense counsel makes an opening statement (unless permitted to reserve).
7. Plaintiff's counsel calls witnesses for the plaintiff.
8. Plaintiff rests.
9. Hear appropriate motions.
10. Defense counsel makes an opening statement if he or she has been permitted to reserve.
11. Defense counsel calls witnesses for the defense.
12. Defense rests.
13. Counsel call rebuttal witnesses.
14. Plaintiff rests on its entire case.
15. Defense rests on its entire case.
16. Consider appropriate motions.
17. Out of the hearing of the jury, rule on counsel's requests for instructions and inform counsel as to the substance of the court's charge. Fed. R. Civ. P. 51(b).
18. Counsel give closing arguments.
19. Charge the jury (see *infra* section 6.07: General instructions to jury at end of civil case). Fed. R. Civ. P. 51.
20. Rule on objections to the charge and make any additional appropriate charge.
21. Instruct the jury to go to the jury room and commence its deliberations.
22. Determine which exhibits are to be sent to the jury room.
23. Have the clerk give the exhibits and the verdict forms to the jury.
24. Recess court during the jury deliberations.
25. Before responding to any communications from the jury, consult with counsel on the record (see *infra* section 6.07: General instructions to jury at end of civil case).

26. If the jury fails to arrive at a verdict before the conclusion of the first day's deliberations, provide for the jurors' overnight sequestration or permit them to separate after instructing them as to their conduct and fixing the time for their return to resume deliberations. Provide for safe-keeping of exhibits.

27. If the jurors report that they cannot agree on a verdict, determine by questioning whether they are hopelessly deadlocked. Do not inquire as to the numerical split of the jury. If you are convinced that the jury is hopelessly deadlocked, declare a mistrial. If you are not so convinced, direct the jurors to resume their deliberations.

28. When the jury has agreed on a verdict, reconvene court and take the verdict (see *infra* section 6.08: Verdict—civil).

29. Poll the jury on the request of either party or on the court's own motion. Fed. R. Civ. P. 48(c).

30. Thank and discharge the jury.

31. Enter judgment upon the verdict. Fed. R. Civ. P. 58.

32. Fix a time for post-trial motions.

33. Adjourn or recess court.

Other FJC sources

Civil Litigation Management Manual 109–15 (Judicial Conference of the United States, 2d ed. 2010)

Effective Use of Courtroom Technology: A Judge's Guide to Pretrial and Trial (2001)

Manual for Complex Litigation, Fourth 131–66 (2004)

William W Schwarzer and Alan Hirsch, The Elements of Case Management: A Pocket Guide for Judges (2d ed. 2006)

6.03 Findings of fact and conclusions of law in civil cases and motions

Fed. R. Civ. P. 41, 52, and 65(d)

A. When required
 1. Fed. R. Civ. P. 52(a)(1) & (2)
    (a) *In all cases tried without a jury or with an advisory jury,* "the court must find the facts specially and state its conclusions of law separately."
    (b) *In granting or refusing interlocutory injunctions,* "the court must similarly state the findings and conclusions that support its action."

    Note that this is in addition to the requirements of Fed. R. Civ. P. 65(d), which requires that "[e]very order granting an injunction and every restraining order shall set forth the reasons for its issuance; shall be specific in terms; shall describe in reasonable detail, and not by reference to the complaint or other document, the act or acts sought to be restrained."

 2. Fed. R. Civ. P. 52(c)—Judgment on Partial Findings

    "If a party has been fully heard on an issue during a nonjury trial and the court finds against the party on that issue, the court may enter judgment against the party . . . on that issue. . . . A judgment on partial findings must be supported by findings of fact and conclusions of law as required by Rule 52(a)."

 3. Fed. R. Civ. P. 41(a)(2)—Voluntary Dismissal

    Plaintiff's motion for voluntary dismissal may be granted "only by court order, on terms that the court considers proper."

B. When not required
 1. *On any motions* (other than those under Fed. R. Civ. P. 52(c)).
    (a) Fed. R. Civ. P. 52(a)(3) states that findings of fact and conclusions of law are "not required . . . when ruling on a motion under Rule 12 or 56 or, unless these rules provide otherwise, on any other motion."
    (b) Fed. R. Civ. P. 12 covers instances when defenses and objections to the pleadings are made and how they are presented—by pleading or motion. Fed. R. Civ. P. 12(c) pertains to a motion for judgment on the pleadings. Rule 12(d) concerns motions for judgment involving "matters outside the pleadings" and refers to Fed. R. Civ. P. 56, which covers summary judgment.
    (c) The exemption of motions, particularly those under Fed. R. Civ. P. 12 and 56, from the requirement of making findings and conclu-

sions means that most motions that are filed can be disposed of by simply stating "granted" or "denied."

[*Note:* Some circuits prefer findings and conclusions on dispositive motions, particularly on motions for summary judgment, and may vacate and remand orders if the district court fails to provide any reasoning on the record for its decision. Judges should be aware that circuit law may require, or strongly urge, detailed findings on some motions.[1]]

C. Form and substance

1. No particular format is required if an opinion or memorandum is filed.

   "The findings and conclusions ... may appear in an opinion or a memorandum of decision filed by the court." Fed. R. Civ. P. 52(a)(1). A memorandum that contains only a list of findings and conclusions is adequate. The findings and conclusions need not be listed separately in an opinion.

2. From the bench

   "The findings and conclusions may be stated on the record after the close of the evidence . . . ." Fed. R. Civ. P. 52(a)(1). It is always quicker and sometimes just as easy to make the findings and conclusions from the bench at the end of the case as it is to take the matter under submission. Be sure that they are put in the record.

3. Requested findings and conclusions submitted by counsel

   Specifically adopting or denying the requested findings and conclusions submitted by counsel is not necessary, as it is in some state courts. Some courts of appeals look with a jaundiced eye on district court findings or conclusions that follow counsel's requests verbatim.

4. Stipulations

   Stipulations by counsel as to the facts are always helpful. Unlike requests, they should be used verbatim. Of course, counsel cannot stipulate as to the applicable law; they can only suggest.

5. Length and style of opinion

   The length and style of the opinion are left to the individual judge, but from the viewpoint of an appellate court, there are certain basic elements that should be included:

---

1. *See, e.g.,* Brewster of Lynchburg, Inc. v. Dial Corp., 33 F.3d 355 (4th Cir. 1994); Pasquino v. Prather, 13 F.3d 1049 (7th Cir. 1994); Thomas v. N.A. Chase Manhattan Bank, 994 F.2d 236, 241 n.6 (5th Cir. 1993); Telectronics Pacing Sys. v. Ventritex, Inc., 982 F.2d 1520, 1526–27 (Fed. Cir. 1992); United States v. Woods, 885 F.2d 352 (6th Cir. 1989); Clay v. Equifax, Inc., 762 F.2d 952 (11th Cir. 1985).

(a) *Jurisdiction.* This is elementary, but sometimes overlooked. The statutory basis should be stated.

(b) *The issues.* It is helpful if the issues are stated at the beginning of the opinion.

(c) *Credibility findings.* These are the exclusive province of the district court. They should be clearly stated. If you do not believe a witness, say so.

(d) *The facts.* If you have a transcript, refer to the pages that contain the evidence on which you rely. If there is no transcript and your opinion is based on your trial notes, say so. Some appellate courts forget that district court judges do not always have the benefit of a written record.

(e) *The law.* There are three basic situations that you will face:

    (i)   the law is well settled;

    (ii) the law is unsettled; or

    (iii) there is no applicable law—the case is one of first impression.

The first situation poses no problem; the second and third may create a fear-of-reversal syndrome. Do not worry about whether you may be reversed. No judge has been impeached for having been reversed. Get on with the opinion and do the best you can. The court of appeals or the Supreme Court is going to have the last word anyhow.

Be sure that someone checks the subsequent history of the cases. It is not a sin to be overruled except for relying on a case that was overruled.

Other FJC sources

Civil Litigation Management Manual 113–15 (Judicial Conference of the United States, 2d ed. 2010)

Manual for Complex Litigation, Fourth 165 (2004)

6.04 Jury selection—civil

The *Benchbook* Committee recognizes that there is no uniform recommended procedure for selecting jurors to serve in criminal or civil cases and that trial judges will develop the patterns or procedures most appropriate for their districts and their courts. Section 6.05, *infra*, however, provides an outline of standard voir dire questions for civil cases. For a sample juror questionnaire, see Sample Forms 42 and 43 in Appendix A of the *Civil Litigation Management Manual* (Judicial Conference of the United States, 2d ed. 2010) (the forms are available only online at http://cwn.fjc.dcn/fjconline/home. nsf/pages/1245).

The 1982 Federal Judicial Center publication *Jury Selection Procedures in United States District Courts,* by Gordon Bermant, contains a detailed discussion of several different methods of jury selection. Copies are available on request. See also the section on jury selection and composition (pp. 580–82) in Judge William W Schwarzer's article "Reforming Jury Trials" in volume 132 of *Federal Rules Decisions* (1990).

Judges should be aware of the cases, beginning with *Batson v. Kentucky*, 476 U.S. 79 (1986), that prohibit peremptory challenges based on race. In *Edmonson v. Leesville Concrete Co.*, 500 U.S. 614 (1991), the Supreme Court extended *Batson* to prohibit private litigants in civil cases from using peremptory challenges to exclude jurors on account of race. Peremptory strikes on the basis of gender are also prohibited. *J.E.B. v. Alabama ex rel. T.B.*, 114 S. Ct. 1419 (1994).

The Supreme Court has left it to the trial courts to develop rules of procedure and evidence for implementing these decisions. It has, however, set out a three-step inquiry for resolving a *Batson* challenge (see *Purkett v. Elem*, 514 U.S. 765, 767–68 (1995):

1. At the first step of the *Batson* inquiry, the burden is on the opponent of a peremptory challenge to make out a prima facie case of discrimination. A prima facie case may be shown where (1) the prospective juror is a member of a cognizable group, (2) the prosecutor used a peremptory strike to remove the juror, and (3) the totality of the circumstances raises an inference that the strike was motivated by the juror's membership in the cognizable group. *Johnson v. California*, 545 U.S. 162, 170 (2005). The burden at this stage is low.[1]

2. If the opponent of the peremptory challenge satisfies the step one prima facie showing, the burden then shifts to the proponent of the

---

1. "[A] defendant satisfies the requirements of *Batson*'s first step by producing evidence sufficient to permit the trial judge to draw an inference that discrimination has occurred." The defendant does not have to show that it was "more likely than not" that discrimination occurred. *Johnson*, 545 U.S. at 170.

strike, who must come forward with a nondiscriminatory explanation of the strike.

3. If the court is satisfied with the neutral explanation offered, it must then proceed to the third step, to determine the ultimate question of intentional discrimination. *Hernandez v. New York*, 500 U.S. 352 (1991). The opponent of the strike has the ultimate burden to show purposeful discrimination. The court may not rest solely upon the neutral explanation offered by the proponent of the strike. Instead, the court must undertake a sensitive inquiry into the circumstantial and direct evidence of intent, *Batson*, 476 U.S. at 93, and evaluate the "persuasiveness of the justification" offered by the proponent of the strike. *Purkett*, 514 U.S. at 768. One method of undertaking such inquiry is to make a "side-by-side comparison" of the reasons given for striking panelists vis-à-vis those who were allowed to serve. *Miller-El v. Dretke*, 545 U.S. 231, 241 (2005).

The *Benchbook* Committee suggests that judges

- conduct the above inquiry on the record but outside of the venire's hearing, to avoid "tainting" the venire by discussions of race, gender, or other characteristics of potential jurors; and

- use a method of jury selection which requires litigants to exercise challenges at sidebar or otherwise outside of the venire's hearing and in which no venire members are dismissed until all of the challenges have been exercised. *See Jury Selection Procedures in United States District Courts, supra.*

These procedures should ensure that prospective jurors are never aware of *Batson* discussions or arguments about challenges, and therefore can draw no adverse inferences by being temporarily dismissed from the venire and then recalled.

Other FJC sources

Civil Litigation Management Manual 106–07 (Judicial Conference of the United States, 2d ed. 2010)

Manual for Complex Litigation, Fourth 150–52 (2004)

For a summary of procedures that courts developed for criminal cases in the first two years after *Batson*, see Bench Comment, 1988, nos. 3 & 4

For a discussion of voir dire practices in light of *Batson*, see Chambers to Chambers, vol. 5, no. 2 (1987)

6.05 Standard voir dire questions—civil

Fed. R. Civ. P. 47(a) provides that the court "may permit the parties or their attorneys to examine prospective jurors or may itself do so." The following outline for an initial in-depth voir dire examination of the entire panel by the court assumes that

1. if there are affirmative responses to any questions, follow-up questions will be addressed to the juror(s) (at sidebar, if such questions concern private or potentially embarrassing matters); and

2. the court and counsel have been furnished with the name, address, age, and occupation of each prospective juror.

If the court conducts the entire examination, it should require counsel to submit proposed voir dire questions before trial to permit the court to incorporate additional questions at the appropriate places in this outline.

Outline

A. Have the jury panel sworn.

B. Explain to the jury panel that the purpose of the voir dire examination is

1. to enable the court to determine whether any prospective juror should be excused for cause; and

2. to enable counsel for the parties to exercise their individual judgment with respect to peremptory challenges—that is, challenges for which counsel need not give a reason.

C. Indicate that the case is expected to take ___ days to try, and ask if this fact presents a special problem to any member of the panel.

D. Briefly describe the case that is about to be tried.

E. Ask if any member of the panel has heard or read anything about the case.

F. Introduce counsel (or have counsel introduce themselves) and ask if any member of the panel or his or her immediate family knows or has had any business dealings with any of the counsel or their law firms.

G. Introduce the parties (or have counsel introduce the parties) and ask if any member of the panel or his or her immediate family

1. is personally acquainted with,

2. is related to,

3. has had business dealings with,

4. is currently or was formerly employed by,

5. has had any other relationship or business connection with, or

6. is a stockholder of any party in the case.

H. Introduce or identify by name, address, and occupation all prospective witnesses (or have counsel do so). Ask if any member of the panel knows any of the prospective witnesses.

I. Ask prospective jurors:

1. Have you ever served as a juror in a criminal or civil case or as a member of a grand jury in either a federal or state court?

2. Have you or has anyone in your immediate family ever participated in a lawsuit as a party or in any other capacity?

3. If you are selected to sit on this case, will you be able to render a verdict solely on the evidence presented at the trial and in the context of the law as I will give it to you in my instructions, disregarding any other ideas, notions, or beliefs about the law that you may have encountered in reaching your verdict?

4. Is there any member of the panel who has any special disability or problem that would make serving as a member of the jury difficult or impossible?

5. [At this point, if the court is conducting the entire examination, ask those questions submitted by counsel that you feel should be propounded. If the questions elicit affirmative responses, ask appropriate follow-up questions.]

6. Having heard the questions put to you by the court, does any other reason suggest itself to you as to why you could not sit on this jury and render a fair verdict based on the evidence presented to you and in the context of the court's instructions to you on the law?

J. 1. If appropriate, permit counsel to conduct additional direct voir dire examination, subject to such time and subject matter limitations as the court deems proper; or

2. Direct counsel to come to the bench, and consult with them as to whether any additional questions should have been asked or whether any were overlooked.

Other FJC sources

Gordon Bermant, Jury Selection Procedures in United States District Courts (1982)

Civil Litigation Management Manual 106–07 (Judicial Conference of the United States 2d ed. 2010)

Civil Litigation Management Manual (Judicial Conference of the United States, 2d ed. 2010), Sample Form 46 in Appendix A.

Manual for Complex Litigation, Fourth 151–52 (2004)

6.06 Preliminary jury instructions— civil case

These suggested instructions are designed to be given following the swearing of the jury. They are general and may require modification in light of the nature of the particular case. They are intended to give the jury, briefly and in understandable language, information to make the trial more meaningful. Other instructions, such as explanations of depositions, interrogatories, and the hearsay rule, may be given at appropriate points during the trial.

Preliminary instructions

Members of the jury: Now that you have been sworn, I will give you some preliminary instructions to guide you in your participation in the trial.

Duty of the jury

It will be your duty to find from the evidence what the facts are. You and you alone will be the judges of the facts. You will then have to apply to those facts the law as the court will give it to you. You must follow that law whether you agree with it or not.

Nothing the court may say or do during the course of the trial is intended to indicate, or should be taken by you as indicating, what your verdict should be.

Evidence

The evidence from which you will find the facts will consist of the testimony of witnesses, documents and other things received into the record as exhibits, and any facts that the lawyers agree to or stipulate to or that the court may instruct you to find.

Certain things are not evidence and must not be considered by you. I will list them for you now.

1. Statements, arguments, and questions by lawyers are not evidence.

2. Objections to questions are not evidence. Lawyers have an obligation to their clients to make objections when they believe evidence being offered is improper under the rules of evidence. You should not be influenced by the objection or by the court's ruling on it. If the objection is sustained, ignore the question. If it is overruled, treat the answer like any other. If you are instructed that some item of evidence is received for a limited purpose only, you must follow that instruction.

3. Testimony that the court has excluded or told you to disregard is not evidence and must not be considered.

4. Anything you may have seen or heard outside the courtroom is not evidence and must be disregarded. You are to decide the case solely on the evidence presented here in the courtroom.

There are two kinds of evidence: direct and circumstantial. Direct evidence is direct proof of a fact, such as testimony of an eyewitness. Circumstantial evidence is proof of facts from which you may infer or conclude that other facts exist. I will give you further instructions on these as well as other matters at the end of the case, but keep in mind that you may consider both kinds of evidence.

It will be up to you to decide which witnesses to believe, which witnesses not to believe, and how much of any witness's testimony to accept or reject. I will give you some guidelines for determining the credibility of witnesses at the end of the case.

Burden of proof

This is a civil case. The plaintiff has the burden of proving his [her] case by what is called the preponderance of the evidence. That means the plaintiff has to produce evidence which, considered in the light of all the facts, leads you to believe that what the plaintiff claims is more likely true than not. To put it differently, if you were to put the plaintiff's and the defendant's evidence on opposite sides of the scales, the plaintiff would have to make the scales tip somewhat on his [her] side. If the plaintiff fails to meet this burden, the verdict must be for the defendant.

Those of you who have sat on criminal cases will have heard of proof beyond a reasonable doubt. That requirement does not apply to a civil case; therefore, you should put it out of your mind.

Summary of applicable law

[*Note:* A summary of the elements may not be appropriate in some cases.]

In this case, the plaintiff claims that _____; the defendant claims that _____. I will give you detailed instructions on the law at the end of the case, and those instructions will control your deliberations and decision. But in order to help you follow the evidence, I will now give you a brief summary of the elements which the plaintiff must prove to make his [her] case: [here summarize the elements].

Conduct of the jury

Now, a few words about your conduct as jurors.

You, as jurors, must decide this case based solely on the evidence presented here within the four walls of this courtroom. This means that during the trial you must not conduct any independent research about this case, the matters in the case, and the individuals or corporations involved in the case. In other words, you should not consult dictionaries or reference materials, search the Internet, websites, or blogs, or use any other electronic tools to obtain information about this case or to help you decide the case. Please do not try to find out information from any source outside the confines of this courtroom.

Until you retire to deliberate, you may not discuss this case with anyone, even your fellow jurors. After you retire to deliberate, you may begin discussing the case with your fellow jurors, but you cannot discuss the case with anyone else until you have returned a verdict and the case is at an end.

I know that many of you use cell phones, Blackberries, the Internet, and other tools of technology. You also must not talk to anyone at any time about this case or use these tools to communicate electronically with anyone about the case. This includes your family and friends. You may not communicate with anyone about the case on your cell phone, through e-mail, Blackberry, iPhone, text messaging, or on Twitter, through any blog or website, including Facebook, Google+, My Space, LinkedIn, or YouTube. You may not use any similar technology of social media, even if I have not specifically mentioned it here. I expect you will inform me as soon as you become aware of another juror's violation of these instructions.[1] A juror who violates these restrictions jeopardizes the fairness of these proceedings, and a mistrial could result, which would require the entire trial process to start over.

Finally, do not form any opinion until all the evidence is in. Keep an open mind until you start your deliberations at the end of the case.

I hope that for all of you this case is interesting and noteworthy.

[If the court decides to allow note taking, add:]

If you want to take notes during the course of the trial, you may do so. However, it is difficult to take detailed notes and pay attention to what the witnesses are saying at the same time. If you do take notes, be sure that your note taking does not interfere with your listening to and considering all of the evidence. Also, if you do take notes, do not discuss them with anyone before you begin your deliberations. Do not take your notes with you at the end of the day—be sure to leave them in the jury room.

---

1. Taken from "Proposed Model Jury Instructions: The Use of Electronic Technology to Conduct Research on or Communicate about a Case," prepared by the Judicial Conference Committee on Court Administration and Case Management (June 2012). *See* Memorandum, "Juror Use of Social Media" from Judge Julie A. Robinson, Chair, Committee on Court Administration and Case Management to all United States District Court Judges (Aug. 6, 2012), *available at* http://jnet.ao.dcn/img/assets/7324/DIR12-074.pdf. *See also* "Strategies for Preventing Jurors' Use of Social Media During Trials and Deliberations," *in* Jurors' Use of Social Media During Trials and Deliberations: A Report to the Judicial Conference Committee on Court Administration and Case Management 5–10 (Federal Judicial Center Nov. 22, 2011), *available at* http://cwn.fjc.dcn/public/pdf.nsf/lookup/DunnJuror.pdf/$file/DunnJuror.pdf.

If you choose *not* to take notes, remember that it is your own individual responsibility to listen carefully to the evidence. You cannot give this responsibility to someone who is taking notes. We depend on the judgment of all members of the jury; you all must remember the evidence in this case.[2]

Course of the trial

The trial will now begin. First, each side may make an opening statement. An opening statement is neither evidence nor argument; it is an outline of what that party intends to prove, offered to help you follow the evidence.

Next, the plaintiff will present his [her] witnesses, and the defendant may cross-examine them. Then the defendant will present his [her] witnesses, and the plaintiff may cross-examine them.

After all the evidence is in, the parties will present their closing arguments to summarize and interpret the evidence for you, and the court will give you instructions on the law.

[*Note:* Some judges may wish to give some instructions before closing arguments. *See* Fed. R. Civ. P. 51(b)(3).]

You will then retire to deliberate on your verdict.

Other FJC sources

Civil Litigation Management Manual 111–12 & Forms 44, 46 (Judicial Conference of the United States, 2d ed. 2010)

Manual for Complex Litigation, Fourth 154–56 (2004)

---

2. For another sample instruction on note taking, see Civil Litigation Management Manual at Appendix A, Form 44 (Judicial Conference of the United States, 2d ed. 2010).

6.07 General instructions to jury at end of civil case

Introductory note

Fed. R. Civ. P. 51(b) outlines the procedure for the submission and consideration of requests by the parties for specific jury instructions. It requires

1. that the court inform counsel before closing arguments of its proposed instructions and its proposed action upon the instructions requested by counsel; and

2. that the court give counsel adequate opportunity outside the hearing of the jury to object to the court's instructions.

There is no prescribed method for the court to settle on its final set of instructions. Some courts hold an on-the-record charge conference with counsel during trial. At that conference, the tendered instructions are discussed and are accepted, rejected, or modified by the court.

Other courts, without holding a charge conference, prepare a set of proposed instructions from those tendered by counsel. These courts then give a copy of the proposed instructions to all counsel and permit counsel to take exception to the instructions. Thereafter, the court may revise its instructions if convinced by counsel in their objections that the instructions should be modified.

Still other courts require counsel to confer during trial and to agree, to the extent that they can, on the instructions that should be given. The court then considers only those instructions upon which the parties cannot agree.

The court may, of course, give an instruction to the jury that neither party has tendered.

While the court is free to ignore tendered instructions and to instruct the jury sua sponte, the usual practice is for the court to formulate the final instructions with the assistance of counsel and principally from the instructions counsel tendered.

Local practice varies as to whether a written copy of the instructions is given to the jury for use during its deliberations. Many courts always give the jury a written copy of the instructions. Some courts have the instructions recorded as they are given in court and permit the jury to play them back in the jury room. Some courts do neither but will repeat some or all of the instructions in response to a request from the jury.

Outline of instructions

Instructions delivered at the end of a case consist of three parts: Instructions on general rules that define and control the jury's duties; statement of rules of law that the jury must apply; and rules and guidelines for jury deliberation and return of verdict.

A. General rules
  1. Outline the duty of the jury
     (a) to find facts from admitted evidence;
     (b) to apply law as given by the court to the facts as found by the jury; and
     (c) to decide the case on the evidence and the law regardless of personal opinions and without bias, prejudice, or sympathy.
  2. Discuss the burden of proof in civil trials and explain how it differs from the burden of proof in criminal trials.
  3. Indicate the evidence to be considered:
     (a) sworn testimony of witnesses;
     (b) exhibits;
     (c) stipulations; and
     (d) facts judicially noticed.
  4. Indicate what is not evidence:
     (a) arguments and statements of counsel;
     (b) questions to witnesses;
     (c) evidence excluded by rulings of the court.
B. Delineate with precision and with specific consideration of the law of your circuit each claim and defense of the parties that is to be submitted to the jury for their consideration.
C. Jury procedure
  1. Selection and duty of the foreperson.
  2. Process of jury deliberation:
     (a) rational discussion of the evidence by all jurors for the purpose of reaching a unanimous verdict;
     (b) each juror is to decide the case for himself or herself in the context of the evidence and the law, with proper consideration of other jurors' views; and
     (c) jurors may reconsider their views if persuaded by rational discussion but not solely for the sake of reaching a unanimous verdict.
  3. Absent a stipulation, the verdict must be unanimous on the issue submitted (Fed. R. Civ. P. 48).
  4. Explain the verdict form, if used.[1]
  5. Jury communications with the court during deliberations must be in writing and signed by the foreperson.

---

1. Consider whether to use a special verdict (Fed. R. Civ. P. 49(a)). It can be a useful device to reduce the risk of having to retry the entire case.

6. The jury must not disclose how it stands numerically or otherwise on the issues submitted.

7. Consider giving the jury the following instruction:

During your deliberations, you must not communicate with or provide any information to anyone by any means about this case. You may not use any electronic device or media, such as a telephone, cell phone, smart phone, iPhone, Blackberry, or computer; the Internet, any Internet service, or any text or instant messaging service; or any Internet chat room, blog, or website, such as Facebook, MySpace, LinkedIn, YouTube, or Twitter, to communicate to anyone any information about this case or to conduct any research about this case until I accept your verdict. In other words, you cannot talk to anyone on the phone, correspond with anyone, or electronically communicate with anyone about this case. You can only discuss the case in the jury room with your fellow jurors during deliberations. I expect you will inform me as soon as you become aware of another juror's violation of these instructions.

You may not use these electronic means to investigate or communicate about the case because it is important that you decide this case based solely on the evidence presented in this courtroom. Information on the Internet or available through social media might be wrong, incomplete, or inaccurate. You are only permitted to discuss the case with your fellow jurors during deliberations because they have seen and heard the same evidence you have. In our judicial system, it is important that you are not influenced by anything or anyone outside of this courtroom. Otherwise, your decision may be based on information known only by you and not your fellow jurors or the parties in the case. This would unfairly and adversely impact the judicial process.[2] If a juror violates these restrictions, it could cause a mistrial, which would require the entire trial process to start over.

---

2. Taken from "Proposed Model Jury Instructions: The Use of Electronic Technology to Conduct Research on or Communicate about a Case," prepared by the Judicial Conference Committee on Court Administration and Case Management (June 2012). *See* Memorandum, "Juror Use of Social Media" from Judge Julie A. Robinson, Chair, Committee on Court Administration and Case Management to all United States District Court Judges (Aug. 6, 2012), *available at* http://jnet.ao.dcn/img/assets/7324/DIR12-074.pdf. *See also* "Strategies for Preventing Jurors' Use of Social Media During Trials and Deliberations," *in* Jurors' Use of Social Media During Trials and Deliberations: A Report to the Judicial Conference Committee on Court Administration and Case Management 5–10 (Federal Judicial Center Nov. 22, 2011), *available at* http://cwn.fjc.dcn/public/pdf.nsf/lookup/DunnJuror.pdf/$file/DunnJuror.pdf.

D. Consider providing the jury with a written copy or transcript of the jury instructions.

Other FJC sources

Civil Litigation Management Manual 111–12 & Forms 44, 47 (Judicial Conference of the United States, 2d ed. 2010)

Manual for Complex Litigation, Fourth 156–59 (2004)

6.08 Verdict—civil

A. Reception of an unsealed verdict
   1. Upon announcement by the jury that it has reached a verdict, have all interested parties convene in open court to receive the verdict.
   2. When court is convened, announce that the jury is ready to return its verdict(s), and instruct the deputy marshal (or bailiff) to have the jurors enter and assume their seats in the jury box.
   3. If not already known, inquire of the jury who speaks as its foreperson.
   4. Ask the foreperson if the jury has unanimously agreed upon its verdict(s). [*Note:* If the response is anything other than an unqualified yes, the jury should be returned without further inquiry to continue its deliberations.]
   5. Instruct the foreperson to hand the verdict form(s) to the clerk to be delivered to you for inspection before publication.
   6. Inspect the verdict(s) to ensure regularity of form. [*Note:* If the verdict form(s) is (are) not properly completed, take appropriate corrective action before publication.]
   7. Explain to the jurors that their verdict(s) will now be "published"— that is, read aloud in open court.
   8. Instruct the jury to pay close attention as the verdict(s) is (are) published; and explain that, following publication, the jury may be "polled"—that each juror may be asked, individually, whether the verdict(s) as published constituted his or her individual verdict(s) in all respects.
   9. Publish the verdict(s) by reading it (them) aloud (or by having the clerk do so).
   10. Upon request of any party, or on your own motion, poll the jury by asking (or by having the clerk ask) each individual juror, by name or number, whether the verdict(s) as published constituted his or her individual verdict(s) in all respects.
   11. If polling verifies unanimity, direct the clerk to file and record the verdict(s), and discharge the jurors with appropriate instructions concerning their future service, if any.
   12. If polling results in any doubt as to unanimity, or if there are inconsistent answers to a special verdict, make no further inquiry and have no further discussions with the jury; rather, confer privately with counsel and determine whether the jury should be returned for further deliberations or a mistrial should be declared.

B. Reception of a sealed verdict

[*Note:* On some occasions an indispensable party may not be available to receive a verdict when the jury reaches agreement. In such cases a sealed verdict may be delivered to the clerk for subsequent "reception" and publication in open court when the jury, the judge, and all necessary parties are present.]

1. Upon announcement by the jury that it has reached a verdict, have all interested and available parties convene in open court and on the record.

2. When court is thus convened, announce that the jury is ready to return its verdict(s), and explain that a sealed verdict will be taken in accordance with the following procedure:

   (a) Instruct the deputy marshal (or bailiff) to usher the jurors into the courtroom to assume their seats in the jury box.

   (b) If not already known, inquire of the jury who speaks as its foreperson.

   (c) Ask the foreperson if the jury has unanimously agreed on its verdict. [*Note:* If the response is anything other than an unqualified yes, the jury should be returned without further inquiry to continue its deliberations.]

   (d) Explain to the jury that a sealed verdict will be taken, and further explain why that procedure has become necessary in the case.

   (e) Poll the jury on the record.

   (f) Direct the clerk to hand a suitable envelope to the foreperson. Instruct the foreperson to place the verdict form(s) in the envelope, to seal the envelope, and to hand it to the clerk for safekeeping.

   (g) Recess the proceedings, instructing the jury and all interested parties to return at a fixed time for the opening and formal reception of the verdict. Instruct that, in the interim, no member of the jury should have any conversation with any other person, including any other juror, concerning the verdict or any other aspect of the case.

   (h) When court is again convened for reception of the verdict, have the clerk hand the sealed envelope to the jury foreperson.

   (i) Instruct the foreperson to open the envelope and verify that the contents consist of the jury's verdict form(s) without modification or alteration of any kind.

   (j) Follow the steps or procedures outlined in paragraphs A.5 through A.12 *supra*.

NOTE
In the event th[e] jury will not be present at the opening of the verdict, it is rec[]ommended tha[t] each juror sign[] verdict form(s)[.]

Other sources on polling the jury

Federal Trial Handbook, Civil, § 79:12 (4th ed.) (2012)

Moore's Federal Practice ¶ 49.07 (3d ed.) (1997)

Wright & Miller, Federal Practice and Procedure, Civil, § 2504 (1998)

Humphries v. District of Columbia, 174 U.S. 190 (1899)

Castleberry v. NRM Corp., 470 F.2d 1113 (10th Cir. 1972)

Other FJC sources

Manual for Complex Litigation, Fourth 160–63 (2004)

6.09 Referrals to magistrate judges (civil matters)

Fed. R. Civ. P. 72 and 73; 28 U.S.C. § 636

Listed below are duties in civil matters that may be referred to magistrate judges. Most districts have local rules or standing orders governing referrals to magistrate judges.

For a more comprehensive listing of the duties magistrate judges may perform, see the *Inventory of United States Magistrate Judge Duties* (December 1999).[1] This inventory is available on request from the Magistrate Judges Division of the Administrative Office of the U.S. Courts and also appears in Chapter 3, "Jurisdiction," of the *Legal Manual for United States Magistrate Judges,* published by the Administrative Office.

A magistrate judge may conduct:

1. All phases of a civil case, with the written consent of the parties.[2] 28 U.S.C. § 636(c)(1); Fed. R. Civ. P. 73. Appeal is to the court of appeals, as in any other civil case. 28 U.S.C. § 636(c)(3); Fed. R. Civ. P. 73(c). See generally *supra* section 6.02: Trial outline—civil.[3]

2. Pretrial matters:

   (a) A magistrate judge may conduct a Rule 16 pretrial conference and hear and determine nondispositive pretrial matters, such as discovery disputes and requests for bifurcation or consolidation. Upon timely objection by a party, a district court shall consider such objections and modify or set aside any portion of the magis-

---

1. The Inventory was updated online in July 2009 and is available at http://jnet.ao.dcn/Judges/Magistrate_Judges/Authority/Inventory.html. The Administrative Office also provides an online web page that summarizes more recent decisions and articles relating to the duties and authority of magistrate judges at http://jnet.ao.dcn/Judges/Magistrate_Judges/Authority/Decisions. html.

2. The Supreme Court recently held that lack of written or express consent might not deprive the magistrate judge of jurisdiction—implied consent was sufficient in a case in which, after being informed of the right to trial before a district judge, a party voluntarily appeared before a magistrate judge and tried the case to conclusion. Roell v. Withrow, 538 U.S. 580, 586–91 (2003) ("although the specific referral procedures in 28 U.S.C. § 636(c)(2) and Federal Rule of Civil Procedure 73(b) are by no means just advisory, the text and structure of the section as a whole suggest that a defect in the referral to a full-time magistrate judge under § 636(c)(2) does not eliminate that magistrate judge's 'civil jurisdiction' under § 636(c)(1) so long as the parties have in fact voluntarily consented"). However, the *Benchbook* Committee believes that *Roell* is an unusual case and strongly recommends that written consent be obtained before proceeding.

3. For an illustrative consent form and order of reference to a magistrate judge, see Civil Litigation Management Manual (Judicial Conference of the United States, 2d ed. 2010), Sample Forms 50–53.

trate judge's order found to be clearly erroneous or contrary to law. 28 U.S.C. § 636(b)(1)(A); Fed. R. Civ. P. 72(a).

(b) A magistrate judge may hear and submit to the district court proposed findings of fact and recommended determinations of dispositive pretrial matters, such as summary judgment motions. A district court must make a de novo determination of those portions of proposed findings and recommendations to which the parties object. 28 U.S.C. § 636(b)(1); Fed. R. Civ. P. 72(b).

See generally *supra* section 6.02: Trial outline—civil.

3. Voir dire, if the parties consent. 28 U.S.C. § 636(c)(1); *Stockler v. Garratt,* 974 F.2d 730 (6th Cir. 1992); *Olympia Hotels Corp. v. Johnson Wax Development Corp.,* 908 F.2d 1363 (7th Cir. 1990). See *supra* section 6.05: Standard voir dire questions—civil.

4. "[A]dditional duties [that] are not inconsistent with the Constitution and laws of the United States." 28 U.S.C. § 636(b)(3). For examples of additional duties and case law on § 636(b)(3), see the *Inventory of United States Magistrate Judge Duties* at 112–40.

Other FJC sources

Civil Litigation Management Manual 150–54 (Judicial Conference of the United States, 2d ed. 2010)

Manual for Complex Litigation, Fourth 117 (2004)

7.01 Contempt—criminal

Fed. R. Crim. P. 42; 18 U.S.C. § 401

Background

The purpose, procedure, and penalty for criminal contempt differ from those for civil contempt. It is essential that the trial judge make clear on the record whether the proceeding is for civil or criminal contempt.

The purpose of criminal contempt is to punish a person for a past act of contempt. Criminal contempt has the characteristics of a crime, and the contemnor is cloaked with the safeguards of one accused of a crime. The purpose of civil contempt is to compel someone to do or not do a certain act.

Case law makes clear that the contempt power is one to be exercised with the greatest restraint and that, in exercising that power, a court should exert only the power needed to achieve the desired end.

Controlling statute and rule

The controlling statute for criminal contempt is 18 U.S.C. § 401. It provides as follows:

> A court of the United States shall have power to punish by fine or imprisonment, at its discretion, such contempt of its authority, and none other, as—
>
> (1) Misbehavior of any person in its presence or so near thereto as to obstruct the administration of justice;
>
> (2) Misbehavior of any of its officers in their official transactions;
>
> (3) Disobedience or resistance to its lawful writ, process, order, rule, decree, or command.

The applicable rule of procedure is Fed. R. Crim. P. 42. That rule, as amended December 1, 2002, provides as follows:

> (a) Disposition After Notice. Any person who commits criminal contempt may be punished for that contempt after prosecution on notice.
>
> > (1) Notice. The court must give the person notice in open court, in an order to show cause, or in an arrest order. The notice must:
> >
> > > (A) state the time and place of the trial;
> > >
> > > (B) allow the defendant a reasonable time to prepare a defense; and
> > >
> > > (C) state the essential facts constituting the charged criminal contempt and describe it as such.
> >
> > (2) Appointing a Prosecutor. The court must request that the contempt be prosecuted by an attorney for the government, unless the interest of justice requires the appointment of another attorney. If the government declines the request, the court must appoint another attorney to prosecute the attempt.

    (3) Trial and Disposition. A person being prosecuted for criminal contempt is entitled to a jury trial in any case in which federal law so provides and must be released or detained as Rule 46 provides. If the criminal contempt involves disrespect toward or criticism of a judge, that judge is disqualified from presiding at the contempt trial or hearing unless the defendant consents. Upon a finding or verdict of guilty, the court must impose the punishment.

(b) Summary Disposition. Notwithstanding any other provision of these rules, the court (other than a magistrate judge) may summarily punish a person who commits criminal contempt in its presence if the judge saw or heard the contemptuous conduct and so certifies; a magistrate judge may summarily punish a person as provided in 28 U.S.C. § 636(e). The contempt order must recite the facts, be signed by the judge, and be filed with the clerk.

Criminal contempt procedures

Fed. R. Crim. P. 42 prescribes two different procedures, depending on whether the judge personally observes the contemptuous conduct and whether immediate action is required.

Procedure when contemptuous conduct is personally observed by the judge and immediate action is required

When you see or hear contemptuous conduct, you may but are not compelled to proceed under Fed. R. Crim. P. 42(b).

This summary procedure is appropriate only when immediate action is needed. It is reserved for conduct that actually disrupts or obstructs court proceedings and for situations in which immediate action is necessary to restore the court's authority. The conduct must be more flagrant than mere disrespect to the judge or an affront to the judge's sense of dignity.[1]

If the conduct (such as shouting in the courtroom) does interfere with court proceedings, proceed as follows:

1. First, warn the person that if a repetition occurs, he or she may be removed from the courtroom or may be found in criminal contempt.

2. If marshals are not already in the courtroom, summon them, so that they will be present if the disruptive conduct is repeated.

3. If the offender repeats the disruptive conduct, order him or her removed from the courtroom.

4. If the conduct is so disruptive that removing the offender is inadequate to reestablish the authority and dignity of the court, follow the Fed. R. Crim. P. 42(b) procedure. [*Note:* In summary proceedings un-

---

1. Summary procedure may also be appropriate when an already imprisoned witness refuses to testify during a criminal trial despite a grant of immunity. *See* United States v. Wilson, 421 U.S. 309 (1975). *See also supra* section 5.04: Handling the recalcitrant witness.

der Rule 42(b), the court may impose a sentence that does not exceed the punishment authorized for a petty offense, i.e., imprisonment of no more than six months or a fine of no more than $5,000 if the contemnor is an individual, $10,000 if the contemnor is an organization. If more severe punishment seems appropriate, the court must proceed by notice under Rule 42(a) and accord the contemnor the right to a jury trial. (Contempt fines exceeding the petty offense limit on organizations have been imposed without the right to a jury trial. See *Muniz v. Hoffman*, 422 U.S. 454 (1975); *United States v. Twentieth Century Fox Film Corp.*, 882 F.2d 656 (2d Cir. 1989); *United States v. Troxler Hosiery Co.*, 681 F.2d 934 (4th Cir. 1982). These cases, however, did not involve summary proceedings under Rule 42(a) (now 42(b)).]

5. Before proceeding, be sure that an adequate number of marshals are in the courtroom.

6. Retire the jury. Have the offender brought before you. (The offender is not entitled to counsel in a summary proceeding.)

7. Advise the offender that you intend to find him or her in criminal contempt for obstructing the administration of justice by reason of [here describe the conduct].

8. Ask the offender if he or she would care to say anything in mitigation.

9. After hearing the offender out, impose sentence in words to this effect:

> I find you in criminal contempt for so conducting yourself in this courtroom that you obstructed the administration of justice. The conduct for which I find you in criminal contempt was [here describe the conduct observed by you]. I sentence you to ____ hour(s) [day(s)] in jail [*or* I fine you $____] for that conduct. [In criminal contempt you cannot both imprison and fine.] The serving of this sentence shall commence at once [*or* shall commence at the conclusion of this trial].

(a) No sentencing guideline has been prescribed for contempt because of the variety of behaviors covered. See U.S.S.G. § 2J1.1, Application Note 1.[2] In the absence of a guideline, the court is to "impose an appropriate sentence, having due regard for the purposes set forth in [18 U.S.C. § 3553(a)(2),] . . . for the relationship of the sentence imposed to sentences prescribed by guidelines applicable to similar offenses and offenders, and to the applica-

---

2. The application notes do, however, provide cross-references to other guidelines for when the contemptuous conduct involves obstruction of justice, willful failure to pay court-ordered child support, or violation of a judicial order enjoining fraudulent behavior.

ble policy statements of the Sentencing Commission." 18 U.S.C. § 3553(b).

(b) It is possible for the court to find a person in summary criminal contempt but to defer commencement of the sentence until the trial ends. In this case, however, using the Fed. R. Crim. P. 42(a) procedure rather than the summary procedure of 42(b) is probably best.

10. You must prepare, sign, and file an order of contempt. This order is intended to permit informed appellate review. The order must contain all that you saw or heard that obstructed the proceedings and by reason of which you found the defendant in contempt. Remember, for your action to be sustained on appeal, the conduct described in your order must constitute an obstruction to the administration of justice. Be sure, therefore, that the order fully and accurately recites all of the obstructive conduct that you saw or heard. The order of contempt must contain your certification that the described conduct was seen or heard by you and was committed in your presence. The form of the order of contempt may be as follows:

> In conformity with Rule 42(b), Federal Rules of Criminal Procedure, I hereby certify that the following was committed in my presence and was seen or heard by me: [Here insert a detailed recital of the acts constituting the contemptuous conduct.]
>
> Because of the foregoing conduct, which obstructed and disrupted the court in its administration of justice, I sentenced [name of contemnor] to hours/days in jail, the said jail sentence to commence [at once/at the conclusion of the trial] [*or* I fined [name of contemnor] $_____].

11. You must date and sign the order of contempt and file it without delay.

Procedure when contemptuous conduct is not personally observed by the judge or when the conduct is observed by the judge but requires no immediate action

If you become aware of conduct that is within the contemplation of 18 U.S.C. § 401 but did not occur in your presence, or if you observed contemptuous conduct but it did not actually disrupt court proceedings, you must proceed under Fed. R. Crim. P. 42(a), which requires that the contempt be prosecuted by notice rather than summarily.

Under Fed. R. Crim. P. 42(a):

1. The notice may be given

    (a) orally by you in open court in the defendant's presence; or

    (b) by an order to show cause; or

    (c) by an order of arrest.

2. If giving oral notice to the defendant in open court is not possible, you should ask the U.S. attorney to prepare for your signature an order to show cause directed to the defendant and ordering the defendant to show cause why he or she should not be found in criminal contempt because of the offending conduct.

3. The notice, whether oral or written, must set down a definite time and place for the hearing and must describe the conduct constituting the charged contempt and describe it as being criminal contempt. You must accord the defendant a reasonable period in which to engage an attorney and prepare a defense.

    Remember that under the rule, another judge must conduct the trial if the contemptuous conduct involved criticism of or disrespect for you, unless the defendant expressly waives the right to trial by another judge.

4. Because a person found guilty of criminal contempt may be imprisoned, the defendant has a right to counsel. If the defendant cannot afford counsel, you must appoint an attorney for him or her.

5. The defendant has a right to a jury trial unless, before trial, you, on your own motion or on the government's motion, limit the maximum sentence that you will impose to the maximum authorized for a petty offense, that is, imprisonment for six months or a fine of $5,000 (for an individual; the fine limit on organizations for petty offenses is $10,000 (*but see Muniz v. Hoffman*, 422 U.S. 454 (1975); *United States v. Twentieth Century Fox Film Corp.*, 882 F.2d 656 (2d Cir. 1989); *United States v. Troxler Hosiery Co.*, 681 F.2d 934 (4th Cir. 1982), allowing contempt fines on organizations in excess of those authorized for petty offenses, without the right to a jury trial).

6. At trial, whether a bench or jury trial, remember that the defendant is being tried for a crime and is entitled to all the protections to which anyone accused of a crime is entitled. The defendant has a right to testify and to call witnesses on his or her own behalf but cannot be compelled to testify. The defendant is to be found guilty only if his or her guilt is proven beyond a reasonable doubt.

7. If found guilty, the defendant should be sentenced in the same manner as any defendant convicted of a crime. You may wish to order a presentence report and to set down the sentencing for a later date.

8. If the defendant has been afforded the right to a jury trial, there is no statutory maximum to the fine or imprisonment that may be imposed. However, you may not impose both imprisonment and a fine. Because of the variety of behaviors covered, no sentencing guideline has been prescribed for contempt. See U.S.S.G. § 2J1.1, Application Note 1.[3] In the absence of a guideline, the court is to "impose an appropriate sentence, having due regard for the purposes set forth in [18 U.S.C. § 3553(a)(2),] . . . for the relationship of the sentence imposed to sentences prescribed by guidelines applicable to similar offenses and offenders, and to the applicable policy statements of the Sentencing Commission." 18 U.S.C. § 3553(b)(1).

Other FJC sources

Manual on Recurring Problems in Criminal Trials 30–43 (Tucker Carrington & Kris Markarian eds., 6th ed. 2010)

---

3. The application notes do, however, provide cross-references to other guidelines for when the contemptuous conduct involves obstruction of justice, willful failure to pay court-ordered child support, or violation of a judicial order enjoining fraudulent behavior.

7.02 Contempt—civil

Fed. R. Crim. P. 42; 18 U.S.C. § 401

Background

The purpose, procedure, and penalty for civil contempt differ from those for criminal contempt. It is essential that the trial judge make clear on the record whether the proceeding is for civil or criminal contempt.

NOTE
If you are dealing with a recalcitrant witness, see *supra* section 5.04: Handling the recalcitrant witness.

The purpose of criminal contempt is to punish a person for a past act of contempt. Criminal contempt has the characteristics of a crime, and the contemnor is cloaked with the safeguards of one accused of a crime. The primary purpose of civil contempt is to compel someone to do or not do a certain act.

Case law makes clear that the contempt power is one to be exercised with the greatest restraint and that, in exercising that power, a court should exert only the power needed to achieve the desired end.

Civil contempt serves one or both of the following purposes:

1. to coerce the contemnor into complying in the future with a court order; or

2. to compensate the complainant for damages resulting from the contemnor's past noncompliance.

Controlling statute and rule

The only statute applying directly to civil contempt is 28 U.S.C. § 1826(a), which applies only to recalcitrant witnesses (see *supra* section 5.04: Handling the recalcitrant witness). However, 18 U.S.C. § 401(3) does have some application to civil contempt, as follows:

> A court of the United States shall have power to punish by fine or imprisonment, at its discretion, such contempt of its authority, and none other, as—
>
> . . . .
>
> (3) Disobedience or resistance to its lawful writ, process, order, rule, decree, or command.

There is no civil rule comparable to Fed. R. Crim. P. 42. In a civil contempt proceeding, you should follow the procedure outlined in Fed. R. Crim. P. 42(a) to the extent that it applies, as follows:

> (a) Disposition After Notice. Any person who commits criminal contempt may be punished for that contempt after prosecution on notice.
>
> > (1) Notice. The court must give the person notice in open court, in an order to show cause, or in an arrest order. The notice must:
> >
> > > (A) state the time and place of the trial;
> > >
> > > (B) allow the defendant a reasonable time to prepare a defense; and

(C) state the essential facts constituting the charged criminal contempt and describe it as such.

(2) Appointing a Prosecutor. The court must request that the contempt be prosecuted by an attorney for the government, unless the interest of justice requires the appointment of another attorney. If the government declines the request, the court must appoint another attorney to prosecute the attempt.

(3) Trial and Disposition. A person being prosecuted for criminal contempt is entitled to a jury trial in any case in which federal law so provides and must be released or detained as Rule 46 provides. If the criminal contempt involves disrespect toward or criticism of a judge, that judge is disqualified from presiding at the contempt trial or hearing unless the defendant consents. Upon a finding or verdict of guilty, the court must impose the punishment.

Civil contempt procedure

The contempt will normally come before you on the petition of a civil litigant seeking the imposition of sanctions by reason of another party's failure to comply with a court order.

When one party petitions to have another found in civil contempt, you should proceed as follows:

1. Set down a time and place for a hearing on the petition. The respondent must be accorded a reasonable period in which to engage an attorney and prepare a defense.

2. Because a person found in civil contempt may be imprisoned, the respondent has a right to counsel. If the respondent desires an attorney but cannot afford one, you must appoint counsel for him or her unless waived (see *supra* section 1.02: Assignment of counsel or pro se representation).

3. The respondent in a civil contempt proceeding has no right to a jury trial, because the respondent, if imprisoned, can secure immediate release by complying with the court's order.

4. The hearing is to be by way of the live testimony of witnesses, not by way of affidavit. Note that the Federal Rules of Evidence apply to contempt proceedings. See Fed. R. Evid. 1101(b).

5. The respondent is to be found in civil contempt only if his or her contempt is established by clear and convincing evidence. In contrast with the procedure for criminal contempt, the respondent's guilt need not be proved beyond a reasonable doubt.

6. If the respondent is found guilty of civil contempt, you have wide discretion in fashioning a remedy.

    (a) You may imprison the contemnor until he or she purges himself or herself of contempt by complying with the court's order, you may impose a prospective conditional fine (such as a certain monetary amount per day) until the contemnor complies with the court's order, or you may both incarcerate the contemnor *and* impose a conditional fine. (There is no statutory ceiling on a conditional fine. You must, however, weigh the financial circumstances of the contemnor in fixing a conditional fine.)

(b) You may in addition impose a fine on the contemnor to be paid to the aggrieved party, to reimburse the party for damages suffered because of the contemnor's conduct. This fine may not, however, exceed the actual damages suffered by the aggrieved party. It may, under certain circumstances, include an award to the aggrieved party of the attorney's fees and costs in bringing the contempt proceeding.

7. If you incarcerate the contemnor or impose a conditional fine, advise the contemnor that he or she may purge himself or herself of contempt by complying with the court's order and that, upon complying, the contemnor will be released from jail and his or her fine, if one was imposed, will stop accumulating.

8. Prepare, sign, and file an Order in Civil Contempt, setting forth your findings of fact, your conclusions of law, and the precise sanctions you have imposed.

Other FJC sources

Manual on Recurring Problems in Criminal Trials 30–33 (Tucker Carrington & Kris Markarian eds., 6th ed. 2010)

7.03 Injunctions

Fed. R. Civ. P. 65

I. Temporary restraining orders

A. Background

Considering an application for a temporary restraining order (TRO) is, by definition, an emergency proceeding of such urgency that relief may be granted ex parte. At the outset, the court should be satisfied that there is truly an emergency and decline to consider the application if there is not. The court should also verify that it has jurisdiction over the matter.

Note that whether or not the TRO is granted, Fed. R. Civ. P. 52(a)(1) & (2) requires the court to "state the findings [of fact] and conclusions [of law] that support its action," and the court's "findings and conclusions may be stated on the record after the close of the evidence or may appear in an opinion or a memorandum of decision filed by the court."

B. TRO without notice

Fed. R. Civ. P. 65(b)(1) permits granting a TRO *without written or oral notice* to the adverse party or the party's attorney[1] only if

1. there are specific facts, shown by affidavit or verified complaint, clearly indicating that immediate and irreparable injury will result to the applicant before the adverse party or his or her attorney can be heard in opposition; and

2. there is a written certification of the attorney's attempts, if any, to give notice, and an explanation of why notice should not be required.

Other factors the court may consider are

1. probability of success on the merits;

2. balance of harm to other interested parties if the TRO is issued against the harm to the applicant if relief is denied; and

3. the public interest.

C. TRO with notice

1. If notice is given, the standards governing issuance of a preliminary injunction are applicable.

2. The petition may be treated like one for a preliminary injunction if there is notice and a hearing, and adequate opportunity is provided for developing legal and factual issues. The court should, however,

---

1. The advisory committee notes stress that "informal notice, which may be communicated to the attorney rather than the adverse party, is to be preferred to no notice at all." Note to 1966 amendment to Fed. R. Crim. P. 65(b).

consider the applicability of Fed. R. Civ. P. 6(c)(1) (requiring fourteen days' notice before hearing on motion, but granting court discretion to modify the time period).

3. If there is notice but no hearing, or a hearing that does not permit adequate opportunity for the development of legal and factual issues, no preliminary injunction may issue.

D. Contents of order

Fed. R. Civ. P. 65(b)(2) provides that if the TRO is granted without notice, the order shall

1. be endorsed with the date and hour of the issuance;
2. be filed forthwith in the clerk's office and entered on the record;
3. define the injury and state why it is irreparable and why the order was granted without notice; and
4. expire by its terms within such time after entry as the court fixes (but no more than fourteen days), unless within the time fixed by the court good cause is shown to extend the order for a like period, or unless the party against whom the order is directed consents to a longer period.

These requirements, particularly with regard to a restraining order's duration, should be applied to a TRO even when notice has been given. In addition, Fed. R. Civ. P. 65(d) provides that every restraining order shall

1. set forth the reasons for its issuance;
2. be specific in terms;
3. describe in reasonable detail, and not by reference to the complaint or other documents, the act or acts to be restrained[2]; and
4. bind only the parties to the action; the parties' officers, agents, servants, employees, and attorneys; and persons in active concert or participation with the parties who receive actual notice of the order.

E. Motion for dissolution after notice

On two days' notice to the party that obtained the TRO without notice, or on such shorter notice as the court may prescribe, the adverse party may appear and contest a TRO that was issued without notice. Fed. R. Civ. P. 65(b)(4).

---

2. Care should be taken to ensure that the terms of the order are clear and specific. As one court phrased it, "a court must craft its orders so that those who seek to obey may know precisely what the court intends to forbid." American Red Cross v. Palm Beach Blood Bank, Inc., 143 F.3d 1407, 1411 (11th Cir. 1998).

F. Security

A TRO may not be issued unless the applicant gives such security as the court fixes. This security requirement does not apply to the United States. Fed. R. Civ. P. 65(c).

G. The hearing record

The hearing on an application for a TRO, including pleadings and evidence taken, becomes a part of the record in the later injunction hearing and need not be repeated.

Whether or not the TRO is granted, Fed. R. Civ. P. 52(a)(1) & (2) requires the court to "state the findings [of fact] and conclusions [of law] that support its action." The court's "findings and conclusions may be stated on the record after the close of the evidence or may appear in an opinion or a memorandum of decision filed by the court."

II. Preliminary injunctions

A. Notice and hearing

A preliminary injunction may not be issued without notice. Fed. R. Civ. P. 65(a)(1). The rule does not specify the form of notice or how much notice is required. However, Fed. R. Civ. P. 6(c)(1) requires that notice of a hearing, and affidavits that support a motion, be provided "at least 14 days before the time specified for the hearing" unless the court provides otherwise. For shorter time periods, and for the form of notice, general considerations of due process and fairness should be applied.

Generally, some kind of hearing will be held, although the form of the hearing will depend upon the record before the court. For example, if there is no disputed issue of fact, the determination of whether to issue the injunction may be made on the papers alone, with or without oral argument. Even if there is a disputed issue of fact, a witness's direct testimony may be presented by way of affidavit and the witness may be subject to cross-examination.

B. Burden of proof

The moving party has the burden of demonstrating entitlement to relief. Rule 65 does not specify the requirements for a preliminary injunction, and they vary from circuit to circuit, but the courts generally consider

1. the likelihood that the moving party will suffer irreparable injury in the absence of a preliminary injunction;
2. the moving party's likelihood of success on the merits;
3. the balance of hardships between the parties (and any relevant non-parties); and

    4. the effect on public policy of granting or denying the preliminary in-
        junction.

Absent extraordinary circumstances, a preliminary injunction will not be issued where an adequate remedy at law exists, that is, where the moving
party could be compensated by money damages. An exception to this general rule exists when it is shown that a money judgment will go unsatisfied
absent equitable relief, such as when the target of the injunction is insolvent
or is likely to transfer or dissipate assets to avoid payment.

C. Preparing for the hearing

Because a decision must be reached quickly and the time to prepare for the
hearing may be brief, it may help the parties and the court if some matters
are addressed before the hearing. The court may, for example,

1. narrow the legal scope of the hearing by eliminating claims, de-
    fenses, and counterclaims that do not relate directly to the decision
    of whether to issue a preliminary injunction;

2. narrow the factual scope of the hearing by directing the parties to
    submit statements of undisputed facts or requests for admission;

3. direct counsel to identify any witnesses in advance, along with the
    substance of their testimony and the exhibits they will sponsor;

4. require that direct testimony be offered in the form of adopted narra-
    tive statements, exchanged in advance, which will be subject to mo-
    tions to strike, to cross-examination, and to redirect at the hearing if
    issues of credibility are presented;

5. direct counsel to exchange proposed exhibits in advance, give notice
    that objections may be treated as waived if not made in writing in ad-
    vance of the hearing, and resolve objections to foundation before the
    hearing;

6. direct counsel to present stipulated summaries or extracts of any
    deposition testimony to be used in lieu of lengthy readings of tran-
    scripts; and

7. direct counsel to submit briefs in advance of the hearing, along with
    proposed findings of fact and conclusions of law.

If the court determines that no substantial factual disputes exist, consider
holding the hearing only on the affidavits.

D. Advancing trial on the merits

At any time before or during the hearing on the motion, trial on the merits
may be advanced and consolidated with the preliminary injunction motion,
on motion or by the court sua sponte. Fed. R. Civ. P. 65(a)(2). It should be
done on notice and might be appropriate when, for example, expedited discovery has produced virtually all of the discovery that would be produced for

trial on the merits. Adequate notice must be provided to allow sufficient preparation for trial, and the court should consider whether the case is sufficiently urgent to give it preference over others. Note that the rule provides that consolidation "must preserve any party's right to a jury trial."

Whether or not consolidation is ordered, "evidence that is received on the motion and that would be admissible at trial becomes part of the trial record and need not be repeated at trial. Fed. R. Civ. P. 65(a)(2). However, the court's findings of fact and conclusions of law made in connection with the motion for preliminary injunction are not binding at the trial and the decision on the merits.

E. Decision and findings

As with a TRO, see *supra* section I.D, Rule 65(d)(1) sets out the form and scope of the order granting an injunction (or restraining order) and notes, inter alia, that such orders shall

1. set forth the reasons for issuance (which should, of course, include a finding of no adequate remedy at law); and

2. describe in reasonable detail and not by reference to other documents the acts to be restrained or compelled. Thus, such an order should adequately inform the reader of the acts that are enjoined or compelled.

In addition, Fed. R. Civ. P. 52(a)(1) & (2) states that when "granting or refusing an interlocutory injunction, the court must . . . state the findings [of fact] and conclusions [of law] that support its action." The court's "findings and conclusions may be stated on the record after the close of the evidence or may appear in an opinion or a memorandum of decision filed by the court."

Note that a preliminary injunction is binding "only upon the parties to the action, their officers, agents, servants, employees, and attorneys, and upon those persons in active concert or participation with them who receive actual notice of the order of personal service or otherwise." Fed. R. Civ. P. 65(d)(2).

F. Security

As with a temporary restraining order, a preliminary injunction generally may not be issued unless the applicant posts security in an amount deemed appropriate by the court in its discretion, although a nominal amount may be required. Fed. R. Civ. P. 65(c). The court may also dispense with security when, for example, the movant has adequate resources to pay damages for a wrongfully issued injunction. If nominal or no security is ordered, the court should explain its reasons. The rule provides that no security shall be required of the government or its officers or agencies.

7.04   Grand jury selection and instructions

Fed. R. Crim. P. 6; 18 U.S.C. §§ 3321, 3331–3333

Procedure

The Jury Act, 28 U.S.C. § 1863(b)(7), states that the district jury plans required by that section may provide that the names of persons summoned for possible grand jury service be kept confidential. In addition, the Judicial Conference of the United States recommended at its session in September 1981 "that the district courts reexamine their jury selection plans . . . to consider whether the names of grand jurors should be excluded from public records." *Report of the Proceedings of the Judicial Conference of the United States* 39–40 (1981). The jury plans of many of the district courts now provide, therefore, that the names of grand jurors be kept confidential. Accordingly, the grand jury must be selected in closed session with only necessary court personnel and attorneys for the government in attendance so that the jurors' names will not be revealed in open court. Fed. R. Crim. P. 6(d) and (e)(5).

The grand jury consists of not fewer than sixteen persons (a quorum) and not more than twenty-three persons. 18 U.S.C. § 3321; Fed. R. Crim. P. 6(a)(1). Alternate grand jurors may be selected. Fed. R. Crim. P. 6(a)(2). After twenty-three persons have been selected as regular members of the grand jury, the usual practice in some districts is to call four to six alternates, who are sworn and instructed with the regular members. These alternates are then excused with the explanation that they will be subject to call, in the order in which they were selected, if it subsequently becomes necessary to excuse one of the regular members and replace that person with an alternate (to facilitate the assemblage of a quorum during the remaining life of the grand jury).

To accommodate the selection of alternates and the possibility of a few excusals for cause, the panel summoned to the courtroom for grand jury selection should consist of thirty to thirty-five persons.

A regular grand jury may serve up to eighteen months, followed by one extension, if that is determined to be in the public interest, for up to six months. Fed. R. Crim. P. 6(g). The usual term varies from district to district. Special grand juries formed pursuant to 18 U.S.C. §§ 3331–3333 may serve, with extensions, up to thirty-six months, and they have the added power of making certain reports under § 3333.

Opening statement to the venire panel

It is a pleasure to welcome you on behalf of the judges of the United States District Court for _____, as potential members of the grand jury for the period _____ through _____.

Although my welcoming remarks are intended for all, only twenty-three of you, plus _____ alternates, will be selected to form this new grand jury. Also, although your term will be for the next _____ months, you will sit as a jury from time to time only when called on by the Office of the U.S. Attorney. I cannot tell you in advance how much time will be involved, but normally you can expect to be called an average of ___ days a month during your term of office.

Federal law requires that we select the grand jury from a pool of persons chosen at random from a fair cross section of the district in which the grand jury is convened. At this time, you are the pool of persons from which that selection is to be made.

The grand jury is involved with criminal matters. It does not concern itself with civil matters. Generally speaking, a criminal matter is one in which the government seeks to enforce a criminal law. By contrast, a civil matter is a court proceeding in which one party seeks to recover money damages or other relief from another party. The trial jury in a criminal matter listens to the evidence offered by the prosecution and defense during trial and renders a verdict of guilty or not guilty. The functions of a grand jury are quite different from those of a trial jury. A grand jury does not determine guilt or innocence. Its sole function is to decide, after hearing the government's evidence and usually without hearing evidence from the defense, whether a person should be indicted and stand trial for a federal crime.

Since the grand jury performs such an important role in protecting rights guaranteed by the Constitution, you should view it as a real privilege and honor to have an opportunity to serve.

We will now proceed with the selection of the grand jury. As the first step in the process, I am going to ask the clerk to call you forward in groups of ___ [usually 12] persons at a time so that I might ask each of you a few questions concerning your possible service as members of the grand jury.

Voir dire examination of the panel

1. Please state your name, occupation, and employer.

   [This information may assist you later in choosing and designating a foreperson and deputy foreperson pursuant to Fed. R. Crim. P. 6(c).]

2. Have any of you ever had, or are any of you currently having, any experience with a grand jury or with other aspects of the criminal justice system—as a witness, a victim, or an indicted person, for example—which might now make it difficult for you to serve impartially if you are selected?

3. Do any of you have any other reason why you cannot or should not serve on the grand jury?

[Excuse any members of the panel whose responses to the voir dire questions dictate that they should be excused for cause.]

Selection and oath

1. Have the clerk call at random the names of twenty-three to twenty-nine persons from the remaining members of the panel. The first twenty-three shall constitute the regular members of the grand jury, and the others (one to six) shall constitute the alternates. After the grand jury and alternates have been chosen, excuse the remaining members of the panel.

2. Designate and appoint a foreperson and deputy foreperson under Fed. R. Crim. P. 6(c).

3. Have the clerk administer the oath:

   Do each of you solemnly swear [affirm] to diligently inquire into and make true presentment or indictment of all such matters and things touching your present grand jury service that are given to you in charge or otherwise come to your knowledge; to keep secret the counsel of the United States, your fellows, and yourselves; and not to present or indict any person through hatred, malice, or ill will, nor to leave any person unpresented or unindicted through fear, favor, or affection or for any reward or hope or promise thereof, but in all your presentments and indictments to present the truth, the whole truth, and nothing but the truth to the best of your skill and understanding? If so, answer "I do."

Grand jury charge[1]

Give the court's charge or instructions to the grand jury (including the alternates):

Ladies and gentlemen:

1. Now that you have been empaneled and sworn as a grand jury, it is the court's responsibility to instruct you as to the law which should govern your actions and your deliberations as grand jurors.

2. The framers of our Federal Constitution deemed the grand jury so important for the administration of justice, they included it in the Bill of Rights. The Fifth Amendment to the United States Constitution provides in part that no person shall be held to answer for a capital or otherwise infamous crime without action by a grand jury. An infamous crime is a serious crime which may be punished by impris-

---

1. This grand jury charge was written by the Benchbook Committee of the Federal Judicial Center and the Court Administration and Case Management Committee of the Judicial Conference of the United States. It was approved in 2005 as a replacement for each group's earlier grand jury charge.

onment for more than one year. The purpose of the grand jury is to determine whether there is sufficient evidence to justify a formal accusation against a person—that is, to determine if there is "probable cause" to believe the person committed a crime. If law enforcement officials were not required to submit to an impartial grand jury proof of guilt as to a proposed charge against a person suspected of having committed a crime, they would be free to arrest a suspect and bring that suspect to trial no matter how little evidence existed to support the charge.

3. The grand jury is an independent body and does not belong to any branch of the government. As members of the grand jury, you, in a very real sense, stand between the government and the person being investigated by the government. A federal grand jury must never be made an instrument of private prejudice, vengeance, or malice. It is your duty to see to it that indictments are returned only against those who you find probable cause to believe are guilty and to see to it that the innocent are not compelled to go to trial.

4. A member of the grand jury who is related by blood or marriage to a person under investigation, or who knows that person well enough to have a biased state of mind as to that person, or is biased for any reason, should not participate in the investigation of that person or in the return of the indictment. This does not mean that if you have an opinion you should not participate in the investigation. However, it does mean that if you have a fixed opinion before you hear any evidence, either on a basis of friendship or ill will or some other similar motivation, you should not participate in that investigation and in voting on the indictment.

5. Sixteen of the twenty-three members of the grand jury constitute a quorum and must be present for the transaction of any business. If fewer than this number are present, even for a moment, the proceedings of the grand jury must stop.

Limitation on the powers of the grand jury

6. Although as grand jurors, you have extensive powers, they are limited in several important respects.

7. You can only investigate conduct which violates federal criminal laws. Criminal activity which violates state law is outside your inquiry. Sometimes, though, the same conduct violates both federal and state law, and this you may properly consider.

8. There is also a geographic limitation on the scope of your inquiries in the exercise of your power. You may inquire only as to federal offenses committed in this district.

9. You cannot judge the wisdom of the criminal laws enacted by Congress, that is, whether or not there should or should not be a federal law designating certain activity as criminal. That is to be determined by Congress and not by you.

10. Furthermore, when deciding whether or not to indict, you should not consider punishment in the event of conviction.

The grand jury's tasks and procedures

11. The cases which you will hear will come before you in various ways. Frequently, suspects are arrested during or shortly after the commission of an alleged crime, and they are taken before a magistrate judge, who then holds a preliminary hearing to determine whether there is probable cause to believe that the person has committed a crime. If the magistrate judge finds such probable cause, he or she will direct that the person be held for the action of the grand jury so that you can independently consider whether there should be an indictment.

12. Other cases will be brought before you by a government attorney—the U.S. attorney or an assistant U.S. attorney—before an arrest but after an investigation has been conducted by a governmental agency, such as the Federal Bureau of Investigation, the Treasury Department, the Drug Enforcement Administration, Postal Authorities, or other federal law enforcement officials.

13. Since the government attorney has the duty of prosecuting persons charged with the commission of federal crimes, the government attorney will present the matters which the government wants you to consider. The government will point out to you the laws which it believes have been violated, and will subpoena for testimony before you such witnesses as the government attorney may consider important and necessary and also any other witnesses that you may request or direct be called before you.

14. If during the course of your hearings, a different crime other than the one you are investigating surfaces, you have the right to pursue this new crime. Although you can subpoena new witnesses and documents, you have no power to employ investigators or to expend federal funds for investigative purposes. If the government attorney refuses to assist you or if you believe he or she is not acting impartially, you may take it up with me or any judge of this court. You may use this power even over the active opposition of the government's attorneys, if you believe it is necessary to do so in the interest of justice.

Evidence

15. The evidence you will consider will normally consist of oral testimony of witnesses and written documents. Each witness will appear before you separately. When the witness first appears before you, the grand jury foreperson will administer to the witness an oath or affirmation to testify truthfully. After this has been accomplished, the witness may be questioned. Ordinarily, the government attorney questions the witness first. Next, the foreperson may question the witness, and then any other members of the grand jury may ask questions. In the event a witness does not speak or understand the English language, an interpreter may be brought into the grand jury room to assist in the questioning.

16. Witnesses should be treated courteously and questions put to them in an orderly fashion. If you have any doubt whether it is proper to ask a particular question, ask the government attorney for advice. If necessary, a ruling may be obtained from the court.

17. You alone decide how many witnesses you want to hear. You can subpoena witnesses from anywhere in the country, directing the government attorney to issue necessary subpoenas. However, persons should not ordinarily be subjected to disruption of their daily lives, harassed, annoyed, or inconvenienced, nor should public funds be expended to bring in witnesses unless you believe they can provide meaningful evidence which will assist you in your investigation.

18. Every witness has certain rights when appearing before a grand jury. Witnesses have the right to refuse to answer any question if the answer would tend to incriminate them and the right to know that anything they say may be used against them. The grand jury should hold no prejudice against a witness who exercises the right against compulsory self-incrimination, and this can play no part in the return of any indictment.

19. Although witnesses are not permitted to have a lawyer present with them in the grand jury room, the law permits witnesses to confer with their lawyer outside of the grand jury room. Since an appearance before a grand jury may present complex legal problems requiring the assistance of a lawyer, you also cannot hold it against a witness if a witness chooses to exercise this right and leaves the grand jury room to confer with an attorney.

20. Ordinarily, neither the person being investigated by the government nor any witnesses on behalf of that person will testify before the grand jury. Upon his or her request, preferably in writing, you may afford that person an opportunity to appear before you. Because the appearance of the person being investigated before you may raise

complicated legal problems, you should seek the government attorney's advice and, if necessary, the court's ruling before his or her appearance is permitted. Before that person testifies, he or she must be advised of his or her rights and required to sign a formal waiver. You should be completely satisfied that the person being investigated understands what he or she is doing. You are not required to summon witnesses which that person may wish to have examined unless probable cause for an indictment may be explained away by their testimony.

21. The determination of whether a witness is telling the truth is something that you must decide. Neither the court nor the prosecutors nor any officers of the court may make this determination for you.

    As you listen to witnesses presented to you in the grand jury room and hear their testimony, remember that you are the judge of each witness's credibility. You may believe the witness's testimony, or you may not believe it, in whole or in part. Determining the credibility of a witness involves a question of fact, not a question of law. It is for you to decide whether you believe the person's testimony. You may consider in that regard whether the witnesses are personally interested in the outcome of the investigation, whether their testimony has been corroborated or supported by other witnesses or circumstances, what opportunity they have had for observing or acquiring knowledge concerning the matters about which they testify, the reasonableness or probability of the testimony they relate to you, and their manner and demeanor in testifying before you.

22. Hearsay is testimony as to facts which are not personally known by the witness but which have been told or related to the witness by persons other than the person being investigated. Hearsay testimony, if deemed by you to be persuasive, may in itself provide a basis for returning an indictment. You must be satisfied only that there is evidence against the accused showing probable cause, even if such evidence is composed of hearsay testimony that might or might not be admissible in evidence at a trial.

23. Frequently, charges are made against more than one person. It will be your duty to examine the evidence as it relates to *each* person, and to make your finding as to *each* person. In other words, where charges are made against more than one person, you may indict all of the persons or only those persons who you believe properly deserve indictment.

Deliberation and vote

24. After you have heard all the evidence you wish to hear in a particular matter, you will then proceed to deliberate as to whether the person

being investigated should be indicted. No one other than your own members or an interpreter necessary to assist a juror who is hearing or speech impaired is to be present while you are deliberating or voting.

25. To return an indictment charging an individual with an offense, it is not necessary that you find that individual guilty beyond a reasonable doubt. You are not a trial jury, and your task is not to decide the guilt or innocence of the person charged. Your task is to determine whether the government's evidence as presented to you is sufficient to cause you to conclude that there is probable cause to believe that the person being investigated committed the offense charged. To put it another way, you should vote to indict where the evidence presented to you is sufficiently strong to warrant a reasonable person's belief that the person being investigated is probably guilty of the offense charged.

26. Each juror has the right to express his or her view of the matter under consideration. Only after all grand jurors have been given full opportunity to be heard will a vote be taken. You may decide after deliberation among yourselves that further evidence should be considered before a vote is taken. In such case you may direct the government attorney to subpoena the additional documents or witnesses you want to consider.

27. When you have decided to vote, the foreperson shall designate a juror as secretary, who will keep a record of the vote, which shall be filed with the clerk of court. The record does not include the names of the jurors but only the number of those voting for the indictment. Remember, at least sixteen jurors must be present at all times, and at least twelve members must vote in favor of an indictment before one may be returned.

28. If twelve or more members of the grand jury, after deliberation, believe that an indictment is warranted, then you will request that the government attorney prepare the formal written indictment if one has not already been prepared and presented to you. The indictment will set forth the date and place of the alleged offense, will assert the circumstances making the alleged conduct criminal, and will identify the criminal statute violated. The foreperson will sign the indictment as a true bill in the space followed by the word "foreperson." It is the duty of the foreperson to sign every indictment, whether the foreperson voted for or against. If fewer than twelve members of the grand jury vote in favor of an indictment which has been submitted to you for your consideration, the foreperson will endorse the indictment "Not a True Bill" and return it to the court and the court will impound it.

29. Indictments which have been signed as a true bill will be presented to a judge [or a magistrate judge] in open court by your foreperson at the conclusion of each deliberative session of the grand jury. In the absence of the foreperson, a deputy foreperson may act in place of the foreperson and perform all functions and duties of the foreperson.

Independence of the grand jury

30. It is extremely important for you to realize that under the United States Constitution, the grand jury is independent of the United States attorney and is not an arm or agent of the Federal Bureau of Investigation, the Drug Enforcement Administration, the Internal Revenue Service, or any governmental agency charged with prosecuting a crime. Simply put, as I have already told you, the grand jury is an independent body and does not belong to any branch of the government.

31. However, as a practical matter, you must work closely with the government attorneys. They will provide you with important service in helping you to find your way when confronted with complex legal matters. It is entirely proper that you should receive this assistance. If past experience is any indication of what to expect in the future, then you can expect candor, honesty, and good faith in matters presented by the government attorneys. However, ultimately, you must depend on your own independent judgment, never becoming an arm of the United States Attorney's Office. The government attorneys are prosecutors. You are not. If the facts suggest that you should not indict, then you should not do so, even in the face of the opposition or statements of the government attorney. You would violate your oath if you merely "rubber-stamped" indictments brought before you by the government representatives.

32. Just as you must maintain your independence in your dealings with the government attorneys, so should your dealings with the court be on a formal basis. If you have a question for the court or desire to make a presentment or return an indictment to the court, you will assemble in the courtroom for these purposes. Moreover, each juror is directed to report immediately to the court any attempt by any person who under any pretense whatsoever addresses or contacts him or her for the purpose of or with the intent to gain any information of any kind concerning the proceedings of the grand jury, or to influence a juror in any manner or for any purpose.

The obligation of secrecy

33. Your proceedings are secret and must remain secret permanently unless and until the court decrees otherwise. You cannot relate to your family, to the news or television reporters, or to anyone that which transpired in the grand jury room. There are several important reasons for this requirement. First, a premature disclosure of grand jury action may frustrate the ends of justice by giving an opportunity to the person being investigated to escape and become a fugitive or to destroy evidence. Second, if the testimony of a witness is disclosed, the witness may be subject to intimidation, retaliation, bodily injury, or other tampering before testifying at trial. Third, the requirement of secrecy protects an innocent person who may have come under investigation but has been cleared by the actions of the grand jury. In the eyes of some, investigation by a grand jury alone carries with it a suggestion of guilt. Thus, great injury can be done to a person's good name even though the person is not indicted. And fourth, the secrecy requirement helps to protect the members of the grand jury themselves from improper contacts by those under investigation. For all these reasons, therefore, the secrecy requirement is of the utmost importance and must be regarded by you as an absolute duty. If you violate your oath of secrecy, you may be subject to punishment.

34. To ensure the secrecy of grand jury proceedings, the law provides that only authorized persons may be in the grand jury room while evidence is being presented. Only the members of the grand jury, the government attorney, the witness under examination, the court reporter, and an interpreter, if required, may be present.

35. If you ultimately vote to return an indictment, the presence of unauthorized persons in the grand jury room could invalidate it. Particularly remember that no person other than the grand jury members themselves or an interpreter necessary to assist a juror who is hearing or speech impaired may be present in the grand jury room while the jurors are deliberating and voting. Although you may disclose matters which occur before the grand jury to attorneys for the government for use by such attorneys in the performance of their duties, you may not disclose the contents of your deliberations and the vote of any juror even to a government attorney.

Conclusion

36. The importance of the service you will perform is demonstrated by the very comprehensive and important oath which you took a short while ago. It is an oath rooted in history, and thousands of your forebears have taken similar oaths. Therefore, as good citizens, you

should be proud to have been selected to assist in the administration of the American system of justice.

37. The government attorney will now accompany you and will assist you in getting organized, after which you may proceed with the business to come before you.

38. The United States marshal and deputy United States marshals will attend to you and be subject to your appropriate orders.

39. You may now retire.

[*Note:* It is suggested that grand jurors be provided either with a written copy of the charge or with the *Handbook for Federal Grand Jurors* (Judicial Conference of the United States and Administrative Office of the U.S. Courts 1986).]

[The remainder of the charge should be given only if the grand jury is a special grand jury being impaneled pursuant to 18 U.S.C. §§ 3331–3334.]

Additional powers of a special grand jury

As stated to you earlier, you are being impaneled as a special grand jury, as distinguished from a regular grand jury.

A regular grand jury is subject to two important restrictions: (1) its term or life is limited to a period of eighteen months, and (2) it can indict someone, on a finding of probable cause, or vote not to indict, but that is the extent of the action it can take; it cannot issue a report concerning its findings.

You, as a special grand jury, will be governed by a different set of rules or laws. First, while your term of service is also fixed at eighteen months (unless a majority of the jury determines sooner that your work has been completed), that term may be extended by the court for up to eighteen additional months. Second, unlike a regular grand jury, you are authorized under certain conditions at the end of your term to submit to the court, if a majority of you so desire, a report concerning your findings as to certain matters.

Specifically, the United States Code, title 18, section 3333, provides as follows:

(a) A special grand jury impaneled by any district court, with the concurrence of a majority of its members, may, upon completion of its original term, or each extension thereof, submit to the court a report—

   (1) concerning noncriminal misconduct, malfeasance, or misfeasance in office involving organized criminal activity by an ap-

pointed public officer or employee as the basis for a recommendation of removal or disciplinary action; or

(2) regarding organized crime conditions in the district.

The U.S. attorney will explain to you in more detail your powers and duties under this law. As you approach the end of your term the court will give you additional instructions if you request, or answer any questions you might have.

7.05   Foreign extradition proceedings

18 U.S.C. §§ 3181–3196

A. Ascertain

1. the identity of the detainee as the individual being demanded by a foreign nation; and

2. whether the detainee is represented by counsel (see *supra* section 1.02: Assignment of counsel or pro se representation). 18 U.S.C. § 3006A(b).

B. Inform the detainee

1. of the charge or charges upon which extradition is sought and by which foreign nation;

2. of the right to a public extradition hearing, 18 U.S.C. § 3189;

3. under what circumstances the United States will pay the costs for subpoenaing material witnesses for the detainee's defense to extradition, 18 U.S.C. § 3191;

4. that at the hearing it will be determined:

(a) whether the detainee is charged with a crime or crimes for which there is a treaty or convention for extradition between the United States and the demanding country, 18 U.S.C. §§ 3181, 3184; see also *Collins v. Loisel,* 259 U.S. 309 (1922);

(b) whether the warrants and documents demanding the prisoner's surrender are properly and legally authenticated, 18 U.S.C. § 3190; and

(c) whether the commission of the crime alleged is established by probable cause such as would justify commitment for trial if the offense had been committed in the United States, 18 U.S.C. § 3184.

C. Obtain a waiver of hearing, hold the hearing, or grant a continuance if necessary (see *supra* section 1.03: Release or detention pending trial).

D. If a hearing is held, determine whether the detainee is extraditable.

E. If the detainee is found extraditable:

1. Commit the detainee to jail under surrender to the demanding nation, unless "special circumstances" justify his or her release on bail. *Wright v. Henkel,* 190 U.S. 40 (1903); *Hu Yau-Leung v. Soscia,* 649 F.2d 914 (2d Cir. 1981).

2. Notify the Secretary of State by filing a certified copy of your findings and a transcript of the proceedings.

F. If the detainee is found not extraditable, notify the Secretary of State by filing an appropriate report certifying to that effect.

NOTE
The Federal Rules of Criminal Procedure are not applicable to extradition proceedings. Fed. R. Crim. P. 1(a)(5)(A).

7.06 Naturalization proceedings

8 U.S.C. §§ 1421, 1443–1448

The Immigration Act of 1990 changed the naturalization process from a judicial proceeding to an administrative proceeding. The following is a brief outline of current naturalization practice. Note that the role of the district court has been curtailed.

Procedure

1. The applicant for naturalization commences the proceeding by filing an application for naturalization with the Attorney General.
2. An employee of the Immigration and Naturalization Service (INS) examines the applicant and determines whether to grant or deny the application. The INS employee may invoke the aid of a district court in subpoenaing the attendance and testimony of witnesses and the production of books, papers, and documents. 8 U.S.C. § 1446(b), (d).
3. If the INS denies the application, the applicant may request a hearing before an immigration officer. 8 U.S.C. § 1447(a).
4. If the immigration officer denies the application, the applicant may seek de novo review in the federal district court. 8 U.S.C. § 1421(c).
5. If the INS fails to make a determination on the application within 120 days of the applicant's interview, the applicant may apply to a district court for a naturalization hearing. The court may determine the matter or remand the matter to the INS with appropriate instructions. 8 U.S.C. § 1447(b).
6. If an application is approved, a district court with jurisdiction under 8 U.S.C. § 1421(b) may administer the oath of allegiance.

Oath of allegiance

The following oath, based on the requirements listed in 8 U.S.C. § 1448(a), is designed for use with groups of applicants and includes various alternatives to bearing arms.

> Do you solemnly swear [affirm] to support the Constitution of the United States; to renounce and abjure absolutely and entirely all allegiance and fidelity to any foreign prince, potentate, state, or sovereignty of which you have previously been a citizen or subject; to support and defend the Constitution and the laws of the United States against all enemies, foreign and domestic; to bear true faith and allegiance to the same; and to bear arms on behalf of the United States when required by law [*or* to perform noncombatant service in the Armed Forces of the United States when required by law, *or* to perform work of national importance under civilian direction when

required by law]? Do you take this obligation freely without any mental reservation or purpose of evasion?

See also the oath provided at 8 C.F.R. § 337.1(a):

> I hereby declare, on oath, that I absolutely and entirely renounce and abjure all allegiance and fidelity to any foreign prince, potentate, state, or sovereignty, of whom or which I have heretofore been a subject or citizen; that I will support and defend the Constitution and laws of the United States of America against all enemies, foreign and domestic; that I will bear true faith and allegiance to the same; that I will bear arms on behalf of the United States when required by the law; that I will perform noncombatant service in the Armed Forces of the United States when required by the law; that I will perform work of national importance under civilian direction when required by the law; and that I take this obligation freely, without any mental reservation or purpose of evasion; so help me God.

[*Note:* If the applicant refuses to bear arms or do noncombatant service in the armed forces, ascertain whether there is "clear and convincing evidence" that the refusal is based on "religious training and belief." 8 U.S.C. § 1448(a).]

An individual may be granted an expedited judicial oath administration ceremony upon demonstrating sufficient cause.

> In determining whether to grant an expedited judicial oath administration ceremony, a court shall consider special circumstances (such as serious illness of the applicant or a member of the applicant's immediate family, permanent disability sufficiently incapacitating as to prevent the applicant's personal appearance at the scheduled ceremony, developmental disability or advanced age, or exigent circumstances relating to travel or employment).

8 U.S.C. § 1448(c).

If the applicant possesses any hereditary title or orders of nobility in any foreign state, he or she must expressly renounce such title or orders of nobility in open court. 8 U.S.C. § 1448(b).

Address (or designate some member of the community to address, or invite some of the newly naturalized citizens to address) the naturalized citizens on the general topic of the meaning of U.S. citizenship and the importance of each citizen's participation in the workings of a democracy. 36 U.S.C. § 154.

7.07 Excluding the public from court proceedings

A. Closing of the courtroom is appropriate upon the court's own motion

1. in proceedings other than an actual trial, for the court to receive testimony from or about grand jury proceedings, argument using such testimony, or discussions of such testimony;

2. when the court receives testimony or argument on grand jury evidence or other sensitive information that is the subject matter of the closure motion;

3. when the court determines it is necessary to protect a child witness from "substantial psychological harm" or when it would "result in the child's inability to effectively communicate," 18 U.S.C. § 3509(e); or

4. when the law requires closure to protect some phase of a juvenile delinquency proceeding (18 U.S.C. § 5038).

B. The steps in closing trial or pretrial proceedings upon motion by a party are as follows:

1. Notice of motion

   Ensure that interested parties, including the media, are given notice and an opportunity to defend against the motion in court. If public notice was given of a scheduled hearing, further notice is not necessarily required. If the motion is ex parte or at an unusual time, the court should delay the hearing until interested parties have been notified.

2. The hearing

   The burden is on the movant seeking closure to show

   (a) that an overriding interest is likely to be prejudiced if closure is *not* granted. Such interests include

       (i)   the defendant's right to a fair trial; and

       (ii) the government's interest in inhibiting disclosure of sensitive information (the court may, sua sponte, close the hearing to receive the preliminary information or proffer);

   (b) that alternatives to closure cannot adequately protect the overriding interest the movant is seeking to protect; and

   (c) that closure will probably be effective in protecting against the perceived danger.

3. Decision by the court
    (a) In a pretrial proceeding, when the moving party asserts that the defendant's right to a fair trial will be prejudiced if hearings are conducted publicly, the court should consider
        (i)   the nature and extent of the publicity to date;
        (ii) the size of the jury pool;
        (iii) the ease of a change of venue;
        (iv) the ability to cure any harm through voir dire;
        (v)   whether the public already has the information; and
        (vi) the impact of further publicity on the publicity that has already occurred.
    (b) In deciding whether alternatives to closure can adequately protect the overriding interest that the movant seeks to protect, the court should consider the following alternatives:
        (i)   granting a continuance;
        (ii)   granting severance;
        (iii) changing the venue;
        (iv)   changing the venire;
        (v)   engaging in further voir dire questioning;
        (vi)   permitting additional peremptory challenges;
        (vii) sequestering the jury; and
        (viii) instructing the jury.
4. Findings and order
    (a) If the court decides to order closure
        (i)   it must make findings that
            (a) without closure, there is a substantial probability that the defendant's right to a fair trial would be impaired;
            (b) steps less drastic than closure would be ineffective in preserving the defendant's right to a fair trial; and
            (c) closure would achieve the desired goal of protecting the defendant's right to a fair trial.
        (ii) the closure must be as narrow as possible;
        (iii) the findings must be on the record; and
        (iv) the findings must be adequate to support an order of closure.
    (b) The order must
        (i)   be no broader than is necessary to protect the interest asserted by the moving party; and

      (ii) be tailored to ensure that proceedings that are closed encompass no more than is actually necessary to protect the interest asserted by the moving party.

  (c) Determine whether the order itself should be sealed.

Other FJC sources

Recent Developments Regarding Standards and Procedures for Barring the Public from the Courtroom During a Criminal Trial, Bench Comment 1984, no. 2

7.08 Oaths

Affirmation in lieu of oath

Any person who has conscientious scruples about taking an oath may be allowed to make an affirmation. See, e.g., Fed. R. Civ. P. 43(b); Fed. R. Crim. P. 1(b)(6). Substitute the words "solemnly affirm" for the words "solemnly swear" at the beginning of the oath and delete the words "so help me God" at the end. (If appropriate, courts may wish to substitute "this I do affirm under the pain and penalties of perjury" for "so help me God" at the end.)

Sample oaths

The following are suggested oaths for several situations. A statutory cite after an oath indicates that the oath is taken directly from the statute.

If the person taking an oath or making an affirmation does not understand English, the oath or affirmation should be in a language he or she understands.

Oath to attorneys

(admission to practice before the court)

I, _____, do solemnly swear [*or* affirm] that to the best of my knowledge and ability I will support and defend the Constitution of the United States against all enemies, foreign and domestic, and that I will bear true faith and allegiance to the same; that I take this obligation freely, without any mental reservation or purpose of evasion; and that I will demean myself as an attorney, proctor, and solicitor of this court uprightly and according to law, so help me God.

Oath to clerks and deputies

(to be made by each clerk of court and all deputies before they assume their duties)

I, _____, having been appointed _____, do solemnly swear [*or* affirm] that I will truly and faithfully enter and record all orders, decrees, judgments, and proceedings of such court, and will faithfully and impartially discharge all other duties of my office according to the best of my abilities and understanding. So help me God.
[28 U.S.C. § 951]

Oath to crier (bailiff)

(may be administered in those districts that employ a temporary court crier)

Do you solemnly swear [*or* affirm] that you will faithfully, impartially, and to the best of your ability discharge the duties of crier [bailiff] of this court, to which office you have been appointed, and will strictly obey all orders of the court and your superiors as crier [bailiff] during the session now being held, so help you God?

Oath to crier (bailiff) to conduct jury to view place

Do you solemnly swear [*or* affirm] that you will, together with the United States Marshal, keep these jurors together and permit no one to talk to them, aside from the guides, nor talk to them yourself regarding the case under consideration, until discharged by the court, so help you God?

Oath to guides to conduct jury to view place

Do each of you solemnly swear [*or* affirm] that you will guide these jurors on an inspection of the _____ involved in this action and that you will permit no one to talk to them, nor talk to them yourselves, regarding the case under consideration, except as instructed by the court, so help you God?

Oath to crier (bailiff) to keep jury during adjournment

Do you solemnly swear [*or* affirm] that you will keep the jurors composing this panel together until the next meeting of this court, and during all other adjournments of the court during the trial of this case; that you will permit no person to speak or communicate with them, nor do so yourself, on any subject connected with the trial; and that you will return them to court at the next meeting thereof, so help you God?

Oath to crier (bailiff) and marshal after cause is submitted

Do you solemnly swear [*or* affirm] that you will keep these jurors together in some private and convenient place and not permit any person to speak to or communicate with them, nor do so yourself unless by order of the court, nor ask whether they have agreed on a verdict, and that you will return them to court when they have so agreed, or when ordered by the court, so help you God?

Oath to defendant

(as to his or her financial ability to employ counsel)

Do you solemnly swear [*or* affirm] that all of the statements you are about to make relative to your financial ability to employ counsel will be the truth, the whole truth, and nothing but the truth, so help you God?

Oath for deposition

Do you solemnly swear [*or* affirm] that all the testimony you are about to give in the matter now in hearing will be the truth, the whole truth, and nothing but the truth, so help you God?

Oath to grand jury foreperson and deputy foreperson

Do you, as foreperson and deputy foreperson of this grand jury, solemnly swear [*or* affirm] that you will diligently inquire into and make true presentment or indictment of all public offenses against the United States committed or triable within this district of which you shall have or can obtain legal evidence; that you will keep your own counsel and that of your fellows and of the United States and will not, except when required in the due course of judicial proceedings, disclose the testimony of any witness examined before you, or anything which you or any other grand juror may have voted on in any matter before you; that you shall present or indict no person through malice, hatred, or ill will, nor leave any person unpresented or unindicted through fear, favor, or affection, or for any reward or for the promise or hope thereof; and that in all your presentments or indictments you shall present the truth, the whole truth, and nothing but the truth to the best of your skill and understanding, so help you God?

Oath to other grand jurors

Do each of you solemnly swear [*or* affirm] that you shall diligently inquire into and make true presentment or indictment of all such matters and things touching your present grand jury service that are given to you in charge or that otherwise come to your knowledge; that you shall keep secret the counsel of the United States, your fellows, and yourselves; that you shall not present or indict any person through hatred, malice, or ill will, or leave any person unpresented or unindicted through fear, favor, or affection or for any reward or for the hope or promise thereof; and that in all your presentments and indictments you shall present the truth, the whole truth, and nothing but the truth to the best of your skill and understanding, so help you God?

or

Do each of you solemnly swear [*or* affirm] that you will well and truly observe on your part the same oath that your foreperson and deputy foreperson have now taken before you on their part, so help you God?

Oath to venirepersons

(to be administered at juror qualification or voir dire)

Do you solemnly swear [*or* affirm] that you will truthfully answer all questions that shall be asked of you regarding your qualifications as a juror in the case now called for trial, so help you God?

Oath to interpreter

(The interpreter's duties include interpreting the oath to the witness, the verbatim questions of the court and counsel, and the answers thereto.)

Do you solemnly swear [*or* affirm] that you will justly, truly, fairly, and impartially act as an interpreter in the case now before the court, so help you God?

[*Note:* In addition to the initial oath, the Tenth Circuit has stated that "before the verdict is announced, [the court] should inquire . . . whether the interpreter abided by her oath to act strictly as an interpreter and not to participate in the deliberations. Ideally, the judge should then question the jurors to the same effect." *United States v. Dempsey*, 830 F.2d 1084, 1092 (10th Cir. 1987).]

Oath to interpreter for a deaf juror[1]

Do you solemnly swear [*or* affirm] that you will accurately interpret from the English language into the sign language understood by the juror, who is deaf, and from that language as used by the juror into the English language; that, while you are present in the jury room during the jury's deliberations, your communications with that juror and the other jurors will be limited to translating for the deaf juror what the other jurors say and for the others what the deaf juror says, so that you will not express any of your own ideas, opinions, or observations or otherwise participate yourself in the jury's deliberations; and that you will keep secret all that you hear in the jury room and will not discuss with anyone the testimony or merits of the case unless ordered differently by the court or authorized by the deaf juror after the trial is finished to disclose anything he or she said during the deliberations, so help you God?

Oath to jurors in civil cases (including condemnation cases)

Do each of you solemnly swear [*or* affirm] that you will well and truly try the matters in issue now on trial and render a true verdict according to the law and the evidence, so help you God?

---

1. This sample oath is based on one given to an interpreter in *New York v. Green*, 561 N.Y.S. 2d 130 (N.Y. County Ct. 1990). It is provided as one example of the form for such an oath.

Oath to jurors in criminal cases

(This oath may also be administered to alternate jurors by substituting for the first line: "Do you, as an alternate juror.")

Do each of you solemnly swear [*or* affirm] that you will well and truly try, and a true deliverance make in, the case now on trial, and render a true verdict according to the law and the evidence, so help you God?

Oath to master

Do you solemnly swear [*or* affirm] that you will well and truly hear and determine the facts and true findings according to the evidence, so help you God?

Oath to reporter or stenographer

(for grand jury proceedings, to be administered by the grand jury foreperson)

Do you solemnly swear [*or* affirm] that you will well and truly take and record the evidence about to be presented to this grand jury; that you will translate such testimony as required; and that you will keep secret all information you receive as reported at these grand jury proceedings, except on order of the court, so help you God?

Oath to witness

Do you solemnly swear [*or* affirm] that all the testimony you are about to give in the case now before the court will be the truth, the whole truth, and nothing but the truth, so help you God?

Oath of allegiance

(naturalization proceedings)

I hereby declare, on oath, that I absolutely and entirely renounce and abjure all allegiance and fidelity to any foreign prince, potentate, state, or sovereignty, of whom or which I have heretofore been a subject or citizen; that I will support and defend the Constitution and laws of the United States of America against all enemies, foreign and domestic; that I will bear true faith and allegiance to the same; that I will bear arms on behalf of the United States when required by the law; that I will perform noncombatant service in the Armed Forces of the United States when required by the law; that I will perform work of national importance under civilian direction when required by the law; and that I take this obligation freely, without any mental reservation or purpose of evasion; so help me God.

[8 C.F.R. § 337.1(a)]

[*Note:* If the petitioner refuses to bear arms, ascertain whether there is "clear and convincing evidence" that the refusal is based on "religious training and belief." If so, the petitioner should be required to take the remainder of the oath, including at least one of the alternatives to bearing arms. 8 U.S.C. § 1448(a). See also 8 C.F.R. § 337.1(b) (may substitute "and solemnly affirm" for "on oath").]

Oath to justices, judges, and magistrate judges

I, _____, do solemnly swear [*or* affirm] that I will administer justice without respect to persons, and do equal right to the poor and to the rich, and that I will faithfully and impartially discharge and perform all the duties incumbent upon me as _____ under the Constitution and laws of the United States. So help me God.
[28 U.S.C. § 453]

Oath to public officials

(given to all individuals, except the President, who are "elected or appointed to an office of honor or profit in the civil service or uniformed services," 5 U.S.C. § 3331)

I, _____, do solemnly swear [*or* affirm] that I will support and defend the Constitution of the United States against all enemies, foreign and domestic; that I will bear true faith and allegiance to the same; that I take this obligation freely, without any mental reservation or purpose of evasion; and that I will well and faithfully discharge the duties of the office on which I am about to enter. So help me God.
[5 U.S.C. § 3331]

Table of authorities

The following is a brief compilation of authorities with respect to taking an oath or making an affirmation.

affirmation—
in lieu of oath

Fed. R. Civ. P. 43(b)
Fed. R. Crim. P. 1(b)(6)

bankruptcy—
authority to administer

11 U.S.C. § 343

clerks and deputies—
oath of office

28 U.S.C. § 951

authority to administer oaths

28 U.S.C. § 953

deposition—
taken before an officer or other person so appointed

Fed. R. Civ. P. 28(a)

grand jury foreperson—
authority to administer oaths

Fed. R. Crim. P. 6(c)

interpreter—to take oath

Fed. R. Evid. 604

interrogatories—
to answer under oath

Fed. R. Civ. P. 33(b)(3)

jurors, alternate—
to take same oath as regular jurors

Fed. R. Crim. P. 24(c)(2)(A)

justices and judges—
oath of office

28 U.S.C. § 453

authority to administer oaths

28 U.S.C. § 459

magistrate judge—
    oath of office   28 U.S.C. § 631(g)
    authority to administer oaths   28 U.S.C. § 636(a)(2)

master—
    may administer oath   Fed. R. Civ. P. 53(c)(1)

naturalization proceedings—
    oath of allegiance   8 U.S.C. § 1448(a)

perjury   18 U.S.C. §§ 1621 and 1623

public officer—
    oath of office   5 U.S.C. § 3331
    authority to administer   5 U.S.C. § 2903

reporter—
    to take oath   28 U.S.C. § 753(a)

waiver of oath   *Wilcoxon v. United States,*
                      231 F.2d 384 (10th Cir. 1956)

witness—
    required to take oath   Fed. R. Evid. 60

Appendix: FJC publications

The Federal Judicial Center publishes numerous manuals, reference works, and monographs on substantive legal topics, including patent, copyright, securities, and admiralty law. It also publishes research reports on criminal litigation and the sentencing process, civil litigation, case management, the history of the federal court system, and federal judicial administration. The Center sends selected publications to new circuit and district judges upon their nomination and to new bankruptcy and magistrate judges upon their appointment. Listed below are publications sent to new district judges.

The Center also has a wide collection of media programs, including Center-produced audio and video programs and commercially produced instructional programs. Many judges find particularly helpful the audio recordings of presentations at Center seminars and workshops.

All Center publications and media programs can be found and ordered through FJC Online, the Center's site on the judiciary's intranet at http://cwn.fjc.dcn. Most publications can also be downloaded from the site, and a growing number of media programs are available in streaming audio and video formats.

Publications sent to new district judges (by topic)

Civil litigation and case management

Awarding Attorneys' Fees and Managing Fee Litigation, Second Edition
2005 (162 pp.)
This monograph explains the doctrinal and case-management aspects of fee awards. It analyzes the law of attorneys' fee awards under fee-shifting statutes, the common fund doctrine and its offspring, and the substantial benefit doctrine, and it addresses an issue of special significance to bankruptcy courts—the propriety of sua sponte review of fee petitions. It also presents a selection of case-management strategies, based on interviews with judges, attorneys, U.S. trustees, and others.

Capital § 2254 Habeas Cases: A Pocket Guide for Judges
2012 (28 pp.)
This pocket guide provides a basic overview of the issues judges can expect to face when assigned a capital habeas case. It begins with appointment of counsel, budgeting concerns, and stays of execution. It then summarizes the primary procedural considerations that affect habeas cases—successive petitions, petition timeliness, exhaustion of state remedies, procedural default, and amending a petition. The guide also addresses substantive considerations for case resolution, evidentiary development, and briefing procedures.

Finally, the guide highlights some of the issues that often arise prior to an execution.

Civil Litigation Management Manual, Second Edition
2010 (220 pp.)
The *Civil Litigation Management Manual* provides trial judges with a handbook on managing civil cases. It sets out a wide array of case-management techniques, beginning with early case screening and concluding with steps for streamlining trials and final disposition. It also discusses a number of special topics, including pro se and high visibility cases, the role of staff, and automated programs that support case management. This new edition incorporates statutory and rules changes and contains updated advice on electronic case management, electronic discovery, and ways of containing costs and expediting cases. The manual, which was produced and is periodically updated pursuant to a requirement set forth in the Civil Justice Reform Act of 1990, is based on the experiences of federal district and magistrate judges and reflects techniques they have developed. It was prepared under the direction of the Judicial Conference Committee on Court Administration and Case Management, with substantial contributions from the Administrative Office of the U.S. Courts and the Federal Judicial Center, and was approved by the Judicial Conference in March 2010. This new edition supersedes the first edition (2001) and the Manual for Litigation Management and Cost and Delay Reduction (1992). Note: Appendices A and C of the manual, including sample procedures and guidelines, orders, and other materials, are only available on line and are not included in the published manual.

Compensatory Damages Issues in Patent Infringement Cases: A Pocket Guide for Federal District Court Judges
2011 (43 pp.)
This is a guide for trial judges to consult when deciding issues of compensatory damages in patent infringement cases. It was prepared by a national committee of experts from the bench, bar, in-house counsel, and academia formed at the request of the chief judge of the U.S. Court of Appeals for the Federal Circuit.

The Elements of Case Management: A Pocket Guide for Judges, Second Edition
2006 (22 pp.)
This is a primer for judges on techniques and methods of case management.

Guide to Judicial Management of Cases in ADR
2001 (193 pp.)
This publication offers guidance to federal trial and bankruptcy courts on when and how to refer appropriate cases to ADR and how to manage cases referred to ADR. The purpose of the guide is not to advocate ADR use, but to

present various approaches that judges and parties may choose to follow when considering and using ADR. The guide identifies areas where there may be disagreement, describing advantages and disadvantages of various approaches. It also alerts readers to emerging trends or what are perceived by many as preferred approaches.

Managing Class Action Litigation: A Pocket Guide for Judges, Third Edition
2010 (55 pp.)
This pocket guide is designed to help federal judges manage the increased number of class action cases filed in or removed to federal courts as a result of the Class Action Fairness Act of 2005 (CAFA). It includes a section on determining federal jurisdiction that incorporates case-management practices and judicial interpretations of CAFA. It also includes suggestions for judicial review and administration of class settlements, especially regarding the disclosure of claims rates and actual payments to class members. This third edition includes an expanded treatment of the notice and claims processes. Revisions are concentrated in Parts III and IV.

Manual for Complex Litigation, Fourth Edition
2004 (798 pp.)
The *Manual for Complex Litigation* describes approaches that trial judges have found useful in managing complex cases. This edition updates the treatment of electronic discovery and other aspects of pretrial management. It also describes major changes in the substantive and procedural law affecting case management in mass tort, class action, intellectual property, employment discrimination, and other types of litigation. A new chapter deals with managing scientific evidence.

Patent Case Management Judicial Guide
2009 (650 pp., currently available on-line only; new edition in progress)
This is a comprehensive, user-friendly, and practical judicial guide for managing patent cases. Although similar in many respects to other forms of complex civil litigation, patent cases pose distinctive case-management challenges, including complex and dynamic technological facts rarely encountered in most other areas of litigation, and unique procedures (such as claim construction hearings) that affect and interact with other aspects of the case (such as summary judgment motions and expert reports). In addition, patent cases often entail distinctive and difficult discovery issues, extensive use of experts, and complex dispositive and pretrial motions practice. The authors surveyed federal judges and describe their approaches and best practices for these and other aspects of patent case management.

Section 1983 Litigation, Second Edition
2008 (239 pp.)
Section 1983 Litigation analyzes the fundamental issues that arise in litigation under 42 U.S.C. § 1983, and the case law interpreting those issues. This edition contains new sections on jury instructions and the Rooker-Feldman Doctrine, new material on retaliatory prosecutions, and expanded coverage on jurisdiction. Research for this edition concluded with the October 2007 Supreme Court Term and covers courts of appeals decisions reported through June 30, 2008.

Ten Steps to Better Case Management: A Guide for Multidistrict Litigation Transferee Judges
2009 (20 pp.)
This guide is intended to help judges to whom an MDL case has been transferred. Congress created the Judicial Panel on Multidistrict Litigation under 28 U.S.C. § 1407 and gave it the responsibility to transfer "civil actions involving one or more common questions of fact" from multiple districts to any single district for coordinated or consolidated pretrial proceedings. The Panel centralizes cases in order to promote the convenient, just, and efficient conduct of the actions. After the Panel transfers cases under § 1407, it exercises virtually no further control over them.

Criminal litigation and sentencing

The Bail Reform Act of 1984, Third Edition
2006 (78 pp.)
This monograph provides a summary of appellate court decisions that interpret provisions of The Bail Reform Act of 1984 on issues of release and detention. This third edition primarily addresses areas that have been changed by statute or case law since the second edition, and cites more recent cases that discuss the substantive issues through June 1, 2006. In addition, the monograph covers practical considerations regarding conditional release, release orders, detention hearings, and waiver. It also includes new material on how the Crime Victims' Rights Act of 2004 affects proceedings under The Bail Reform Act.

The Crime Victims' Rights Act of 2004 and the Federal Courts
2008 (31 pp.)
The Crime Victims' Rights Act (CVRA), effective Oct. 30, 2004, and mainly codified at 18 U.S.C. § 3771, expands the rights of federal crime victims and the role of federal judges in enforcing those rights. This paper provides an overview of key provisions of the CVRA; notes on the CVRA's potential application at various stages of criminal proceedings, keyed to relevant sections of the *Benchbook for U.S. District Court Judges*; potential issues that may

arise under the CVRA; summaries of cases applying the CVRA; and the text of § 3771.

Manual on Recurring Problems in Criminal Trials, Sixth Edition
2010 (101 pp.)
This manual outlines the law governing many of the specific issues and procedural matters that arise frequently in criminal trials. This sixth edition added new material and revised the organization and format to enhance usability. Among the topics covered are pro se representation, jury-related matters, disclosure, evidentiary issues, contempt, confessions, and multiple defendants. Circuit splits are also noted. The manual has been updated to include cases decided during the Supreme Court's October 2009 Term, and district and appellate case summaries through July 1, 2010.

Ethics and Codes of Conduct

Judicial Disqualification: An Analysis of Federal Law, Second Edition
2010 (140 pp.)
Judicial Disqualification outlines the statutory framework of federal judicial disqualification law under 28 U.S.C. §§ 455, 144, 47, and 2106. The monograph substantially revises and expands on the first edition, and analyzes the case law, with a focus both on substantive disqualification standards and procedural requirements. It features a revised organizational structure and includes new material, as well as updated cases.

Maintaining the Public Trust: Ethics for Federal Judicial Law Clerks, Third Edition
2012 (36 pp.)
This pamphlet provides an overview of law clerks' ethical obligations as well as resources they can consult for further information. It covers topics such as confidentiality, conflicts of interest, political activities, online activities, and gifts, and it includes examples that illustrate challenges law clerks may face. It also has an Ethics Checklist for Federal Judicial Law Clerks, which helps law clerks identify ethics problems that may arise.

Federal judicial administration

Deskbook for Chief Judges of U.S. District Courts, Third Edition
2003 (138 pp.)
(Sent to chief judges only)
A detailed reference for chief judges of federal district courts, the *Deskbook* describes the position of chief judges within the system of federal judicial administration as well as their specific roles and responsibilities with respect to national and regional bodies of judicial administration; other judges, officers, and employees of the district court; various functions of the court; and external groups such as the bar, the media, and the public. It includes cita-

tions to statutory requirements and Judicial Conference and Administrative Office policies.

A New Judge's Introduction to Federal Judicial Administration
2003 (20 pp.)
This brief pamphlet describes the major agencies that administer the federal courts on the national, regional, and local levels and summarizes their primary functions. It covers, for example, the circuit judicial councils, the circuit conferences, the Judicial Conference of the United States and its committees, the Administrative Office of the U.S. Courts, and the Federal Judicial Center.

General references

Benchbook for U.S. District Court Judges, Sixth Edition
2013
An ongoing compilation of information that federal district judges have found useful for immediate bench or chambers reference, the *Benchbook* contains sections on such topics as assignment of counsel, taking guilty pleas, sentencing procedure, standard voir dire questions, and contempt proceedings. It is prepared under the guidance of experienced district judges and is produced in loose-leaf format for easy supplementation.

Conducting Job Interviews: A Guide for Federal Judges
1999 (29 pp.)
This guide describes an interviewing process that is simple, effective, and fair and gives examples of questions to help determine whether job candidates have the knowledge, skills, and abilities necessary for the position. The guide may be helpful to judges as they select law clerks, and to chief judges and other judges who are in the process of selecting unit executives.

Confidential Discovery: A Pocket Guide on Protective Orders
2012 (21 pp.)
Among the reasons that courts issue protective orders in both civil and criminal cases is to keep discovery confidential on a showing of good cause. Experience has proved that confidentiality protective orders grease the wheels of discovery in many cases. The protective orders discussed in this pocket guide are different from sealing orders that protect the courts' own records and protective orders that protect information from discovery. Among the topics addressed here are blanket orders, stipulated orders, and designating discovery for attorney eyes only.

A Guide to the Preservation of Federal Judges' Papers, Second Edition
2009 (89 pp.)
Federal judges' papers provide an important documentary record of judges' careers and the work of the federal courts. This guide describes how students of the federal courts use judges' papers and offers guidelines for judges' selection of a repository to house a collection. It also offers recommendations for the management of documents in chambers.

Guide to Research in Federal Judicial History
2010 (227 pp.)
This guide describes the records of the federal courts, as well as records of Congress and the executive branch, that are relevant to researching federal judicial history.

Judicial Writing Manual
1991 (41 pp.)
(New edition in progress)
(3 copies, including 2 for law clerks)
The Center prepared this manual to help judges organize opinions and improve their opinion writing. Drawing on interviews with twenty-four experienced judges, and guided by a board of editors comprising judges, law professors, and writers, the manual offers advice on writing tailored to the needs of the federal judiciary.

Keeping Government Secrets: A Pocket Guide for Judges on the State-Secrets Privilege, the Classified Information Procedures Act, and Court Security Officers
2007 (44 pp.)
Most federal judges come into contact with classified information infrequently, if at all, but when they do, they are faced with the dilemma of how to protect government secrets in the context of an otherwise public proceeding. This pocket guide is designed to familiarize federal judges with statutes and procedures established to help public courts protect government secrets when they are called upon to do so. The guide provides information about the Classified Information Procedures Act (CIPA), information security officers, and secure storage facilities.

Law Clerk Handbook, Second Edition
2007 (137 pp.)
This handbook provides an overview of chambers operations and the work of the federal courts. It replaces the *Chambers Handbook for Judges' Law Clerks and Secretaries* (1994).

Managing Discovery of Electronic Information: A Pocket Guide for Judges, Second Edition
2012 (48 pp.)
This pocket guide helps federal judges manage the discovery of electronically stored information (ESI). It encourages judges to actively manage cases that involve ESI through early intervention and sustained supervision and to use the many tools available to them—case-management conferences and orders, limits on discovery, tiered or phased discovery, sampling, cost shifting, and, if necessary, sanctions—to facilitate cooperation among opposing lawyers and to ensure that discovery is fair, reasonable, and proportional to each case. It covers issues unique to the discovery of ESI, including its scope, the allocation of costs, the form of production, the waiver of privilege and work product protection, the preservation of data, and spoliation.

Reference Manual on Scientific Evidence, Third Edition
2011 (1034 pp.)
(Published jointly by the National Academy of Sciences© and the Federal Judicial Center)
The *Reference Manual on Scientific Evidence* assists judges in managing cases involving complex scientific and technical evidence by describing the basic tenets of key scientific fields from which legal evidence is typically derived and by providing examples of cases in which that evidence has been used.

Judges faced with disputes over the admissibility of scientific and technical evidence refer to the manual to help them better understand and evaluate the relevance, reliability, and usefulness of the evidence being proffered. The manual is not intended to tell judges what is good science and what is not. Instead, it serves to help judges identify issues on which experts are likely to differ and to guide the inquiry of the court in seeking an informed resolution of the conflict.

Sealing Court Records and Proceedings: A Pocket Guide
2010 (26 pp.)
Court case records and proceedings are presumptively public, but occasionally there are compelling reasons for keeping all or parts of them confidential, sometimes permanently but often only temporarily. This pocket guide summarizes the case law on sealing records and proceedings and presents a useful procedural checklist of seven principles to follow when denying public access.

Index

Index

www.ingramcontent.com/pod-product-compliance
Lightning Source LLC
Chambersburg PA
CBHW061342210326
41598CB00035B/5855